INTERVIEW AND INDICATORS IN PSYCHOANALYSIS AND PSYCHOTHERAPY

D1600488

INTERVIEW AND INDICATORS IN PSYCHOANALYSIS AND PSYCHOTHERAPY

Antonio Pérez-Sánchez

KARNAC

First published in 2012 by
Karnac Books Ltd
118 Finchley Road, London NW3 5HT

British Library Cataloguing in Publication Data

A C.I.P. for this book is available from the British Library

ISBN 978 1 78049 129 5

Edited, designed and produced by The Studio Publishing Services Ltd
www.publishingservicesuk.co.uk
e-mail: studio@publishingservicesuk.co.uk

www.karnacbooks.com

CONTENTS

ACKNOWLEDGEMENTS

The conception of this book has taken place over a period of several years, stemming from different professional experiences, for which reason I should like to offer my gratitude to those people who, in one way or another, took part in them. First and foremost, the patients with whom I have worked personally, as well as those whose cases I have come to know through supervisions with colleagues. A first outline of the idea of psychodynamic indicators was presented at a conference of the Catalan Association of Psychoanalytic Psychotherapy, in 1995. Later, I developed these ideas in several seminars, such as those held in Palma de Mallorca over the course of a year, with a group of specialists from the Balearic Islands Mental Health Association at the request of Isabel Salvador, to whom I offer my sincere gratitude. Another great stimulus for the study both of indicators and of interview was the work carried out over several years with a group of psychotherapists in the San Andrés Mental Health Centre (Barcelona). I should like to express special gratitude to my colleagues, Santiago Surís, María Trías, and María Call, who have been so generous as to allow me access to their clinical material presented during supervisions. I should not like to forget the students who took part in the seminars I gave at the Barcelona Psychoanalytic Institute.

For the English version of the book, I have to add some acknowledgements. Luis Martín Cabré and Anna Minieri wrote respective reviews of the Spanish version, which allowed me to insert some modifications in order to clarify ideas. Laura Etchegoyen read the English version of Chapter Eight and gave me some helpful comments. I must also offer my gratitude to Sharon Raeburn, who put me in contact with Karnac Books, and to Jacqueline Amati Mehler, who was kind and generous enough to write the Foreword, despite the short time available. I must not forget Stefan Bolognini, Serge Frisch, and Bernard Reich for reading the book and giving their support. Maggie Evans, my English teacher, helped me to translate the first version of Chapter Eight and the Introduction. My gratitude also goes to Caroline Williamson, the translator of the entire book, except for Chapter Eight and the Introduction, which she edited. She carried out her work with a lot of patience and professionalism, creating, in my opinion, a very good English version.

Finally, although the English version is essentially true to the Spanish original, in the process of re-reading the original, taking into account my experience of seminars in which I presented my ideas as they appeared in the book, I noticed some inaccuracies and confused ideas, which I have now rewritten in an attempt to achieve better clarity. So, my thanks also go to the students of the Spanish Psychoanalytical Society where I gave these seminars.

ABOUT THE AUTHOR

Antonio Pérez-Sánchez is a psychiatrist and psychoanalyst. He is a training analyst and supervisor of the Spanish Psychoanalytical Society (a component society of the International Psychoanalytic Association) and he teaches at the Barcelona Psychoanalytic Institute. He was the president of the Spanish Psychoanalytical Society from January 2008 until January 2012. He has worked in psychiatric hospitals and outpatients departments for many years, and now works in private practice as a psychoanalyst and a psychotherapist. He has written papers on psychological phenomena from a psychoanalytic perspective, including envy, psychic truth, forgiveness, and time. He has also written papers on the subject of psychotherapeutic and psychoanalytic technique, and is the author of three books published in Spanish: *Elementos de Psicoterapia Breve Psicoanalítica* (Elements of Brief Psychoanalytic Psychotherapy) (1992), *Prácticas Psicoterapéuticas: Psicoanálisis Aplicado a la Asistencia Pública* (Psychotherapeutic Practices: Applied Psychoanalysis in Public Mental Health Care) (1996), and *Análisis Terminable* (Terminable Analysis: A Study in Ending the Psychoanalytic Process) (1997).

To my children, Guillermo and Julia

Jacqueline Amati-Mehler[1]

In his Introduction, the author states the reasons for writing a book about intake interviews in psychoanalysis and in psychotherapy. He wonders whether the insufficient attention paid until quite recently by psychiatrists and psychoanalysts to the study of the intake interviews might be attributed to defensive reactions—essentially anxiety, negation, and idealization—on the part of either potential patients or the interviewers that would result in fewer referrals to psychodynamic therapies. Indeed, other authors have dealt with these issues when questioning or trying to explore the possible reasons for the decreasing demand for psychoanalysis and the generally diminishing interest of young people in applying for psychoanalytic training

As quoted by Møller (2011), many authors have emphasised the role played by analysts themselves, and their anxieties during the first encounters with a new patient. Rothstein's opinion is that the exclusion of patients from analysis has more to do with the analyst, his internal setting, and his eventual lack of confidence in the analytic process (Rothstein, 1998).

This is a subject that has continued to be a core issue in the arena of debate, especially within the European psychoanalytic societies. A working party on the subject has been functioning over the past few years in the European Psychoanalytical Federation. Whereas the initial aims regarded the exploration of how psychoanalysts deal with potential new patients and the issues involved in the interplay between them, the title was then changed to "initiating psychoanalysis", thus implying the transformation of the couple's first encounters into the development of a psychoanalytic process.

Pérez-Sánchez's endeavour is far more ambitious and, indeed, this book offers much more than can be inferred from its overall title or, for that matter, from the headings of its nine chapters. His main aim is to reconsider the core issues involved in the dynamics and technique of what he calls psychodynamic interviews in public mental health services, while not forgetting private practice, in order to establish the best therapeutic indication according to the patient's needs; he does not fail to mention as well the conscious or unconscious disposition of the interviewer to engage with a particular patient in a working psychodynamic process.

In the case of psychoanalysts, whether in public services or private practice, this outlook necessarily touches upon the criteria of analysability that vary according to the implicit or explicit theories that each analyst might have developed, and that will influence the kind of therapeutic indication that ensues from the interview/s. The author carefully examines the process and motivations involved in the analyst's choice of whether to take charge of the patient himself or to refer him/her to a colleague. Countertransference and its working through, indeed somewhat neglected until recent years, is crucial for our understanding of those cases in which the analyst's countertransference is the target for strong projections or projective identifications of psychotic parts, part and parcel of psychoneurotic organisations as well. Pérez-Sánchez further provides a detailed exploration of the delicate implications of the eventual indication to the patient. In his role as a psychiatrist, psychoanalyst, and psychotherapist working in private practice as well as in public health services, the author shares with the readers his clinical experience in the area of intake encounters and the far-reaching implications of detecting the factors involved. The richness of his work derives from this careful exploration of the multiple facets involved, claiming the reader's attention throughout the book.

The outline of the author's conceptions of the mind is mainly based on the views of Freud, Klein, and Bion, and precedes the outline of the therapeutic aims of mental health practitioners. The discussion examines the different possible therapeutic goals as well as the factors determining which of them are considered to be accessible. The theoretical and clinical sources chosen by the author focus on the relational experience of patients with their primary and meaningful external objects that determine the internal objects vicissitudes and the personality. Mechanisms such as projective identification (Klein, 1946) and Bion's container–contained model, as well as the constant interaction between fragmentation–disintegration and integration, are discussed. Last, but not least, the concept of unconscious phantasy is highlighted. An important point is the emphasis that Pérez-Sánchez puts on psychic "change" rather than on "cure". He sees the first as a nonending process that unveils the historical biography within the continuous "here-and-now" when in analysis.

Pérez-Sánchez does not present himself as a specialist in psychotherapy or as a psychoanalyst to whom people are referred as potential patients for one or the other treatment. Although he is a psychoanalyst, a member of a component society of the IPA (Spanish Psychoanalytical Society), he wishes his book to be of use also to nonspecialists; that is, professionals who operate in the field of public health care and who, in his opinion, should be able to establish the right treatment indication. He thinks that if the psychiatrists and psychotherapists who operate in public services have the opportunity to learn and be adequately supervised in the course of experiencing intake interviews, many more patients might be orientated towards undertaking a psychodynamic therapy, whether it be psychoanalysis, psychoanalytic psychotherapy, a brief time-limited therapy or a supportive psychotherapy. This challenging and ambitious aim compels readers to a deeper clinical and theoretical reflection on such matters, especially because the author believes that the scarcity of resources in public services rules out the option of indicating a psychotherapy.

Two consequences then ensue. The first concerns an ethical problem regarding what the potential patient will be told about his situation and how this will be conveyed to him/her; emphasis on the "wording" according to different pathologies and circumstances is examined and discussed through the presentation of clinical material. The second consequence is the possibility of a patient being deprived of potential help if not fully understood, or if countertransference reactions on the part of the interviewer interfere with an adequate exploratory function—part and parcel of the intake interviews. Pérez-Sánchez feels that the lack of adequate indications for either psychotherapy or psychoanalysis on the part of professionals operating in the realm of public healthcare institutions might be one of the factors leading to few referrals for psychoanalysis. He presents a brief statement about the differences between the aims of psychoanalysis and of psychotherapy, according to the relevance of (a) symptomatic relief; (b) symptom-focused treatment; (c) clarifying interpersonal conflicts; (d) clarifying external and internal conflicts; (e) psychic change through the understanding of internal relational and transferential conflicts. The personal aspects in relation to the therapist's implicit and explicit theories, the aspects regarding the patient and those concerning social facts, are not overlooked by the author when considering which of these aims, implying technical differences, is attainable. All these issues are briefly mentioned at the beginning of the book and are illustrated throughout with clinical material and the discussion of the underlying meanings.

When discussing the interview technique and its dynamics, Pérez-Sánchez uses the expression "psychodynamic interview", without neglecting the importance of developing "diagnostic" or "evaluation" capacities so as to launch a larger group of professionals who will then be able to perform such functions and, eventually, indicate the most appropriate treatment. The essential issue discussed here is the understanding of the dynamics that are put on to the stage *"when one person seeks the help of another"*. The core issue regards anxiety common to both interviewer and interviewed. A psychodynamic interview presupposes a special aptitude on the part of the interviewer in public services *to detect unconscious workings of the mind* in a setting that differs from a private situation in which a patient might already have been referred to an analyst with a precise indication for psychoanalysis. Interviews in public health services constitute a particularly sensitive issue because, besides the impact of two people who meet for the first time face-to-face, there is also an institution that has a role in establishing its particular setting and strategies. The only aspect common to both settings is that of an asymmetric situation in which one person asks another one for help. The therapist is constantly alerted to, and must be aware of, the issues inherent to dependence *vs.* independence. An important point strongly stressed by Pérez-Sánchez is the necessary technical devices used in the interview, entailing the clarification of its explorative aims and, thus, differing from treatment, regardless of the fact that sometimes an interview itself can have a therapeutic effect. Idealisation and omnipotence risk blurring the differences between diagnostic and therapeutic situations, the latter implying insight, the former a relief through its cathartic effect. The transformation of a diagnostic interview to a therapeutic one is discussed in depth through a clinical vignette.

Transference and countertransference are discussed from the perspective of the different primitive infantile and adult levels at play in the exchange with the interviewer, which constantly challenge the identity of the interviewer as well as that of the patient. In my experience, which coincides with that of Pérez-Sánchez, in cases where early psychic areas of psychotic functioning come up, all too often psychotherapists or analysts will declare these patients to be non-analysable; if they are accepted for therapy, it will most likely be within a face-to-face setting with low frequency of sessions. As Parsons (2006) says, there is a countertransference reaction to the analytic process itself, in as much as it touches upon the very depth of our own functioning when faced with archaic and primitive contents. Pérez-Sánchez does not fail to discuss with deep insight the latent primitive pre- or para-verbal components of communication as an important road—through projection and projective identification—to understanding the deepest unconscious levels that call for countertransferential working through on the part of the therapist.

Emphasis is put on a careful understanding of the patient's general attitudes and ways of establishing relations within the asymmetrical setting. Another crucial issue regards the kind of, or the opportunity for, interventions made during intake interviews, whether interpretative or not. One of the controversies concerns whether one can or should use interpretations during the first interview, regardless of the fact that transference as well as countertransference issues might be at stake even as early as during the telephone encounter of the voices when the request for an appointment is settled. I tend to agree with Pérez-Sánchez, who focuses on what led the patient to request help, and on encouraging the curiosity of the patient to explore further and give meaning to the pain and distress that are being brought to our attention. The aims of the interview from a diagnostic perspective are also examined, with a view to investigating the psychic state of the patient within a relational situation: his or her fantasies, attitudes, and the different kinds of anxieties and/or defences raised by the encounter. For Pérez-Sánchez, it is important to explore the psychodynamics of the clinical history and its proper use and understanding in regard to its quantity and quality, but especially the ways in which it is provided by the patient, whether redundantly or leaving out important issues such as dreams or sexual life.

Pérez-Sánchez focuses on the importance of clarifying to the patient that psychotherapy and psychoanalysis are different procedures, and he stresses how this will also depend on "the stance the therapist takes on this matter", again dealt with more extensively in the last two chapters. As mentioned above, I believe that this part of the book is fundamental, especially because, in our present days, there is a conceptual as well as a clinical confusion between the aim, the dynamics, and the technique of both therapeutic procedures. I share Pérez-Sánchez's view that while psychoanalytically orientated psychotherapy is a method that applies the theories underlying psychoanalysis, the therapeutic practice differs from that of psychoanalysis. The latter method takes into consideration such factors as the depth of levels involved, the frequency of sessions, and the use of the couch.

In Chapter Five, the author provides a very detailed verbatim presentation of case material of intake interviews, amplifying in a very useful, pragmatic, and pedagogical way (I am, here, using this term in its positive sense) many of the items mentioned above. In fact, each piece of the patient's communications is intercalated by a paragraph in which the salient aspects of the patient's words give rise to hypotheses about the possible underlying problems and conflicts, whether overt or hidden. Different aspects are taken into consideration, such as present life problems and attempts to highlight historical unworked-through traumatic experiences.

An original proposal, which certainly might give rise to controversial opinions, regards particular cases in which a "time limited" (one year) psychotherapeutic experience with three follow-up interviews during the following year are offered in order to explore specific problems. These and other interviewing experiences form part of a teaching procedure through supervised working groups, with a view to grasping the psychodynamic aspects at play in the interviews.

The unveiling of the psychopathology includes an exploration of the arena of object relations, defences, and phantasies. However, following Freud's statement, Pérez-Sánchez reminds us that it is not only the illness that indicates the kind of therapy advised, but an estimate of the whole personality. What are emphasised are the potential possibilities of establishing a therapeutic alliance with the therapist, and, as we know, the capacity of the analyst to work with that particular patient is just as fundamental. In other words, the main issue is whether a working couple can result from the patient–therapist encounter.

Following this, the author then goes on to propose, in Chapters Six and Seven, what he calls "psychodynamic indicators"—indicators that should enable the therapist to build a personality profile of whether or not a patient is suitable for psychoanalytic psychodynamic treatment (psychotherapy or psychoanalysis). The theoretical bases of the indicators are the Freudian concept of ambivalence in psychic life, as well as the dual forces present in it: in favour of life (life tendencies) and against life (tendencies towards death). Some of Bion's ideas are also taken into consideration in order to build the concept of the indicators. The indicators are built through the convergence of the data from three areas: the patient's psychopathology, biography, and data coming from the interaction of the patient with the analyst (or psychotherapist) in the interview itself. The author places much importance on the latter data. For instance, when the patient is talking about his/ her relationship with other people (particularly with the most important figures in his/her life) it is important to confront this version with how the patient is relating to the therapist in the interview.

The last two chapters of the book provide an opportunity to explore the importance of the problems dealt with from the inspired perspective of a colleague as he shares with readers his vast experience as a psychiatrist, psychotherapist, and psychoanalyst working in different private and public settings, but, nevertheless, constantly tuned in to an internal psychoanalytic listening. I should like to stress the importance that runs throughout Pérez-Sánchez's book of distinguishing psychoanalytic or psychodynamic listening from *doing* psychoanalysis. The author's endeavour, devoid of ideological partisanship, is to disclose the complexity of the theoretical and clinical boundaries between different professional identities and practices. This is particularly meaningful nowadays, when training flexibilities and the blurring of boundaries between different therapies, professional identities, and institutional organisations are at the core of the arena of debate.

The merit of Pérez-Sánchez's effort lies in illustrating the common ground that allows for important possible convergences, while, at the same time, he concentrates attention on the differences, and especially on safeguarding the specificity of the psychoanalytic method. In fact, Chapter Eight is entitled "Specificity of psychoanalysis and psychoanalytic psychotherapy" and Chapter Nine focuses on "The choice of indication: psychotherapy or psychoanalysis". In Chapter Eight, Pérez-Sánchez's first observation regards the fact that "whatever options are chosen will depend on the therapist's idea of the specificity characterising each one of them . . .", about which there is no unanimous consensus. He refers to relevant quotations from Freud, in which, while defining the psychoanalytic specificity, he also gives birth to psychoanalytic psychotherapy in order to extend access to therapy to more people. However, post-Freudian developments, carefully described by Pérez-Sánchez, have led analysts to consider as analysable a number of patients who were excluded by Freud and continue to be considered non-analysable by many analysts today. I have often had occasion to remark and write about the anxiety that serious borderline or psychotic patients cause in us.

The author comments on the importance of associating the "here and now" interpretations to the classical Freudian description of transference. After an excursus into the history of those who, through the years, have defended the specificity of, and difference between, psychoanalysis and psychotherapy and of those who have challenged it, Pérez-Sánchez's position (which I wholeheartedly share) is that ". . . it is possible to make efforts to stipulate certain criteria in order to define when a procedure is closer to one end of the scale or the other". I believe that in every analytic process we might momentarily make a psychotherapeutic intervention. The essential is to recognise this and to try to understand what motivated it. And this is the author's endeavour in this important chapter. While theoretical discrepancies might be missing when examining the case material of a specific case, it is the aims, the technical and dynamic devices dealt with in previous chapters, that introduce divergences.

The premises for the task announced in the title of Chapter Nine are the premises for creating a psychoanalytic therapeutic modality dealing with observation, the specific setting, the understanding and working through of the vicissitudes within the analytic couple related to past experiences, interpretations, resistance to change, and the modalities of working them through. All these aspects are dealt with from the perspective of self and object representations and how they set up the psychoanalytic scenario shared by patient and analyst. Furthermore, as Pérez-Sanchez sees it—and it would be difficult to disagree with him—". . . the clinical material that gives content to the psychoanalytic process is determined by the characteristics of the method".

A *psychotherapeutic* process develops in psychotherapy also, but the experiences of linking and the observation of the internal psychic reality are less intense and are frequently orientated towards working in reference to "zonal" areas of the ego; extra-therapeutic transferences are more likely to be explored as attention might be more concerned with external past and present objects. An important remark, in my opinion, regards highlighting, as the author does, the risk of giving priority to transference interpretations in a once-a-week session that involves mobilising in the patient anxieties related to deep primitive levels that might be difficult to contain and resolve in low frequency therapy. Furthermore, this is so regardless of whether the therapist is an analyst or not.

In the final part of Chapter Nine, the author discusses the difficult subject of choosing the right indication: psychoanalysis or psychotherapy. He analyses in detail the factors that are relevant and that determine the choice of one or the other. Every part of this chapter, as in the previous one, refers to issues dealt with before and that are "here and now" linked together in what appears to be a very refined gradual construction of Pérez-Sánchez's thinking and purpose, whether or not one agrees with his tenets. In either case, his considerations invite readers to ponder a deepening of the problems put forward in regard to intake interviews—the "entrance hall", if I may use a metaphor, necessary to come in and explore one's internal home, provided the method is adequate and leads to the best indication. We should also not forget that Pérez-Sánchez's concern, announced at the beginning of the book, coincides with that of many psychoanalysts today who work on first encounters as a way of acquiring more competence in leading patients towards psychodynamic therapy. The author is concerned with the internal facts that condition the encounters, but we should not forget that external conditions connected with the confusion of methods and professional identities have rendered this task extremely crucial, and this adds to the value of the items dealt with in this book.

Among the factors explored in this chapter when assessing the suitability of one or another method, besides the ones dealt with before, the following items are also discussed: capacities of insight, the capacity to freely associate, the capacity to establish contact with infantile primitive levels, and the kind of defences used. Pérez-Sánchez reminds us, rightly so in my view, that today it would be difficult to maintain that psychotic patients cannot establish a transference, or that one should not approach psychotic levels in neurotic patients. In other words, it is important to be able to evaluate the capacity of the patient to work through the pain that might accompany insight, or to consider the need to leave out zones that would then lead us to indicate a psychotherapy. This opens up the discussion and the divergences about how each psychoanalyst or psychotherapist deals with the indication, essentially according to psychopathological considerations. While many analysts will analyse psychotic patients, we know, as mentioned above, that most will tend to see them as being suitable for psychotherapy with low frequency sessions, a totally opposite choice from that of many others, such as Rosenfeld, who considered that an analytic setting is possible with psychotic patients. Throughout the book, Pérez-Sánchez cautions the readers by pointing out the importance of blind spots in the interviewers that obscure the possibility of working through the countertransference reaction to the benefit of the therapeutic process.

Last, but not least, besides the resistances of the practitioners themselves that are mentioned above, an important resistance derives from a "lack of conviction in the psychoanalytic method". This contributes to a general confusion about what is the specificity of psychoanalysis when today, in fact, we know that any "talking cure" tends to be called analysis.

An interesting question deals with the possible transformation of psychotherapy into a psychoanalytic process. This raises important issues. Should it be conducted by the same therapist (provided he/she is an analyst). What can the advantages or inconveniences be related to? What does the change of setting imply? The author gives a clinical example with a patient who began a psychotherapy face-to-face, twice a week, and after a year moved to a four sessions a week psychoanlysis on the couch.

In conclusion, the great merit of this book—besides its clinical and theoretical value—consists in the author's rebuttal of simplifications as well as his avoidance of divergence. In a period in which, for many years, we have been talking about the crisis of psychoanalysis, this book has reinforced something that I have believed for a long time: that while our discipline is thriving, it is perhaps psychoanalysts themselves who are in crisis. Without side-stepping convergences and divergences about the specificity of the psychoanalytic method and about how it differs from psychotherapy (a recurrent theme in the IPA), Pérez-Sánchez goes far beyond his declared purpose of simply attempting to deal with the aims, dynamics, and technique of first intake interviews.

Note

1.   Jacqueline Amati Mehler is a training and supervising analyst, past president of the Italian Psychoanalytic Association, and past secretary of the International Psychoanalytic Association.

Introduction

Why should anyone write a book about interview in psychoanalysis and psychotherapy? For years, my professional life has been devoted to both areas. In public healthcare, I have worked as a psychiatrist and, whenever possible, as a psychotherapist, as the director of a therapeutic mental health team, and as a supervisor. In the private sphere, I have worked as a psychoanalyst and psychotherapist, and also as a supervisor. Taking this into account, the experience I have gathered in both areas has led me to the conclusion that the importance conceded to diagnostic interviews is still insufficient, and, as a result, the technique used has not been developed, at least in my opinion, to a satisfactory degree. For this reason I consider it a topic worthy of re-examination.

I think it would be fitting to go back to the criticism made at the beginning of the 1960s by Enid and Michael Balint (1961). These authors point out that neither psychiatrists nor psychoanalysts paid enough attention to the study of the interview. If we stop to study the diagnostic interview, they say, we see that it is complex enough to question the validity of tools commonly used by psychiatrists and psychoanalysts. Therefore, they state, the negligence of specialists in both fields towards interviews must be the consequence of a defensive reaction. They specify two defences that are built up: negation and idealisation. Concerning negation, both specialists behave as if the interview did not present any particular problem. As for idealisation, this is present in psychiatrists because of their confidence in their system of diagnostic evaluation, consisting of the accumulation of data, acting under the principle of "the more the better", and the subsequent pinning on of a diagnostic label; in psychoanalysts, the idealisation springs from their adoption of the Freudian technical recommendation that the analyst should act as a mirror reflecting the patient's image. What is more, in the latter, we should add the fact that the aim of the interviews consists of evaluating the "analysabil-ity" of the patient to take charge of his case or refer him[1] to another analyst. Another reason for idealisation is that when psychoanalysts carry out a fundamentally therapeutic task, they tend to neglect the importance of clinical diagnosis and concentrate their efforts on polishing their therapeutic technique.

Obviously, since the 1960s, a great deal has been written, and some of these texts have rubbed off on to the specialists. Nevertheless, I feel that not enough attention has been paid to their work in the psycho-analytic milieu. For example, in a widely renowned handbook on psychoanalytic technique (Etchegoyen, 1999), they are not mentioned. It is likely that their rich contributions had not been given their full due perhaps because their conclusions came from direct experience with GPs in the development of several kinds of "psychotherapy" (although this term might not be the most accurate one; a better name might be "psychotherapeutic attitudes", or "psychotherapeutic com-ponents in medical practice", so as not to create confusion with psychotherapy carried out by the specialists specifically trained to this end). But if we put aside the field in which these studies were carried out, we see that the teaching contained within them is of great help for psychodynamic interviews in general, including those that set out to evaluate the possible recommendation for psychotherapy or psychoanalysis.

Consequently, despite all the years that have gone by, I think it is possible to state, broadly speaking, but without much margin for error, that the essence of the criticism offered by the British analysts from the Tavistock Clinic is still valid. The specialist from a Mental Health Centre, whether a psychiatrist, a psychologist, or a social worker, is normally more concerned essentially with establishing a diagnosis, but with the accent on their respective psychiatric, psychological, or psychosocial perspective. Such a diagnosis, however, will be considerably determined by two factors: in which category the patient fits according to the labels available, and which treatment corresponds to the chosen label. In the case of the private practice of psychotherapists or psychoanalysts, many of the patients referred to them might have been recommended for some kind of treatment based on psychoanalysis, in which case we are happy simply to find signs to support this recommendation. On occasion, if the patient has been referred by an experienced colleague, hardly any effort is needed to establish the diagnosis; all they need is to get down to work as soon as possible. There is a risk of error in both situations, although of a different nature, as we shall go into later. To briefly summarise, we could say, on the one hand, that the accumulation of data does not always give an accurate picture of the patient, but, on the contrary, might contribute to creating a confusing image, the result of which is a difficult-to-capture profile. On the other hand, the attitude of not conducting a thorough diagnostic interview might incur the risk of setting off on a course of psychotherapy or psychoanalysis involving excessive or unnecessary efforts on behalf of patient and therapist. What is more, the work involved by the therapist in drawing up a diagnosis will allow him to capture fundamental aspects of the patient's personality, which might be confirmed or expanded upon during the process of treatment.

But even if the technique of the psychiatric or medical interview is considered of little use by the psychotherapist or psychoanalyst, this does not justify ignoring it. Not paying sufficient attention to the first interviews with the patient might lead to error, such as recommending psychotherapy or psychoanalysis without sufficient acquaintance with the patient's case beforehand, simply leaving this to develop during treatment. We have to admit that, in our case, this is a very special interview, because it is halfway between the psychiatric interview and the attitude of psychoanalytic listening; on the one hand, it is necessary to gather significant data relating to the patient's personality and symptoms, and, on the other, the therapist needs to adopt a receptive position in an atmosphere conducive to the patient's spontaneity. But neither the psychiatric interview nor the psychoanalytic attitude required for the sessions will be adequate. Therefore, we need another technical tool, one necessarily based on psychoanalysis.

Although excellent contributions have been made to this end, which I will mention later on in this book, now I will take into account only those I consider fundamental. My aim in this work is to try to contribute to a reconsideration of the importance of the psychodynamic interview.

Balint's work with general practitioners not only contributed to the development of a tool to help them do their work better, introducing psychological elements to the patient–doctor relationship, but he probably also stimulated the doctors' interest in considering specific psychotherapeutic and psychoanalytic aids. For instance, the case described by Balint in his work on focal psychotherapy (Balint & Ornstein, 1972) had been referred to him by a GP. That should make us realise the importance of psychotherapeutic recommendations being given not only by psychotherapists, but also by GPs. The same applies to psychoanalysis itself, in which recommendation should not be restricted to psychoanalysts, but should be extended more frequently to psychotherapists. This dynamic is reversed with psychoanalysts who, after an adequate diagnostic interview, have acquired enough elements to choose the best type of help for the patient, which, as should be obvious, is not necessarily psychoanalysis. If experience, with the help of supervisions, is essential to acquiring a solid training for choosing the correct treatment, in this book I set out to provide tools to complement or to delve deeper into that experience.

The book deals essentially with two issues. First, the understanding of the dynamic and technique of the interviews held with patients to evaluate whether they need psychotherapy or psychoanalysis. The second issue deals with what I shall call *psychodynamic indicators*: a series of data which can be observed in what the patient has to say and in the dynamic of the relationship between patient and therapist during the first interviews. The observable data come from three sources: psychopathological, biographical, and those emerging from the interview itself. The indicators are paired according to opposing elements: sane/insane, adult/infantile, pain/pleasure, sincerity/lie, truth/falsity, link/separation and masculine/feminine. With this proposal, I am not attempting to cancel out or substitute other indication criteria already established from a psychodynamic perspective. Rather, I am trying to offer a complement to them.

I should like to draw attention to a curious fact. The recommendations for psychoanalytic psychotherapy and for psychoanalysis are usually dealt with separately in most publications. However, in professional practice, both in psychotherapy and in psychoanalysis, there exists a growing tendency to shade out, or even delete, the dividing line. This is one of the reasons why in this book I deal with psychotherapeutic practices and psychoanalysis together, so that, side by side, what is common and what is different will come to light and help to indicate which approach should be adopted. This is specifically dealt with in Chapter Eight. What is more, the study of interview and psychodynamic indicators as a common field for psychotherapy and psychoanalysis automatically opens up a whole range of psychotherapeutic procedures to be indicated for the patient's needs. In this way, we can avoid an interview with the exclusive aim of establishing the "analysability" of the patient, or, on the other hand, the interview that only contemplates the indication of some kind of psychotherapy, with no consideration of psychoanalysis.

As there is a large amount of clinical material in the book, to preserve the privacy of patients, I have avoided any external reference that could identify them in any way. And when I necessarily refer to certain external circumstances of their lives, I have endeavoured to modify these in order to continue to preserve their anonymity.

While this book was in translation, a new publication has appeared, titled *Initiating Psychoanalysis: Perspectives* (Reith, Lagerlof, Crick, Moller, & Skale, 2012), which includes the topic I am dealing with. This publication forms part of the work carried out by colleagues from the European Psychoanalytic Federation, members of the Working Party on Initiating Psychoanalysis (WPIP), co-ordinated by Bernard Reith. So, while I cannot make any comment about this interesting book, I thought it apt to mention it.

Note

1. Throughout the text I have used "he" or "him" to refer to the patient or professional of either sex for the sake of simplicity and clarity.

CHAPTER ONE

Therapeutic aims and indication in mental health

Outline of a conception of the mind

The attainment of therapeutic aims in mental health presupposes a notion of psychic life that determines how these aims are shaped. For this reason, I consider it necessary, before any clinical proposal, for us to establish a definition of our theoretical points of departure. As the particular model of the mind that I support has already been stated elsewhere, I refer the reader to that quotation for a broader understanding (Pérez-Sánchez, 1996a). For now, I shall simply make a brief allusion to its principal ideas. This model is based on the Freud–Klein–Bion theoretical axis. The fact that, from birth, the individual lives "in relation" to, or within, the context of relationship, implies that the construction of his personality is, in large part, determined by the relational vicissitudes that accompany him throughout his growth (although those pertaining to the early years take on particular relevance), and which, obviously, has its roots in certain specific fundamental biological conditions. For this reason, psychoanalysis has valued the importance of traumatic experience and illness occurring during early stages of life. Today, however, we accord even more value to the kind (or quality) of the continuous relationship that

1

is sustained day after day, during those years, with early parental figures. The result of the confluence and the interaction between these external figures and the individual's lived experience of, and reactions to, them is the construction of certain images, or, more specifically, what we call *internal objects*. Within this interaction, the processes of projection and introjection play a fundamental role. Such processes are sustained by unconscious phantasies; one of the most prominent being that of "projective identification" (as described by Klein, 1946). The development of this concept by post-Kleinian authors—in particular by Bion (1962, 1970)—has given rise to the container–contained model. That which the individual cannot contain must be experienced through the other so that they can metabolise it and return it in a tolerable way. Thus, one learns to contain the pain concomitant to the experiences necessary for growth. There is, furthermore, a constant interaction between the tendency towards splitting and fragmentation of experience ($\rightarrow$Ps) on the one hand, and the tendency towards union, articulation and integration of experience ($\rightarrow$D)[1] on the other. The mind is in continual interplay between Ps and D, which Bion sets out in his Ps$\leftrightarrow$D formula. However, if a change takes place by which growth predominates, from this balance between the Ps$\rightarrow$ and $\rightarrow$D mental states must be inferred a predominance of the latter, or, rather, a sufficient capacity to restore it. A further concept to bear in mind is that of the basic anxieties, which can be summarised into three distinct types: integration (or linking) or depressive and persecutory anxieties, both described by Klein (1935, 1946), and the catastrophic anxieties indicated by Bion (1970), all of which I have discussed elsewhere (Pérez-Sánchez, 2001).

Of equal importance is the above-mentioned concept of "unconscious phantasy", which can be defined as the unconscious level underlying the individual's every mental and behavioural activity, the content of which derives from dramatisations between the component elements of his internal world. Furthermore,

> [Another] basic criterion, for psychoanalysis, is that the recognition of psychic reality should bring with it a certain degree of emotional pain which must be tolerated. This recognition is the starting point for the growth and development of the individual. The inability to tolerate pain leads to forms of defence: the greater the intolerance, the more pronounced and radical the defence. (Pérez-Sánchez, 1996a, p. 34, translated for this edition)

This point seeks to draw a fundamental distinction between degrees of pathology and health in the organisation of the personality; where suffering is linked to a mental organisation which tends towards destructiveness, or, on the contrary, where it is geared towards the constructive.

The purpose of any therapeutic intervention, from a psychoanalytic perspective, consists of promoting psychic or relational change *vs.* the cure. That is to say, the creation or development of a mental space more able to contain the experiences necessary for personal growth, *vs.* the idea of suppressing the symptom, or rather, the pain, without further ado.

I prefer to use the word "change" instead of "cure", because, from a psychodynamic perspective, the cure is a concept that sustains omnipotent fantasies, not only in the patient, but also in the therapist. For this reason, we consciously do not talk of "the cure", but instead use expressions to the effect that the intervention, performed *with* the patient, has effected some change in his relationships and in his internal world. Thus, we speak of "progress", of "improvement", of "growth", and, ultimately, of "psychic change". We would suggest that psychic change takes place when the individual has been able to expand his mental space more adequately to contain his experiences and emotional life, particularly those experiences involving pain. This entails having achieved a greater integration of the distinct aspects of his self and of his objects (or internal images that have formed in him throughout his relational history), along with an acceptance of the need for, at the same time as tolerating autonomy from, the other. This is a never-ending process, and, as such, the therapeutic goal is achieved, to some extent, when the patient discovers or gets to know his mode of relating to his obstacles as well as his potentialities,[2] is willing to continue this task (thereby also discovering the endless nature of it), and is, thus, able to benefit from the resultant satisfaction and mental enrichment.

Psychoanalysis is currently of the view that the patient's route to understanding does not always need to lead back, ultimately, to the vicissitudes of his biography, but depends upon how this becomes manifest "here and now", in the relationship with the therapist, and throughout the course of a long process of continual "here and nows". This is not because of any denial of the patient's history, but precisely because this history is inscribed in the kind of relationship that unfolds in the present, before and with the professional.

It is this psychoanalytical understanding of the patient's mental life which permits its theoretical and technical foundations to be more widely applied to areas other than the analytical session, albeit with the appropriate modifications. These can range from understanding and conducting a diagnostic interview to varying forms of psychoanalytically orientated psychotherapy and psychoanalysis itself.

Therapeutic aims in mental health

The fact that I have begun the book with a chapter on therapeutic aims in mental health, in the generic sense, is owing to my belief that the psychodynamic interview, conducted by a professional in that field of health, is implicitly determined by the aims that professional has in mind at the time of his encounter with the patient. That is to say, I do not position myself as a specialist in psychotherapy and psychoanalysis to whom patients are referred as potential candidates for one of these treatments. My intention is that this book should also be of use to those who, without being specialists, might find themselves in the position of having to assess or rule out an indication for psychological treatment. Sometimes, by excess or by defect, mistakes are made. For example, a psychotic patient or a serious borderline case with fair verbal communication skills and a certain capacity for intellectual understanding might be referred for psychotherapy. This raises unrealistic expectations, as what we then find is that the patient is highly intolerant to the mental pain concomitant to the therapeutic process. Conversely, there are patients with less serious clinical manifestations, which all the same prove disruptive to their lives because of the suffering they cause, but who possess remarkable personal qualities, and for this very reason the option of in-depth psychotherapy or psychoanalysis is dismissed, opting instead perhaps for intermittent or occasional help in the belief that they will be able to overcome their problems on the merits of their own resources. As I stated in the introduction, I am able to make these observations through my dual professional experience in both public and private healthcare. This circumstance has enabled me to make the observation that we often dismiss the option of an indication for psychotherapy or even psychoanalysis in the case of public healthcare, given the limited resources available for this kind of treatment. I believe, however, that healthcare professionals have a duty to establish the right treatment indication for every patient, whatever their background. What to do from there is another matter. Should the patient be told if institutional conditions make such a prescription unfeasible? This raises ethical issues, in the sense of whether patients should be referred to private healthcare, with the patient assuming the costs, or whether we should simply not make such an option available. In any case, failing to put forward the appropriate indication will not resolve any of these issues. My experience has left me with the impression that this has long been a very decisive reality for healthcare professionals, one which prevents them, unconsciously, from making an appropriate assessment in the case of many patients for whom long-term psycho-therapeutic help would have been beneficial. The progressive im-provement seen in the public health service in Spain during the 1980s and 1990s in terms of the recognition of psychotherapy has, unfortu-nately, been somewhat reversed over the past ten to fifteen years. Consequently, I believe that the reluctance to establish an indication for psychotherapy—not to mention for psychoanalysis—on the part of the professionals themselves in the arena of public health might be one of the factors why there are so few indications for psychoanalysis. Another problem could reside in the fact that the indication might not be made correctly. That is to say, even when the treatment that has been advised is the right one, this information has not been passed on appropriately during the evaluative interviews. Hence, also the need to highlight the importance of these interviews, towards which this book also aims to contribute.

In a broad sense, the therapeutic aims in the treatment of mental pathology are diverse, spanning an entire spectrum ranging from clin-ical or symptomatic improvement at one end, to psychic change, which might effectuate some personality modification (relating to the patient's potentialities and obstacles—his pathology—in coping with internal and external reality) at the other. In psychoanalytically orien-tated psychotherapy, one might differentiate between "therapeutic" aims in the strict sense of the word and "analytical" aims, both of which are always present, although to varying degrees. To give a very brief outline, by "therapeutic aims" I mean those aims which seek to achieve symptomatic relief or to mitigate the patient's emotional suffering. By "analytical aims", I mean the aspiration for the patient to attain greater knowledge of his mental life, which can then lead to psychic changes, in the sense of growth. The "analytical" aims presuppose the inclusion of the therapeutic, but in so far as these are not sought directly, but as a consequence derived from achieving the former. So, within the range of the psychoanalytic psychotherapies, the closer we are to the supportive psychotherapies, the greater the predominance of "therapeutic aims" there will be in relation to the analytical, while for psychoanalysis proper, the latter will take centre stage.

Types of therapeutic aim in mental health

Here I shall set out some of the potential therapeutic aims, as outlined in Table 1.1, which might be established as much from the patient's request as from the therapist's proposal.

Symptomatic relief

The patient complains of a specific discomfort linked to situations, circumstances, or concrete aspects of his body or life. That is, he complains of suffering from a set of specific symptoms and requests therapeutic intervention in order to eliminate them. The traditional medical model is able to respond to this type of aim. This conception of therapeutic aims derives from a simplistic approach to the reality of falling ill (and not just psychically ill).

Table 1.1.   Therapeutic aims in mental health.

Symptomatic relief

Symptom-focused treatment

Clarifying external interpersonal conflicts

Clarifying and understanding external relational conflicts and underlying internal conflicts

Partial psychical changes in personality (understanding of internal, relational and transferential conflicts)

Fundamental psychical changes, which might involve changes in personality

---

As a rough outline, we can establish two distinct areas of clinical symptoms: those structured around anxiety and those around depression. Regarding the former, these can manifest as somatic expressions such as attacks of breathlessness, palpitations, sweating, dizziness, and so on. These episodes can occur unexpectedly (for the patient, at least) or can be associated with specific situations. Some of these expressions are rational: the result of facing a difficult situation (an exam, a job interview, or a first date, for example), but are disproportionately severe, at least for the assumed capabilities of the patient, to the extent that he cannot control the emotional impact of the situation and the anxiety spills over. Equally, anxiety might arise when faced with situations that are recognised as anxiety-generating, as they coincide temporally with the beginning of the attack, while the meaning of what has caused it remains unknown to the patient (in the case of phobias to specific situations). In addition, it might be that the anxiety is not linked to any identifiable event or circumstance, but establishes itself within the person in an insidious way, without him knowing why, as is the case with generalised anxiety.

In terms of the pathological states that revolve around the depressive symptomatic constellation, this might also involve clinical symptoms "related" by the patient himself to a (recent) event in his life, such as a separation or significant loss—temporary or permanent— but to which the reaction is so intense that it is beyond the patient's ability to control it. Or there again, it might be a depression that is apparently unrelated to anything as far as the patient is aware. The manifest symptoms might be sadness, despondency, listlessness, lack of strength to cope with routine activities, and so on.

At this level of aim, the therapeutic aspiration consists of eliminating or diminishing the intensity of the symptom. For example, one patient will complain of various symptoms such as neck stiffness or migraine; another will lament his inability to travel by underground train or to take the elevator. It is important to consider the degree of invalidation and suffering that the symptom brings about in the individual's life. The symptoms, as we know, can manifest themselves either within a very small and localised area, as occurs in cases of somatisations confined to a particular organ, or they can affect the personality in a generalised way. The more localised the symptom, the more of a tendency there will be to put forward this type of therapeutic aim as the most suitable. The more diffuse the discomfort, which can be said to be emotional suffering owing to generalised anxiety that is not acute but persistent; or to depression that has become chronic; the more difficult it is to treat. However, as we know, from a psychodynamic perspective, any symptom should be assessed in the context of the personality, as much in order to understand it, as to be able to approximate a prognosis.

Symptom-focused treatment

Here the aim is based upon a consideration of the symptom itself as the problem. The clearest case is that of the phobia, for example, and the aim lies in the manner in which it is confronted and attempts are made to overcome it rationally. Some schools of psychiatry, such as the cognitive and behavioural, often make this the focus of their attention.

From a psychodynamic perspective, we believe that, *for the patient, the symptom acquires the status of an object*, which is generally persecutory, and with which a particular type of relationship must be formed wherever some of the variants of the different relational patterns established by the patient with his primal internal objects are in place. Anxiety or depression is either "controlled" or it "takes control of one"; these are common expressions used by patients, thus anthropomorphising the unpleasant emotion, or, rather, presenting it as if someone were inflicting this on them. In the case of somatisations, where the symptom has a more or less precise physical location (a neck-ache or a headache, for example), the cementing of the relationship as if dealing with a person is clearer to see: "The pain does not leave me alone"; "The pain does what it wants, it comes and goes", and so on. At this level of aim, however, and without a psychodynamic understanding, the therapeutic aspiration would involve drawing on common sense, rationalisation, repetition of behaviour, and force of will in order to overcome the symptom.

Clarifying external interpersonal conflicts

The therapeutic aim in this case links the symptoms with relational problems that are clearly manifest. Such issues might involve a couple with marital problems, for example, or a person who does not get along with his boss, in both cases with the resultant symptomatological accompaniment of anxiety or depression. When the therapeutic aim is confined to the level of manifest problems, without any psycho-dynamic consideration, it suffices to appeal to rational and cognitive arguments to address the problem. This is not a central aim of psycho-analytically orientated psycho-therapy, although this type of clarification might be useful during this kind of therapy, particularly if it is a supportive psychotherapy, or what I call psychodynamically based psychotherapeutic interviews.

Clarifying and understanding relational conflicts and underlying internal conflicts

From this aim on we are now, in fact, entering into the field of the psychoanalytic psychotherapies proper. Here, our endeavour is for the patient to acquire some knowledge of the unconscious conflicts underlying the manifest ones; but the focus is limited to the particular issue or conflict under consideration. Under this umbrella, we can fully include supportive psychotherapy (ST) as well as brief psycho-analytic psychotherapy (BPP), although the latter could be placed as much in this section as in the next, depending on the potentialities and psychopathology of the patient, on the one hand, and the therapist's capabilities, on the other.

Partial psychical changes in personality (understanding of internal, relational, and transferential conflicts)

Here, the aims go beyond the symptoms and our relational and psychodynamic understanding of them, in the sense that changes are sought—though they might be partial—in several aspects of the patient's personality. One of the aims at this level includes under-standing the transference relationship, if only partially. The under-standing of internal conflicts, the patient's internal world, is given prevalence over external conflicts. Brief psychotherapy might belong to this group of aims, as previously mentioned, although they are more suited to long-term psychoanalytic psychotherapy.

Fundamental psychical changes involving changes in personality

In this case, the aims go far beyond symptomatic relief and resolution of external problems or conflicts, and even partially internal conflicts.

To some extent, this presupposes that the above aims are encompassed, although obviously not *per se*, but as a consequence of prioritising this level of aim. This is because priority is determined by the development of self-knowledge—that is, knowledge of one's inner reality—and, consequently, by a better understanding of one's external reality. This must presuppose some modification in the patient's mental organisation: that is, in how his object relationship is organised and the anxieties and defences which accompany it. This level of therapeutic aim might at times occur in psychoanalytic psychotherapy, depending on the patient's psychopathology and the therapist's capabilities. But the most suitable conditions to approach the achievement of this aim are those provided by psychoanalysis proper.

In fact, the change that we are attempting to encourage with the help of psychoanalysis is that which corresponds to what Bion defines as a mentally healthy person; "[one who] is able to gain strength and consolation and the material through which he can achieve mental development through his contact with reality, no matter if this reality is painful or not" (Bion, 1992, p. 192). This implies that to achieve the aims that we have called "analytical", that is to say, to understand what is hindering contact with our internal reality, should comprise symptomatic relief, but does not entail the disappearance of the pain inevitable as a result of contact with reality. That said, it would be inappropriate to pursue analytical aims that do not bring "strength and consolation"—symptomatic relief—at some time or another during the analytic process.

An example: As a first request, a patient asks for couples' counselling as he and his wife are having difficulties (Table 1.1, aim: clarifying interpersonal conflicts). Obviously, the therapist conditions his therapeutic response to the presence of the spouse, but it soon becomes apparent that she has no interest, or she does not see the situation as being troubled enough to require professional help. The patient admits that, in any case, he does need help (Table 1.1, aim: *understanding the internal conflicts underlying the external ones*). He suffers from anxiety and feelings of dissatisfaction in his affective life, resulting in feelings of dejection (Table 1.1, aim: *symptomatic relief*) relating exclusively to his married life to the extent that, were this resolved, he would feel well. Initially, the veiled request was for the professional to intervene in order to "fix" the couple. If the wife did not wish to take part, he wanted help to be provided individually to him, but with that aim. He was made aware of the impossibility of the request, which he understood. It was pointed out to him that, in any case, his personal difficulties would need to be examined in light of how they manifest themselves in his marital relationship. The patient then explained that some time ago he had consulted a urologist because of an impotence problem (Table 1.1, aim: *symptomatic relief* without any other coexisting therapeutic aims, in so far as aspirations were centred upon resolving the issue exclusively linked to the particular symptom, that is, the genital organ demonstrating the impotence). However, the response given to him by that particular specialist (who prescribed anxiolytic and antidepressant medication) did not satisfy him (which implicitly presupposes an unconscious aspiration towards the therapeutic aims of *clarifying external interpersonal conflicts* and *clarifying and understanding external relational conflicts and underlying internal conflicts*, Table 1.1.). At that point he went to a psychotherapist, although with an initial request of couples' counselling. This, of course, masked the true request of dealing with issues of not only sexual but also mental "potency" in his relationships, especially with his partner. He was able to accept this when I pointed this out to him, thus commencing a psychoanalytic psychotherapy at a frequency of two sessions per week.

From the point of view of the feasibility of psychotherapeutic treatment, it is important to establish the existing degree of agreement or divergence between the patient's therapeutic aims, as expressed (consciously and unconsciously) in his request, and those the therapist is able to provide in the light of data obtained from the diagnostic interviews. The simple reason for this is that psychotherapy requires patient collaboration. However, it is likely that, at the beginning of psychotherapy, therapist and patient will only partially share aims (both therapeutic and analytical), but during the course of treatment it is expected that the field of agreement will increasingly overlap.

Factors determining the type of aim attainable

What is it that determines whether one aim or another is sought and achieved? We might include the following factors: the patient, the therapist, the technique attainable, and the "containing therapeutic structure", as outlined in Table 1.2.

Table 1.2.   Factors determining the type of aim attainable.

Therapeutic aims according to the patient

Therapeutic aims according to the therapist:
  (a) depending on the psychological or psychiatric school belonged to
  (b) depending on the therapist's training and experience
  (c) Depending on the therapist's personality

Therapeutic aims according to technique

Therapeutic aims and containing therapeutic structure

Therapeutic aims according to:
  (a) vital reduction of the symptom or psychopathology for which consultation is sought
  (b) expected therapeutic results
  (c) cost of treatment

Therapeutic aims according to the patient

These aims are ascertained by the request made by the patient at the consultation. The patient asks for relief from anxiety, depression, or mental suffering. That said, from a psychoanalytic perspective, we listen to his request beyond that which is explicitly expressed (we shall see this in more detail when we come to consider the *psychodynamic indicators*). In other words, a patient might be asking, on the one hand, that the therapist "extract" from him the troublesome symptoms he is experiencing; but, on the other hand, he might provide data that indicates an interest, a curiosity, and even some need to know what it is that can be causing his current state. These are the patients who, before the consultation, question themselves about their relationships, their mental life, who observe what is happening to them by trying to draw conclusions, and so on. The opposite might also occur; that patients with an apparent desire to know themselves in order to change might, in fact, be hoping that the therapist will take charge of their discomfort.

I assess the request for help made by the patient not only at the beginning of the interview, but also in *how that request evolves* during the interview. In my view, this is its most important aspect, as other authors have also noted (Liberman, 1980, for example). During the course of the diagnostic interviews, through interaction with the therapist, the patient might grasp and be receptive to the attitude of the therapist whose concern is not only his symptoms, but who also takes into account other aspects of his personality.

Therapeutic aims according to the therapist

Here, several possibilities can be distinguished:

- *Depending on the psychological or psychiatric school belonged to.* For example, to mention the most common schools of thought in our area, the biological, the cognitive–behavioural, the systemic, and the psychoanalytic. If the therapist belongs to the first school, it is unlikely his aims will go beyond Table 1.1's *symptomatic relief* and, in part, *symptom-focused treatment*. The cognitive– behavioural school of thought will be concerned with *clarifying external interpersonal conflicts, symptom-focused treatment,* and *symptomatic relief* (Table 1.1) (I believe in that order), and the systemic school with *clarifying and understanding external relational conflicts and underlying internal conflicts, symptom-focused treatment,* and *symptomatic relief.* Within the psychoanalytic school, we might have different options, depending on the type of psycho- therapy: psychoanalytic psychotherapy and psychoanalysis might focus on Table 1.1's *fundamental psychical changes which might involve changes in personality, clarifying and understanding external relational conflicts and underlying internal conflicts, symp- tom-focused treatment,* and *symptomatic relief* (I will elaborate further on the differences in aim and other questions between these two modalities in Chapter Eight). Brief psychoanalytic psychotherapy would tend to focus on *clarifying and understand- ing external relational conflicts and underlying internal conflicts, symptom-focused treatment,* and *symptomatic relief* (Table 1.1), and so on.
- *Depending on the therapist's training and experience.* If we assume that the therapist subscribes to the school of psychoanalytically based psychotherapies, then the aims that might be put forward will depend on the degree of experience the therapist has in these psychotherapies. That is, a therapist with experience solely in psychoanalytic psychotherapy might find it difficult to carry out the aims of brief psychoanalytic psychotherapy. In particular, to carry out an intense treatment, such as that favoured by the

conditions of psychoanalysis, will require the proper experience and training.

- *Depending on the therapist's personality.* This factor is not often considered to be a determining one, since the psychotherapist's training and his own therapeutic experience should adequately equip him to achieve the expected aims in any patient who is a suitable candidate for psychotherapy. However, when this concerns patients with a serious psychopathology, even were they able to meet the conditions to justify the strain of a psychotherapeutic and even a psychoanalytic experience, if the therapist is already treating another patient with a similar pathology, he must assess the burden this will entail and the impact of taking it on.

Another point to consider is whether these aims should be formulated at all. In long-term psychoanalytic psychotherapy and in psychoanalysis, the therapeutic aim is not made explicit, in contrast to what occurs in cognitive therapies or brief psychoanalytic psychotherapies. In any case, I am of the opinion that *in any psychoanalytic psychotherapy there must be an effort made on the part of the therapist to establish a dynamic diagnosis of the patient's fundamental conflicts.* This implicitly involves establishing aims. For example, a patient who has a dependent relationship with his partner, and who, via that relationship, is reactivating a troubled relationship with one or both parental figures, will prompt us to orientate treatment (and I use the word "orientate" in the sense of what a compass needle does, rather than actively directing) towards an understanding of that troubled earlier relationship. In the case of brief psychoanalytic psychotherapy, one of its features is the making explicit of a focus for therapy, which, obviously, will determine the aims to be achieved.

Therapeutic aims according to technique

It is clear that with a psychopharmacological therapeutic intervention alone, we would not seek any of the aims from Table 1.1's *clarifying external interpersonal conflicts* onwards. That said, even within the psychoanalytic psychotherapies, the respective setting for each of them determines the therapeutic potential. For example, a psychoanalyst who has one session a week with a patient is unlikely to achieve the aims of *fundamental psychical changes which might involve changes in personality* (Table 1.1). Furthermore, what is likely to occur if he *acts* (an apt expression in the psychoanalytic sense of the term *acting-out*), seeking to attain these aims, using techniques specific to psycho-analytic treatment proper (i.e., the systematic interpretation of the transference and primitive levels of the mind), is that this will give rise to complications in the patient, with unpredictable side-effects.

I, therefore, believe that the aims of any psychotherapy are also determined by the potentialities of the setting. From a psychoanalytic perspective, a fundamental conception, in accord with Bion (1962), is that the learning that leads to change is that which is realised through *experience*, as we have already said. Consequently, depending upon the intensity of the therapeutic experience, the changes that take place will be more or less fundamental or structural to the personality. The intensity of the experience is determined by the setting and the type of link that is established. The setting that comprises a once-weekly session and for treatment lasting one year, as in the case of the brief psychoanalytic psychotherapy I have been practising, for example, enables *some* experience from which the patient can learn through taking cognisance of what happens to him in his self, in the relation-ships he has with his current surroundings, and in his relationship with the therapist. Obviously, this will be different again from the experience of four or five sessions each week, where the intensity of the link and the potential for deployment of various transferences with the professional are much greater, as well as the potential for the analysis and working through of these transferences.

Therapeutic aims and containing therapeutic structure.

I have dealt in more detail elsewhere with what I call the "containing therapeutic structure" (Pérez-Sánchez, 1996a). Just to recapitulate the central idea, this was conceptualised from the field of public health-care, which, I think, is fairly self-evident. When one works in an insti-tutional environment with the participation of other professionals and with patients who require diverse therapeutic interventions, it would seem necessary to organise this set of elements in the optimum way, so as to provide a context conducive to the realisation of a given ther-apeutic task. It is this set of appropriately articulated people and resources that I call the containing therapeutic structure. To refer more immediately to the field of psychotherapy, the containing structure might be less complex, provided we are not dealing with seriously ill patients. But, at all events, certain elements are still required. This will depend upon whether therapy takes place within the public or private sphere. If within the former, it will be conditional upon the existence or non-existence of a therapeutic team, with its spaces of articulation (referral sessions and clinical sessions), as well as a support structure in the form of supervision for difficult cases and psychotherapies in progress, and so on. Within the latter, the professional might work alone or in a team, and benefit from the help of a supervisor, and so on. In such a way, continuing training through seminars and courses constitutes a component, albeit an indirect one, of the containing structure. In order to contain an emotional psychotherapeutic experience, we need an appropriate container; and the structure of that container will be of greater or lesser complexity depending on the intensity of the pathology, or rather, the psychic pain it generates. Thus, in the psychotherapeutic or psychoanalytic treatment of a psychotic patient, even in the private sphere, in the few cases where treatment is carried out it usually requires co-therapeutic elements, such as a psychiatrist who takes charge of the psychopharmacological treatment or routine care of family members.

Therapeutic aims with regard to the correlation between the reduction of the symptom, expected therapeutic results, and cost of treatment

We might need to evaluate the correlation between these three factors in order to determine the most suitable therapeutic aims: the degree of reduction of the symptoms in the patient's life, the expected therapeutic results, and the emotional and financial cost of treatment. This is a question of technical necessity and, above all, of ethical implications.

- *Vital reduction of the symptom or psychopathology for which consultation is sought.* This refers to the degree of disruption to the patient's life—for him and for those around him—as a result of his psychopathology.
- *Expected therapeutic results.* The therapist's experience could also be taken into account in assessing this factor. Clearly, it is very difficult to predict results accurately enough for this factor to determine the therapeutic aim. However, I think it is valid to

consider it, if treatment has been under way for some time and results have been poor or very scarce in terms of the other two factors. For example, when the symptom is not very restrictive to the patient, as in the case of a particular claustrophobia which prevents him from entering lifts or travelling by underground railway, in a depressive personality structure in whom some resolution has been achieved, and who otherwise has a satisfactory enough love and work life, or, rather, it is in so far as he has learnt to live with these limitations. In such a case we may consider terminating treatment, where the aim had been to resolve the symptom and the conflict tied to the phobia. If the phobic symptom is related to very primitive anxieties, it would be advisable to accept the therapeutic aim achieved; that is, having alleviated the depression, thus helping the patient to understand aspects of his self that are related to it. This, of course, applies to cases where a more intense treatment is not possible.

- *Cost of treatment.* I use the term "cost" in a broad sense, meaning both the mental economics of patient and therapist as well as the material economics, whether in the arena of private or public healthcare.

Notes

1. As we know, this is Bion's spelling, which takes its initials from the paranoid–schizoid position (Ps) and the depressive position (D), as described by Klein in 1935 and 1946, respectively.
2. Translator's note: I have used the term "potentialities" in the sense of the term used by Balint and Balint (1961), to refer to the range of the patient's strengths, capacities, and capabilities.

CHAPTER TWO

Interview technique and dynamic

The interview dynamic

W ithin the psychoanalytic field, the interview has been used adjectivally in various ways, depending on the author or professional milieu in which it was conceptualised. I have collected together some of these expressions here: the *psychiatric interview* (Balint & Balint, 1961; Sullivan, 1954), in texts aimed at professionals in psychiatry and general practice; the *psychological interview* (Bleger, 1971), to highlight the psychological dimension of the professional encounter between two people; the *psychoanalytic interview*, used to refer to the interview conducted for the purpose of formulating an indication for psychoanalytic treatment (Etchegoyen, 1999), or otherwise to indicate that it is an interview inspired by psychoanalytic theory but the aim of which is to establish a structural diagnosis for the patient (Aguilar, Oliva, & Marzani, 1998). In another sense, Enid and Michael Balint speak of the interview according to however it is conducted by the medical practitioner, psychiatrist, or psychoanalyst (Balint & Balint, 1961). The term *diagnostic* or *evaluative interview* is also used for the indication for psychoanalytic psychotherapy or psychoanalysis (Liberman, 1980); or the term *psychoanalytically based diagnostic interview*, in the field of child therapy (Mitjavila, 1991; Torras de Béa, 1991), which deals with the interview as a preliminary phase to the beginning of psychoanalytic psychotherapy. Here, I shall predominantly use the expression *psychodynamic interview*, although I shall also use the adjectives *diagnostic* or *evaluative*. I have chosen this designation mindful of the fact that it might serve as a treatment tool not only for use by the psychoanalyst, but by any professional in the field of psychology or psychotherapy, thus creating more opportunities for therapeutic indication, so as to ensure that the indication for psychoanalysis is not exclusive to the psychoanalyst, or that of psychotherapy to the psychotherapist. It is another matter entirely whether the interviewer considers he has the tools, the training, and the availability required to carry out the treatment indicated, and, if not, whether he will refer the patient to another professional.

In this chapter we will attempt to reach an understanding of the "psychology" of the interview (Bleger, 1971) or the analysis of it; that is to say, the dynamic that occurs when one person seeks the help of another. To do this we must examine each of the participants of the relationship, and then the relationship itself that is established between the two. There are some elements that are common to both and others that differentiate them. What is common, and fundamental, to both is the fact that this is a new experience and, consequently, a source of anxiety. Sullivan, in his now classic work, *The Psychiatric Interview* (1954), emphasises the importance of assessing anxiety in both interviewee and psychiatrist, given that this forms part of the relationship and therefore must also be an object of study. In addition to anxiety, the participants share a common task: that of attempting to give a significant "form" to the request that one of them—the patient—is making, that is to say, to arrive at a diagnosis. But each person, in turn, brings particular characteristics to the relationship that are unique to them, as well as a psychopathology in the patient's case, and certain sufficient mental conditions in the therapist's case, which presupposes that his very psychopathology will be sufficiently contained so as not interfere too much in his function.

Therefore, although we consider patient and therapist to be a couple that forms in order to work together, the result of this task depends upon the specific and differentiated qualities of each of the participants. In this sense, I agree with Etchegoyen in that the therapy's potential does not depend, strictly speaking, on the therapeutic couple as, "if other variables are constant, the best analyst [or thera-pist] always forms the best couple" (Etchegoyen, 1999, p. 56); or in other words, a difficult patient will be difficult with any professional. Obviously, the greater experience, technical ability and personal skills a professional has, the more manageable the relationship will be during the interview, even to the extent of making psychotherapeutic or psychoanalytic treatment viable. But it is not the relationship with the professional which gives rise to the challenges and obstacles, but the patient's psychopathology. Taking this aspect into account, we shall now consider each of the members of this relationship in the interview situation. In the following chapters we shall assess other aspects of the personality and psychopathology of the interviewee.

The interviewee (in relation to the interviewer):
anxieties, defences and expectations

When a person decides to consult a mental health professional, of his own volition or upon the advice of someone else, to a greater or lesser extent a certain configuration of what he wishes, hopes, or fears to find in the interview will inevitably arise in his mind. The predomi-nant type of object relation, or, rather, the most significant modalities employed to relate to his objects, will activate an entire series of phan-tasies, anxieties, and defences relating to this encounter, even from the very first telephone call. A person who seeks consultation often does so for very diffuse reasons. Let us assume, as a primary issue, that he is doing so because there is emotional suffering that he wishes to erad-icate. Obviously, expectations will vary if the request made by the patient is specifically for psychotherapy or psychoanalysis having been referred by another professional, or otherwise if he is familiar with such help through his socio-familiar background, or, if, on the other hand, the patient is seeking consultation in order to relieve anxi-ety or to get help for the depression he is suffering from, for example.

At all events, this involves a first encounter with a person hitherto unknown to him. This reality comprises sufficient elements to estab-lish a type of relationship in which the components of suspicion—the paranoid components—have a substantial presence. One assumes that this fact is slightly softened by the patient deciding to go to a particu-lar professional based on information provided to him by people he trusts. But while this has enabled him to take the step of making the request, it is inevitably he alone who will have to confirm the capabilities and the goodness of the professional, on the basis of his own experience of the interview, in order to mitigate these anxieties. At the other extreme, to adopt the position of harbouring blind faith in the professional because the patient places complete trust in the person who referred him is to shield contact with the immediate reality afforded by his own personal experience of the therapist. This would be a defensive means of avoiding the novelty of the encounter and the corresponding paranoid anxieties.

As I was saying, during this first encounter the patient will deploy some of the predominant forms of object relation in his mental organisation. Note that it is not always the first presentation that is the conclusive one, neither does it even always carry the most weight; hence, the importance of not rushing to establish a psychodynamic diagnosis in the very first interview. As we shall see, it is important to wait for a second and perhaps a third interview, if necessary, in order to have a somewhat more complete idea of the patient. Yet, the putting into action of a particular object relationship is supported and stimulated, in part, by the attitude adopted by the professional. Faced with a professional with a rather more assertive attitude, a patient who tends to be inhibited towards authority figures will respond more timidly and fearfully, while, faced with a therapist with characteristics that could be described as "maternal object", the same patient will be more comfortable, with more chance of expressing himself.

The phantasies and defences engendered by that first encounter with the professional can be extremely varied, depending, and I iterate, on the type of object relationship that is predominant at that moment. At first, the patient operates on an adult level of relationship, with realistic expectations of the professional seeing him in order to help him with his discomfort. But, at the same time, there is another level underlying this one, an infantile and even primitive level, with unconscious phantasies such as thinking that the professional will cure him in such a radical way that his life will change completely (omnipotent phantasies, by projecting such a huge healing ability on to the professional). Or, conversely, the fantasy that his discomfort is so great or difficult to understand that he does not expect any professional to be able to resolve it (self-omnipotent phantasies, by projecting impotence into the professional).

The interviewer (in relation to the interviewee):
anxieties, defences, and expectations

The psychodynamic interview—especially if the prospect exists of referring or establishing the indication for psychoanalytically based psychological help—presupposes a particular aptitude in the interviewer, which is different to that required in other interviews, including the psychiatric interview *sensu stricto*. Specifically, we are trying to gather a series of data that we consider to be rooted in the individual's unconscious. In order to gather this information, the therapist must demonstrate an inherent receptivity and ability not learnt in any textbook, which involves being open to the contact between his unconscious and that of the patient. Furthermore, depending on the place where the encounter takes place, the information the professional possesses beforehand will vary. So, in the context of a public health institution, the prior determining factors will be multiple. If we are dealing with a first visit after discharge from psychiatric hospitalisation, even when we have no prior knowledge of any possible psychiatric reports, this is very likely to determine the professional's expectations in terms of dealing with a serious and most probably psychotic patient. Very different will the expectation be in the case of an appointment made at the professional's private consulting room to see a patient referred with an "indication" for psychoanalysis. The external data from each of these extreme example cases speaks eloquently enough for the therapist's expectations to approximate the reality. However, despite such external realities, only confirmation by the professional himself through the diagnostic experience with the patient will enable him to have his almost final word, if not the final one. And this is not because we would, therefore, modify our initial expectations, in terms of making an indication for psychoanalysis for the patient recently discharged from hospital, and sending the patient referred by the colleague to a psychiatrist (although, incidentally, it would not be the first time this had happened, in both cases). But the pertinence of the examples serves to clear the professional's mind, to approximate the well-known Bionian recommendation, "without memory or desire" (Bion, 1970). Only in such a way can we come close to the real possibilities for help for each of the patients mentioned. Even though the psychotic patient will probably not impel us to give an indication for psychoanalysis, he might allow us to observe his potentialities which warrant an indication for some other form of psychoanalytically based psychotherapeutic help. While for the second patient—the one referred to us by the colleague—it might be that psychoanalysis is not needed or is not feasible, but that some form of psychoanalytic psychotherapy is.

For that reason, the therapist's aptitude, in "separating" as far as possible the determinants of external reality, is imperative in order to be receptive to the patient's projections, through which he will transmit aspects of his unconscious mental life to us. Yet, at the same time, the therapist is always attentive, using his cognitive functions to think, to discriminate between the data provided, to register it, and, when appropriate, to take the appropriate line of investigation, and so on. This type of receptivity should also enable him to gather some of the unspoken data, since these correspond to primitive levels that cannot be put into words, at least not at that moment. Together with this receptivity, certain intuitive skills are also required.

Each patient is unique. This truism, which should be kept in mind in general practice, acquires particular relevance, so to speak, in the field of mental health. Each new patient means a new situation for the professional, in which his knowledge, his capacity to tolerate the patient's projections and tendencies towards omnipotent reactions will be put to the test.

During the course of the interview, the therapist will oscillate with regard to the degree and quality of anxiety that is mobilised. At first, when the professional shakes the hand of a patient whom he is seeing for the first time, he is likely to show some confidence and poise in his attitude. He is "on his own turf", in his own consulting room, under ideal interview conditions, planned over some time; he has accumulated a certain degree of clinical experience, and so on. Therefore, he has good reason to feel happy to introduce himself to the patient as the professional who is able to offer him help for the problem he is "bringing".

But once they sit down, if we are in a psychodynamic interview, that is to say, one that we do not seek to lead or to "protocolise", but instead offer ourselves receptively to listen to what the person sitting before us has brought to us, then things start to become otherwise. "Tell me, what prompted you to make this consultation?" or "What's been happening?" or any other question of this kind can serve to break an initial silence, spoken in a tone and accompanied by an attitude that are as receptive as possible to help counter the patient's fears. These small displays can be of some help in overcoming the enormous obstacles that intervene in this new situation. We rely on the patient's collaboration, starting with what has prompted him to come and the emotional suffering he is experiencing, to overcome these initial obstacles so he ends up "jumping in the deep end". It is true that the patient I am describing is one out of many others whose reaction might be different. Obviously, and I stress, there are as many different reactions as there are patients. For example, take the patient who no sooner than sitting down will start talking, scarcely even waiting for a gesture from the therapist. To evaluate the significance of this behaviour we might have to wait until the end of the interview, and even the next. Then we will be able to assess whether we are dealing with a person with little ability to contain the slightest anxiety, or it might be that the situation he is experiencing is extremely difficult, or he finds himself in a state of confusion with the therapist, to the extent that it is as if there were no interlocutor at all, but that he is simply part of the patient himself.

In any case, during the first quarter of the interview, when the patient has been able to explain what brought him to seek consultation, the therapist begins to reconstruct in his mind a certain type of person. I say *re*construct, because inevitably, as I have said previously, from the time of the initial telephone consultation up until the point where the therapist has seen and heard how the patient presents himself once in the consulting room, he has been forming a picture of the patient, as hazy as it might have been. Now, when he listens to the account of the patient's ailments and their accompanying circumstances, that image is likely to be corrected. But those early pieces of information provided by the patient are often inadequate, or in any case, as occasionally happens, even though the data speaks eloquently about his personality profile, it is possible that it does not yet make enough impact on the therapist to enable him to register the information cognitively and give it meaning. And so, at that moment, the professional is faced with a person who has explained some of the things that concern him, but of which the therapist does not possess sufficient elements to reach an understanding of that person's mental functioning, much less to give an answer or a comment which might be significant. What to do, then? Quite simply, we must tolerate the anxiety that this generates and continue with the interview. This might be a moment—and there could be many of this kind throughout the course of the interview—in which the type of intervention that the therapist makes can determine the interview, in the sense that it might help to advance the exploration of something that has been mentioned, or raise new questions. Or, on the contrary, the therapist might make a comment that proves defensive in the sense of moving both patient and therapist away from new "significant" pieces of information. Too long a silence, if the patient stops talking and does not know how to proceed, can generate excessive anxiety that blocks communication. In contrast, a hasty intervention on the part of the therapist can inhibit the patient's contact with aspects of his story, his account, which, although anxiety-generating, need to be verbalised.

Thus, the therapist's basic anxiety lies in his concern for knowing about the patient and his personality from the information he provides, regardless of theoretical prejudices or the image previously established from the limited information he was able to glean from him before the interview. As we have seen, this information might come from a telephone conversation, or from the background information supplied by the professional making the referral. Or, if being seen for the first time, it might also come from what the patient's external image suggests: the way he dresses, his manners, his way of greeting, of talking, and so on. In however small a way, all of this informs us enough to stimulate a certain image of the patient within us, which, during the course of the interviews, will need to be corrected or readjusted to a greater or lesser extent, as I have stressed.

Faced with that anxiety, the therapist might have the tendency to evacuate it, or to get rid of it by deploying various forms of defence: from claiming that he already knows the patient's problem, when he has barely heard the beginning of his story, responding with precise indications, which would be precipitous, to introducing a large number of questions to guide the interview, whereby the patient has little chance to speak freely. In both cases, the therapist will have tried to "fit" the patient into the image that has been moulded for him. The interviewer's defensive reactions might take the form of any of the known psychic defences. Bleger (1971) describes some of the most frequent, such as the phobic attitude; the desire to go fast and avoid stopping at questions which might be thorny, in themselves or by their uncertainty; or, conversely, the defence might have an obsessive character, by stopping at as many of the details as possible, which slows down and hinders the spontaneous progress of the interview.

Dynamics of the relationship (transference and countertransference)

Broadly speaking, we could say that between patient and therapist a relationship is established which is determined, essentially, by the coexistence of two levels of communication and experience: an adult level and an infantile level. Although both are present in both participants of the encounter, it is assumed that the professional will have sufficient personal maturity and technical preparation to ensure that the adult level predominates over the infantile. Similarly, in the patient, even when the latter is more evident, even markedly so, we rely upon the adult part of his personality, which we will need to be able to detect, even in seriously ill patients, for collaboration to be possible. Although both levels are always intertwined, for greater expository clarity I shall describe them separately.

Although I refer to the interviewee and interviewer separately, in order to focus attention on one or other of the participants, I have inevitably done this taking into account the relationship between the two. Now, turning to the relationship, something similar happens, but in reverse: we speak of the relationship, but we do so from the perspective of one or other of the participants.

We might distinguish an adult level of communication in which there is an exchange between the contributions of the interviewee and the interviewer. This refers, first, to the collaboration volunteered by the patient in discussing the conscious motive for his request. And, on the part of the professional, it includes his interventions during the course of the interview in order to enable its progress and, ultimately, the therapy he is prepared to indicate. In terms of the therapist, the content of this section ties in with the *aims of the interview*, a theme that we shall develop in Chapter Three.

Here we shall deal with the latent levels of communication in the relationship between patient and therapist. Of these levels, we are concerned with observing the infantile and most primitive in the mind of the patient (the transference relationship), but, in the same way, those latent levels in the therapist that are activated by what the patient communicates (the countertransference relationship).

Primitive level of communication

It is likely that the first thing that the person making the consultation will show to us is his physical form, his bearing, that is to say, his bodily ego, and with it, something of the way in which he treats it: the clothing he chooses to wear; the care, or otherwise, he takes in wearing it. At the same time, the patient displays an attitude: a pose, certain gestures, facial expressions, the behaviour of his entire body in general. As this presentation occurs within minutes, the therapist will not have had time to notice every single one of these details, but will simply have captured an overall perception of that physical figure, which provokes an initial response to the implicit question that existed, more or less consciously, somewhere in his mind: "What is this person like? To what extent will he match up to the rough image I have sketched of him?" Of course, this perceptive and sensory encounter will inevitably have some impact on the therapist, in his task of fleetingly contrasting these images: between the phantasised and the real, embodied and present. Consequently, this will awaken an emotional reaction in him which could be favourable or unfavourable (apparently), indifferent, or one of rejection. Then, the patient speaks to us. And he uses a language that is unique to him: rich or poor, accurate or vague, concise or long-winded, and so on. He will use the particular dialect reflecting his social and familial status and the singularity of his own personal characteristics.

Together with his verbal manifestations, we "listen to" the *para-verbal* components that accompany them: his timbre of voice, the cadence, the tone of his words, the musicality of his phrases and of his entire speech as a whole. We also observe the *non-verbal* expressions, in addition to the bodily expressions we have already noted; those accompanying the patient's verbal account, to emphasise what he says at certain moments or, in contrast, the absence of physical accompaniment, as if the person speaking were someone alien to the body sustaining that voice. In this way, the silences interspersed between the narrations are expressive: the moment at which they occur, their duration, whether they are reflective or are indicative of a blockage caused by excessive anxiety.

All of this data is presented or "offered" to us (to use Balint's expression, referring to the symptoms exhibited by the patient to his doctor) on a secondary plane, or background, of communication. The primary plane, or foreground, is taken up by the manifest verbal recounting carried out by the patient in order to explain, for example, why he is asking for help or the suffering that has prompted him to make the consultation. But behind this communication, the data transmitted by that form of expression which escapes the verbal come flooding out, many of which surface simultaneously. All of this makes it difficult to record and even more difficult to accurately recall every detail. Neither do we need to do so. What concerns us is to be receptive, in the sense we have conveyed, so that these signs can reach us and help us to form an image of the patient.

Why is that communication so important? Precisely because, from a psychoanalytic perspective, this is one of the routes by which the unconscious is externalised. This is the case in as much as these manifestations are occurring within a given relationship, that is to say, one that is directed towards the professional. And this is one of the qualities of the communications occurring in the interview: that they are determined, to some extent—as we have already qualified—by the *person* towards whom they are directed. Yet, from this perspective, that *person*, for the patient, is not just the professional with a name and a few specific attributes, about whom, at that moment, the patient knows nothing, or at best has gleaned some scant information. That *person*, above all during this first contact, is essentially an object of projection, towards whom is transferred an entire series of attributes and defects belonging to the nature of the patient's own internal objects. What is more, he becomes the object of the projected attributes and shortcomings of the patient's very *self*.

Clearly we are referring to that phenomenon, which exists in every relationship and which was discovered by psychoanalysis, that we call *transference*. But regardless of the contents thereof, to which we shall also turn our attention later on, what we wish to emphasise here is that this is a particular form of communication that transcends words, which will reinforce or contradict them. It is a form of communication through which the patient attempts to convey certain aspects, emotions, or states of his mental life in a way that would not suffice with words alone for the interlocutor to grasp their meaning at their deepest dimension. I am now referring, as the reader might have gathered, to another significant phenomenon that I mentioned in the previous chapter: *projective identification*, as described by Klein (1946), but later expanded and broadened by other analysts, in particular Bion (1962). The unique feature of this form of communication is that it enables the recipient to experience "first hand" what the patient is experiencing, which, therefore, goes beyond mere cognitive understanding.

As we know today, especially since Bion's aforementioned work, *Learning from Experience*, this type of communication takes its model from that which is established between infant and mother before verbal language has been developed, and yet the existence of some form of communication is so vital, since nothing less than the very life of the infant is at stake; if the baby cannot make itself understood in relation to its most basic needs, how would these needs be met?

As I mentioned previously, this type of communication occurs in the background in a subtle way, often displaying several of its manifestations at once. It is clear, then, that as much as we try to be attentive to perceive every one of these, it simply would not be possible. The receptor organs of sensory perception are not sufficient to gather such information. Consequently, what is needed is some other type of receptor apparatus in the person who is listening; an apparatus that, without sacrificing the information provided by the sensory organs, can unite them, thereby giving them a "common sense". If such communication originates in the patient from his unconscious levels and emerges in a near-direct way, it must be captured on a similarly unconscious level, but now in the therapist. However, in so far as such phenomena have only been able to be communicated by means of the unconscious level, it is clear that we are dealing with matters that have not sufficiently reached consciousness, have not been verbalised, and, as such, neither can they, in the first instance, be grasped on a cognitive level by the therapist. The only possible way for the therapist to receive them, and I stress this, is "unconsciously". The emotional state that is created along with this is what we call *countertransference*. But, precisely because they involve unelaborated or unprocessed mental elements, they often create some kind of "mental turbulence" in the mind of the therapist who receives and experiences them. In my opinion, this expression, used by Bion (1977a), is very appropriate, since we are dealing with emotions or partial mental states that, with their characteristics of the primitive, the unprocessed, and so on, represent a dissonance in terms of one's very own mental organisation.

However, the fact that an individual should need to produce this unconscious level of communication that we call projective identification, to the point of using the most diverse ways and means to make its intensity patently clear, does not mean that it always reaches its target, that is to say, the interlocutor's unconscious. And this is another problem, exemplified very well by Bion himself in reference to mothers who cannot tolerate projective identifications in relation to their infants, which brings about a disruption in their communication (Bion, 1959). We assume that the professional, owing to his personal psychotherapeutic or psychoanalytic experience and theoretical training, will be well able to avoid rejecting the patient's projective identifications, but given how arduous this task is, he does not always achieve it. The question lies in being able to recognise them, if such an attitude is repeated. The therapist's mental state faced with this type of communication, to continue the analogy of Bion's mother–infant relationship, is comparable to that shown by the mother who is attentive to the needs of her infant: a state that is not only cognitive and sensory, but, on the basis of these, opens up a certain receptivity and capacity for intuition which, in turn, enable a greater degree of precision in relation to the communications of the infant. As we know, to give a name to this state that is similar to dreaming, Bion uses the French expression *reverie*, which seems more accurate.

Adult level of communication

Both components of the encounter, patient and therapist, bring to the interview a series of reflections, ideas, and thoughts that they try to put into words in order to make them intelligible to the interlocutor, with the aim of making communication viable. The patient sets out that of which he is conscious, his suffering, symptoms, a particular account of his life story, and his version of himself and others, and is at pains to make this comprehensible to the therapist. The degree of patient collaboration, when placing his adult self in the service of the interview, will depend on a number of factors, as we shall see in our discussion of the *indicators*.

The therapist, in turn, brings knowledge and experience, which are not particularly helpful at first, as they must be measured against the specific and singular experience of his relationship with this particular patient. He relies on certain general guidelines concerning the aims of the interview, which I shall address in Chapter Three. He makes a note of certain suggestions to help the patient specify or clarify certain questions. Finally, he proposes the appropriate type of therapeutic indication to the patient, giving reasons for his decision.

Obviously, that adult level of communication is essential in order to accept the conditions in which the interview takes place. In the case of severely ill patients, the collaboration of relatives or significant others may be required to take on the role of the auxiliary ego.

Anxiety as prime mover in the interview

We have already mentioned the fact that every interview is a source of anxiety, as much for the patient as for the interviewer, and that defences will inevitably be raised in an attempt to mitigate this anxiety. It is to be hoped that the defensive phantasies created, in both participants, are not so powerful as to eliminate any trace of anxiety. If this were the case, we would find we had a devitalised, poor, and flat relationship, unable to generate motivation enough to make the efforts necessary to enable the interview to progress, let alone to set out some kind of future therapeutic task.

As we have also mentioned, the interview is a new experience for both the interviewee and the interviewer, and any new situation, finding ourselves before a person we are consulting for the first time, awakens paranoid anxieties. Let us explore this in a little more detail. What is it that is feared? Why should the therapist, from whom in principle help is received, however unknown he is to the patient, be at the same time someone to be feared—albeit unconsciously? Arguably, because the patient projects into him the undesirable parts of himself, be they persecutory internal objects or aspects of the patient's own self that he would rather did not belong to him. And yet, precisely in so far as these are unconscious processes, they are, to a greater or lesser extent, unknown. I think Bion's reflection (1977b) could be helpful to us, when he states that the total personality that we see of the patient has at some time, consciously or unconsciously, opted to choose a particular view or vertex from which to see the view, in such a way that is acceptable to it. This involves the "inhibition of the capacity to see the views that one does not want to see" (Bion, 1977b, p. 52). He adds that the psychotic patient might be anxious to suppress, be blind to, or unaware of, what the sane person is able to see, which also forms part of himself. Thus, Bion is able to state that:

> . . . the character is psychosis minus neurosis, or psychosis minus sanity or sanity (rationality) minus neurosis or minus psychosis. The important thing is not that a patient is a borderline psychotic, or a psychotic, or a neurotic, but that he is a total character *minus* . . . (1977b, p. 52)

For the professional, this then raises the question of *minus what?* is this patient. What is he lacking in himself that he is unable to recognise? Bion goes on to point out that it is in the course of transit, in changing from what the patient considers himself to be—from his particular vertex—to what he can become, or, rather, recognise, that there is a moment of vulnerability. It seems evident that from being a character *minus* certain aspects to becoming another in which the *minus* is less, as we now include those unwanted aspects of ourselves, might be a source of considerable anxiety. Hence, in my opinion, the interview constitutes one of such moments of vulnerability for the patient, as he is presenting himself before a professional whose therapeutic intervention to alleviate his suffering must inevitably include some kind of modification to the patient's personality. I think this might help us to understand how extremely delicate a situation the first interview is for the patient making the consultation.

But we must, likewise, consider the position of the therapist. Except that, initially, there is less at stake for him, and, furthermore, he has more tools and resources at his disposal and is "on his own turf"—which, on the other hand, could become an obstacle, as we have seen, if he utilises this in a defensive way. I believe that the professional's vulnerable point can be found in the risk that their ability as such could be called into question. Any new interview with a new patient constitutes a kind of evaluation or test that will validate or invalidate the interviewer's professional ability.

Interview technique

The interview setting

From the point of view of the container–contained model described in Chapter One, any professional activity demands certain working conditions that constitute the container within which the relationship will be developed. It is a good idea to inform the patient of such conditions. First, of the *aim of the interview*: to obtain the necessary data about the emotional or relationship difficulties which prompted him to make the consultation, in order to establish the appropriate type of help. If this point is not made clear, it might be that some patients will tend to establish a fusional relationship from the outset, as if treatment had already started, which can then give rise to frustration if it is not

considered suitable to begin psychotherapy with the same professional who saw him at interview. For this reason, it would seem
appropriate to clearly differentiate a diagnostic stage, with the
required interviews, from the beginning of the therapeutic process
proper. The approximate duration period I usually use for interviews
is between forty-five minutes and one hour, not exceeding one hour
and a quarter; exceptionally, one hour and a half. As for the number
of interviews required to establish the diagnosis and treatment indication, this could vary, depending on the patient and the experience
of the therapist. It is my opinion that two or three interviews are
usually sufficient to gain this knowledge, although in some cases it
might be necessary to hold one or two further interviews. Finally, it is
part of the professional's duty of care to express an opinion on the
type of help he considers to be the most suitable and to give reasons
justifying his decision.

I assess the type of relationship that the patient establishes with the
setting from the very first interview, as an important piece of information to take into account. The patient's punctuality or lateness
regarding the agreed time; his concern for the end of the session or,
conversely, his being pressured by it, thus providing large quantities
of material in order to delay the end of the interview; the way the
patient sits: either on the edge of the chair or completely "installed"
in it; stiffly or with complete nonchalance, and so on. Similarly, any
observation or verbalisation made about the consulting room or the
therapist is significant, as well as the patient's reaction to the therapist's proposal to continue the next interviews as necessary: whether
he accepts obediently or co-operatively, or if he immediately objects,
and so on. Clearly, the physical arrangement of the room during an
interview for diagnostic purposes should be *face to face*, even when the
patient makes a request for psychoanalysis.

Some comment should also be made on forms of address.[1] While
contemporary social relationships tend to generalise familiarity, as an
expression of a stance in favour of the democratisation of relationships
and equality among people, I think that this deserves some consideration when it comes to the psychodynamic interview. One patient,
during his first telephone call to arrange an interview with me, tried to
establish a climate of apparent cordiality by using the informal form
tú, as if we knew one another. Apparently, he considered that he had
the right to do so by having obtained my number from one of my

colleagues, who in turn was an acquaintance of his. During the tele-phone conversation, I kept using the formal *usted*, without, of course, getting into any discussion of his form of address towards me. Once in the interview, I continued to address him formally, as *usted*, and, with-out making any comment, the patient started to use this form also. In the third interview, he asked me about it, saying something to the effect of what was happening with the *usted* and the *tú*, as if it were of the utmost importance. I gave him an explanation. I did not restrict myself to telling him that that was the way I worked, as if it were a matter of rules or simply the therapist's personal habit. Although true, this would have been an inadequate response from a technical point of view. I explained that it might appear that informal address (address-ing each other as *tú*) creates a climate of greater trust, closeness, and familiarity, but, in reality, this was not befitting of the relationship or the task we were setting out to achieve. For, although it was to be hoped that we would gradually acquire that mutual trust, at that time he did not know me, or I him. Furthermore, and most importantly, the formal *usted* enables a climate of a certain distance to be established, which is necessary in order to address issues that neither I nor he knew much about, which was the reason he was seeking help. These were, therefore, questions relating to him that we should treat "with respect", each from his respective position.

The explanation in itself, made in a perfectly ordinary way, demonstrates that the formal address (*usted*) does not seek to establish a social and hierarchical distance, but the professional distance required to carry out this therapy. At the same time, it implicitly determines the existence of an asymmetry of function. The patient's response, in the case above, was to understand what was said to him, without trying to defend himself against it with rationalisations.

Types of interview according to aim

The diagnostic interview

The purpose of the diagnostic interview lies in gaining sufficient knowledge of the patient to establish a "diagnosis" of the problem for which he is seeking consultation, as well as of his personality. Although, rather than use the term *diagnosis*, we should say some *knowledge* of the patient's psychopathology and personality. At the same time, if the professional who conducts the interview is available to take on the potential psychological treatment that might be indicated, the interview will fulfil the implicit aim of initiating a relationship with the prospect of continuity. If this is not the case, the patient should be informed promptly of any possible referral. This factor can determine the interview for each of the participants. The patient, driven by anxiety and the need to find a relationship offering him containment, will begin the interview as if treatment had already begun. The therapist, in turn, can also slip into that relationship, forgetting the fundamental aim of the interview and, as such, neglecting the technical command necessary. For example, he might avoid investigating certain pieces of information, which are as yet unknown but essential in order to establish the relevant diagnosis and indication, opting instead to delve disproportionately into only a few of the areas that have emerged.

The guidance and referral interview

In this interview it is known from the outset, both on the part of the professional and the patient, that the professional conducting the interview will not be able to take on any potential treatment required, and that its purpose is evaluative with a view to referral to another professional. Although this is a difficult interview, given that its transitory nature hinders the emotional involvement and trust required to provide the necessary information in order to establish the diagnosis and indication, it is, however, hoped that sufficient linking takes place to achieve this end. To this is added the further problem of making the referral to one particular professional as opposed to another. The argument for presenting the customary list of professionals to the patient is one that simply does not seem to hold water. Based on what criteria does the patient choose? Based on gender? On how nice or otherwise their names sound? And why give several names? The advantages are not clear. Instead, I can only see the disadvantages, in accord with Etchegoyen (1999). Once again, under the pretext of giving greater freedom to the patient, he is subjected to a situation that, in fact, makes things more difficult for him and that stimulates omnipotent fantasies, since whether to choose one and reject others is placed in his hands. This has occasionally led to some patients secretly carrying out several interviews with different therapists, in order to then choose between them. In any case, if the interview, although transitory, has enabled the professional to clarify the right type of therapeutic indication for the patient, then the question arises of how to convey this conclusion to the patient. It is not an easy task, and quite often the manner of dealing with it has served to strengthen the patient's resistances, resulting in the referral being aborted. For example, if a professional makes an indication for psychoanalysis but he himself is not convinced of the benefits of it, it is clear that, although the words utilised formally communicate the idea that "you need psychoanalysis", they will have been contaminated by certain countertransferential objections. Conversely, an excessively warm or enthusiastic recommendation might be perceived by the patient as an imposition or as overwhelming pressure, which will provoke a flight reaction, at least momentarily.

The therapeutic interview

Any diagnostic interview that fulfils its function will involve therapeutic factors, a matter upon which several authors agree. Given the breadth that I have afforded the subject, I shall discuss this separately in Chapter Four.

Types of interview according to technique

Free interview

In this type of interview, it is hoped the patient's attitude will be one of "free association", although guided by the therapist. I do not think we can, strictly speaking, use the term "free association" in the same way as that which takes place in the analytical session. Nevertheless, the type of communication we expect from the patient is not guided by a set of questions, but by his own needs. In that respect, a certain amount of free association is already determined by the suffering or discomfort that has motivated the consultation. For the therapist's part, his attitude is one of floating attention, while being able to make exploratory interventions during the interview when required, that is, on the basis of the material provided by the patient. This, therefore, requires particular tact to be able to follow closely what the patient is saying, but intervening if necessary to enable him to continue, without, however, setting the pace too much. The fact that this free interview character predominates is to enable the patient to introduce himself and to show what he deems necessary, or, conversely, his defences against it.

The semi-structured interview

In my experience, I adopt this type of interview as a technique once the patient has spoken as spontaneously as possible during the first meeting. At this point, I am aiming to orientate this second interview based on the data that has not been provided in the first interview, but that I consider important in order to make a diagnosis. However, from a psychodynamic perspective, structuring the interview does not mean a set of questions, lest we lose the accompanying nuances when the patient presents the same information in a more spontaneous way. In this sense, I think that Sullivan's invaluable contribution on the subject of the interview departs somewhat from psychoanalytic postulates, owing to its technical considerations of how the interview should be managed. Sullivan (1954, p. 38) proposes a very structured and scheduled type of interview, to the point that one of its stages consists of "detailed inquiry", by which he restricts the climate of spontaneity for the patient and limits a certain amount of the free association that, although not to the same degree as in the analytic session, as I have already said, I believe is also necessary in the interview.

As I have just said, this type of semi-structured interview generally seems necessary to me after the first interview has taken place. It is possible, however, that even during the first interview, in the case of a patient with good communication skills, after a certain time we have enough data from what he has provided spontaneously to then introduce some questions for guidance, or advance our exploration of certain questions that are still pending, even though we might finish exploring them in the next. If the first meeting passes without us having had this opportunity because the patient has needed to take the time for his spontaneous production, it might be useful, at the end of the session, to anticipate that in the next we will need some more information about x, and I will mention the information that he has not provided or only partially provided; for example, "about your childhood, your relationships and sex life, your dreams, and so on". I endeavour to state the above aspects explicitly, which, as I will set out later, I consider to be fundamental. In this way, at the beginning of the second interview, the patient will have several matters to talk about, after having been able to think about, remember, get in touch with, and even make certain enquiries into them in the interval between the first and second interviews.

The interviewer's function as participant observer

The dynamic established in any interview where someone is making a consultation to seek the services of a professional acquires particular relevance when the aim is to establish the suitability of a person for psychological help and even to specify, within this interview, which type of help would be the right one for them. Therefore, an essential function of the interviewer is to participate in the relationship with the interviewee in such a way that he not only enables the existing dynamic to be externalised, but also that he is available to access this dynamic, even at levels that cannot be manifested verbally, as we set out above. This requires of the interviewer an attitude that has been called that of the *participant observer*, a term used by Sullivan (1954), who says that

> . . . we cannot make any sense of, for example, the motor movements of another person except on the basis of behaviour that is meaningful to us—that is, on the basis of what we have experienced, done ourselves, or seen done under circumstances in which its purpose, its motivation, or at least the intentions behind it were communicated to us. . . . Therefore, the psychiatrist has an inescapable, inextricable involvement in all that goes on in the interview. (Sullivan, 1954, p. 18)

In order to differentiate *professional understanding* from that provided by any person, or *private understanding*, Balint and Balint (1961), point out that this is based on the professional's capacity to make a double effort: first, he must be able to identify with the patient, that is, to place himself in a position as if it were he himself being observed, but then he must be able to put this identification to one side and be an objective professional; although, put in such a way, it might seem that the process of identification is a question of will that simply requires the professional to actively engage in imagining what it would be like to be in the position of the person being observed. I think that the concept of projective identification, that I explained above, might give a more accurate account of the reality we seek to

describe; that is to say, what takes place would be a projective identification on the part of the patient, faced with which the therapist acts
in a receptive way, by tolerating his projections. It is in this sense that
Bleger (1971) defines the role of "participant observer", which he also
includes as an essential function of the interviewer.

Therefore, by the attitude of "participant observer", I understand
this to mean, on the one hand, that the professional is receptive to the
verbal and non-verbal communication that comes to him via the
patient's projections and speech, and on the other hand, that he endeavours to observe and to understand what is being said to him. Or,
rather, that one part of the professional adopts the stance of the
observer who is *outside* of the relationship between interviewee and
interviewer, by observing the dynamics and the course of it, while
another part is involved in that relationship. In other words, the
professional is at one moment immersed in what the patient is
communicating, and the next adopts a stance of a certain distance and
observes what he has just heard and perceived. This is what Bleger
(1971) calls *dynamic* or *functional dissociation*, in the sense that the
processes of introjection and projection are continually in play. In fact,
as Bion says in relation to the interpretative capabilities of the analyst,
we cannot take in all of the ideas suggested to us by the extremely
complex situation that unfolds before us whenever the patient shows
himself to us at a particular moment, as "[T]he human personality
exists as a whole; we have to split that personality to formulate several
possible ideas or interpretations" (Bion, 1977b, p. 46). Bion calls this
non-pathological splitting, and I believe that this is also most closely
corresponds to the attitude of the therapist during the interview.

In fact, in so far as during the course of the interview we endeavour to make contact with the emotional and cognitive life of the
patient, we will not cease to be in some way immersed in what is
being transmitted to us. As such, the *observer* function is partially—
one might say necessarily—affected by the *participant* function. Once
the interview is finished, it is then that the professional can put a
certain distance between what he has experienced together with the
patient and develop the observer function from another perspective,
in solitude. Only now will he be able to rationalise, in the sense of
thinking about and giving meaning to what he has gathered from the
patient, in his *memory*. The italics allude to an idea of memory that is
not confined only to volitional and cognitive recall, but is also an idea

of memory on the basis of sensations and feelings that have been caught (fast) in our psyche.

From a psychodynamic perspective, other functions that fall to the interviewer include taking responsibility for establishing the appropriate conditions of the setting to carry out the interview; helping to modulate the interviewee's anxiety in a way that enables its containment, that is to say, for it to be bearable, but without seeking to ignore or to suppress it; collecting the data provided by the interview, and, finally, providing the indication for the help that he considers relevant in a way that is understandable to the interviewee.

Interviewer interventions

The interviewer's interventions must facilitate the patient's task of communicating everything he is able to, and that can be contained in the interview. Therefore, I try not to force the patient beyond what he considers to be enough, if he does not feel strong enough or able enough to express it or make it manifest. As I have said, I prefer the first interview to be as free as the patient can tolerate, in order to allow the most genuine aspects of himself to emerge, or, conversely, the defences that hide them. However, when difficulties in communication arise, and I see that it is necessary to make some intervention to help unblock the situation, I try to make my interventions as broad as possible so as not to determine the course of the patient's mental contents.

Let us take a look at the attitude of the interviewer in two extreme examples, such as I see and often carry out. The first case relates to a withdrawn patient with difficulties in communicating, who is unaccustomed to speaking about himself and being spoken to, with a passive attitude whereby he hopes to be walked through the interview step-by-step. In short, for whom the experience of speaking about himself becomes something that is extremely painful. Pain of this type might produce one of two reactions: emotional withdrawal and apparent disinterest, such as a defensive stance, as if the patient finds it all beyond him and, as such, does not feel the need to have to talk, hoping that the concern of the therapist will drive the interview, or, otherwise, it will cause the patient to feel acute anxiety, experiencing intense conflict between his desire to talk and the blockage. In the first case, I think that the therapist's attitude must consist of pointing out that situation to the patient: that it seems as though he is somewhat disconnected from the interview, although adding that perhaps this is because of the many fears he might have, such as that of feeling judged by something he might say. In the second case, the patient inhibited by anxiety, as a therapist, I try to be very careful not to fall into the position of taking charge of the entire direction of the interview by means of pre-formulated questions, one after the other. Instead, I restrict myself to helping the patient on the basis of any small interventions I might make. As always, to assess whether the degree of inhibition noted in the first interview is so pronounced that it might make psychotherapy very painful, we will have to wait until the second interview to observe what state the patient is in when he returns. If he continues in the same way, we might think that the relationship experienced with the professional in the first interview has not left the "trace" of a relationship of (some degree of) trust and that, for the moment, there seems to be some obstacle, which augurs badly in terms of the viability of an indication for psychological treatment, at least at that time. The problem will be clearer if the blockage persists for a third interview.

The opposite example would be that of the *"evacuative" patient*, who requires no intervention by the therapist to speak throughout the entire encounter. Here, there might be the risk of letting the individual express himself with no interruption to his communication. I say that it is a risk because it can happen that the entire course of the interview elapses in this way. As a consequence, the type of relationship that we have offered the patient might have stimulated the following fantasies: either that the therapist is someone who is incapable of setting boundaries, which makes it difficult to put one's trust in him; or, otherwise, that he is someone who does not care what the patient is saying to him, since he has left the patient alone talking, with the consequent feeling of abandonment. In such a way, what might initially meet a need to alleviate the immediate urgency to "evacuate" the anxieties besetting the patient then becomes a bad experience. Therefore, in such cases, while I understand this need to "evacuate" motivated by intolerable anxiety, I will try to respect it to a certain point, but, right from the first interview, I will place little "checks" on that tendency. The technique can be simple, such as from time to time introducing a comment based on what the patient has said in order to reinforce an idea or to relate to him that what he says is understood, and so on. So, I give indications to show that I am following the patient's discourse and at the same time I assert my presence as some-one who is capable of saying something, not a mere "recipient" who only listens. In the second interview, I will seek to make more precise interventions on a number of issues that, as a professional carrying out a diagnostic interview, it is my concern to know.

As we shall see, when we move on to a discussion of the indica-tors, that the patient's response to the therapist's interventions consti-tutes a significant piece of information in assessing his suitability with a view to psychotherapy. I include within this the therapist's inter-pretations as much as any other type of intervention, as anodyne and neutral as they might be.

Non-interpretative interventions

These comprise all of the gestures made by the interviewer in order to facilitate the patient's communication. If we are in the first interview, these interventions could range from the first question, "Why are you seeking consultation?", or "What prompted you to ask for help?", or simply, "Tell me, what's been happening?" Then I try to track the patient's communication as far as possible with my interventions in order to emphasise something; to recall a piece of information that was promised and then forgotten, although I will retain that forget-fulness as something meaningful; or to encourage the patient to continue talking about some other aspect he considers relevant and that he has not yet mentioned. If we are now in the second interview, my intention is to encourage the exploration of those areas of the patient's relational life and personality that have not yet appeared in the first interview.

Interpretative interventions

Material permitting, and when it appears that the patient will be able to tolerate it, if I understand something of the unconscious dynamic or I capture some unconscious phantasy, I attempt, as a test, to formu-late an interpretation that I will usually raise in the form of a question. The question reflects my—as yet—insufficient knowledge of the patient, as well as my wish to suggest it as a proposal for investiga-tion, inviting the patient to consider it. It is not that his answer will be definitive in itself, but it is one more piece of information to add to the others. I shall return to this subject when I go on to talk about the *complementary indicators.*

The evolution of the interview: stages, number of interviews

The course of the interview cannot be predetermined, as, clearly, it depends on each patient. Broadly speaking, however, we might establish three distinct stages. A *first stage,* in which the prevailing climate is one of anxiety faced with the new situation, as much for the patient as for the professional. The absence of at least a minimum of anxiety in both, but especially in the patient, indicates a very defensive attitude. As we already said in the section on the interview dynamic, a certain degree of anxiety is necessary; it is the prime mover that can enable obstacles arising in the interview to be overcome. In this first stage, anxieties might be confusional or persecutory. Depending on the degree of psychopathology in the patient, this will last for longer or shorter a time. If we think about a person who might be a candidate for psychotherapy, one would hope that this state does not last too long. After a silence, during which the patient does not know where to start and hopes that the therapist will be the one to make suggestions, some might perhaps request this specifically. If the therapist responds with a generic invitation for the patient to discuss what is troubling him and what led him to make the consultation, the patient may seize the initiative and begin to relate his reasons for the consultation. Some are so driven by the anxiety of the "here and now" that they will not be able to begin their account of their problems and discomforts until they have clarified certain issues relating to the therapist's personality or the treatment that might be applicable to them. They might ask, for example, about the professional's qualifications, whether he is a doctor, a psychiatrist or a psychologist, since being treated by one or other professional sustains different phantasies; or they might ask what type of treatment will be indicated for them, how long it will last, and so on. In relation to the first questions, I refer them, first, to any information they might have about me, and I clarify any misunderstandings provided they are relevant to the professional requirements of the interview. As for questions about the type of treatment, the duration, and so on, I explain that we cannot know which indication will be appropriate until we have some knowledge of the request and of the patient's personality.

Once these early anxieties have been modulated, and the patient is put back on track regarding the therapist, with a modicum of trust in the relationship, we enter a *second stage* that revolves around the patient setting out his difficulties and problems, in whatever order he considers best, helped by the therapist. One assumes that this will take place in a first interview in which we are adopting the open interview technique.

Finally, we enter a *third stage* in which we prepare for the time to say goodbye and the conditions under which we will establish the continuity of the relationship. Here, again, the patient's attitude is usually indicative of certain aspects of his personality, particularly in terms of his capacity to tolerate separation and his gratification or not as a result of what he has received in the interview, as well as his capacity to wait until the next meeting. In general terms, one interview is usually not sufficient to assess a person's mental state and potentialities with the aim of establishing a therapeutic indication. If the professional is not available to take the treatment on, as we have already seen, it is advisable for him to produce a summary using the information already obtained, outlining the problems and the suitability of a specific type of help—psychotherapeutic or psychoanalytic—and co-ordinate the referral to another colleague.

As we have maintained, in accord with Liberman (1980), it is important to conduct a second or a third interview, in the sense that we can then compare and contrast the patient's attitude between one and another. It is likely that in the first interview, for the reasons we have already mentioned, as it is a new experience, the anxieties that hinder communication will be very present, or they might otherwise stimulate significant defences that will mask the patient's potentialities as much as his difficulties. Furthermore, I consider it essential to observe what attitude the patient adopts in relation to his experience of the first interview. That is to say, has he taken into account the data that he provided, or that the therapist was able to point out to him? Some will declare, "I've been thinking about what you said", or "When you suggested that we could talk about my childhood today, as we did not do so in the previous interview, I have thought about such and such . . .", or "I asked my mother [or other family member] about certain things from my early childhood", and so on. It is also significant if the patient lets us know how the first meeting affected him: whether he felt relieved, or if it was not what he expected, or if he does not say anything explicitly, but some vestige of those feelings comes to light now. Has the patient kept the interview in mind during the interval between the two, or has he completely disregarded it? In the same way, during that time, the therapist—consciously or unconsciously—will have borne the patient in mind in some way, which he will hope to check in the next encounter to see whether what this has awakened in him is confirmed or not. It would, therefore, be prudent to take the first version we hold of the patient as somewhat provisional, the result of a first interview, which will be contrasted with the successive "images" that might continue to arise in subsequent interviews.

Post-interview: recording data

As I have said before, the observer function carried out by the interviewer during the interview simultaneously entails being a "participant" of that experience. Consequently, the interviewer's capacity to reflect upon the wealth of data he has received during this time is limited by that emotional involvement. Not until the interview is over will the therapist be able to make fuller use of his intellectual capabilities and professional expertise to attempt to carry out, that is, to consciously formulate, an assessment of the patient.

I believe that the systematic written recording of data during the interview itself is a device that interferes with both of the actors. The professional, because it deprives him of the openness necessary in terms of his attention being directed towards what the patient is exhibiting, and also because transcribing in the patient's presence hinders the emotional receptivity necessary for the patient's projections. In terms of the patient, he might feel as though he is the object of a bureaucratic relationship, which will establish itself as a barrier between the professional and the patient, despite him being consciously able to justify it. It is likely that, for the professional starting out as an interviewer, the resource of simultaneous transcription of the interview will act as a support that could ease the emotional impact of the situation. But I do not think that it is a resource that should be used for too long. In my opinion, it is preferable to "jump straight into" the interview, relying on the capacity of one's own *memory* (I explained the meaning of the italics earlier) and on the understanding and support of one's supervisors and teachers. I deal with this subject more thoroughly elsewhere (Pérez-Sánchez, 1997), in terms of reviewing the difficulties and benefits provided by the task of making notes once the interview is finished.

The diagnostic process

In the same way that we speak of a psychotherapeutic process, so we can legitimately do so in relation to the diagnosis, despite its relative brevity. If we understand that the diagnosis, as we shall see further on, consists of developing a certain knowledge about the patient's illness or key aspects of his personality, then, clearly, to achieve this one must have had some direct experience of these things in the relationship with him. This experience should include some moment of separation between patient and therapist, in such a way that the alternation between being together and being separated can be experienced before the next meeting, whereby we once again take up the activity of getting to know the patient. This time that elapses, this fixing of sequences in the relationship, is what gives rise to a development or a process in that relationship, although here, in the diagnostic interviews, such a process is limited by certain aims—that I will expand upon in the next chapter—which may be summarised in terms of reaching a sufficient knowledge of the patient to make an indication for the most suitable type of help. Thus, one may also legitimately speak of a diagnostic process, which, like any process, has its various sequences over the course of time.

Along general lines, the stages we have discussed above could be summarised into two broad moments of the diagnostic process. One would be that of obtaining data, or *indicators*, such as I shall call them, which enable the correct therapeutic referral to be made. The other moment is the therapeutic choice made by the professional and how this is formulated to the patient.

As I have emphasised, I believe a distinction should be made between the diagnostic process and initiation of the therapeutic process proper. On the one hand, in order to avoid the patient being installed in a relationship with the professional without knowing under which conditions and with what aims it has been established, but also for the therapist, to avoid being carried along by that inertia of the patient who assumes that the therapeutic relationship has begun, which perhaps has prevented him from going to the effort required to make a psychodynamic diagnosis, that is to say, to obtain a profile of the patient's personality and the basic questions of his pathology.

Note

1. Translator's note: The author is referring to the polite or formal *usted* vs. the informal *tú* form of the personal pronoun "you". In Spanish, the basic rule—with some exceptions—is that *tú* is used for anyone with whom one is on first-name terms, while *usted* is used in roughly the same way as the French *vous* and the German *Sie*.

CHAPTER THREE

Aims of the interview

s we have already pointed out, along general lines the aim of
an interview involves an evaluation, that is to say, a "diagnosis" of the interviewee in order to weigh up the request he is
making and the response that this requires of the professional. As
such, it is my understanding that the task of the psychoanalytically
based diagnostic interview inevitably carries with it not only a knowledge of the psychological and psychopathological aspects of the
patient's personality, but also knowledge of what, ultimately, the
most suitable therapeutic option will be. For this reason, in so far as
we consider the interview to be founded on the relationship that is
established between the two people involved—as we have seen—the
aims will be determined, in part, by the probable purpose of that relationship. There will be a difference if the professional is able to take
charge of that person's continuity of care, or if he knows beforehand
that he will have to refer him to another professional.

In the first case, the diagnostic interview will have as its aim to
gather the data required in order to arrive at a diagnosis—the "psychodynamic"—and, furthermore, from that moment on, to show what kind
of relationship that is likely to be established later in the help that will
be offered. In the second case, only the first phase will be necessary.

49

We cannot stress enough the significance acquired by these first contacts with the patient in the diagnostic interview, since, as we have seen (in the previous chapter), the functioning of the primitive level of the mind, by means of the mechanism of projective identification, places the purpose of the interviews squarely in the hands of the professional. This might, as such, orientate the course of the interview and subsequent referral in one direction or another in a conscious way, but the professional's attitude and emotional responses, however subtle or obvious, will be data that the patient will collect together and take into account when it comes to deciding upon, or trusting in, the proposed therapeutic approach.

For that reason, I think it is important to examine which methods used to conduct the interview are consistent with help of a psycho-dynamic nature, if this is considered to be the most suitable option. And this must be borne in mind from the outset, precisely because of the emotional intensity those first moments acquire. It is a common fact that, long after beginning psychotherapy, the patient remembers certain attitudes and comments made by the therapist which were not sufficiently clarified by him, or were misunderstood by the patient, and which have kept the latter convinced of what is, in fact, a miscon-ception about the personality of the therapist or the functioning of the treatment.

Clearly, clarifying such matters forms part of the therapist's task, since, to some extent, the perceptions of the patient had been some-what distorted by the predominance of those anxieties and primitive mental mechanisms. But what I wish to emphasise here is the impor-tance of those first contacts and the precautions the professional needs to take so that his attitude remains consistent with that typical of a psychoanalytically focused helping relationship.

As we said earlier, it is important to differentiate between the period in which the professional relates to the patient with the aim of assess-ing the type of therapeutic indication that will be the most suitable— that is to say, the diagnostic process—and the period in which he enters into and continues with the agreement to proceed with the chosen treatment, although at times the line is not always so clear. The pres-sure placed upon the therapist by the patient to give immediate answers to his problems does not allow for the minimum time that is required for any diagnostic process. But if that pressure and the con-comitant anxiety can be tolerated and contained, it is clear that the aim of a relationship for the purposes of diagnosis and that of a relationship for psychotherapy are not one and the same, and, therefore, must be kept distinct. Nevertheless, if we stop to examine the diagnostic process and the psychotherapeutic process, as we will do in detail in the next chapter, they might not turn out to be as different as they could at first appear. For this reason it is also necessary for the therapist to make an effort, within that continuity brought about by the diagnostic and therapeutic processes, to establish a marker between the two, which indicates that from a certain point we are entering into a different phase: that of treatment. We derive this marker from the offer of the therapeutic indication given by the professional, and the patient's explicit agreement in accepting it: that is, by the therapeutic contract.

Definition of the diagnostic interview.

The purpose of the diagnostic interview can be neatly described by the etymological sense of the word *diagnosis*, both in the sense of "that which enables differentiation", as well as of "I know" (Corominas, 1976 (translated for this edition)); or, rather, it is the knowledge which enables me to discriminate, or distinguish, a certain personality in terms of its specific characteristics. Similarly, the *New Oxford English Dictionary* (1998) gives the word's origin as late seventeenth century modern Latin, from the Greek *diagignoskein*, "to distinguish or discern", from *dia*, meaning "apart" and *gignoskein*, meaning "to recognise or know". In this sense, and in agreement with Aguilar, Oliva, and Marzani (1998), we can say that, contrary to what occurs during the psychiatric diagnosis, which highlights the common features of patients in order to isolate differential nosological entities, the psychoanalytic diagnosis "highlights the distinguishing features which personalise the patient" (Aguilar, Oliva, & Marzani, 1998, p. 26 (translated for this edition)).

The diagnostic interview is, therefore, orientated towards the activity of knowing or investigating the mental state of the patient or person consulting as it is shown in his relationship with the professional. There are three areas from which we may attempt to gather the most significant data from the patient: the psychopathological, the biographical, and that of the interview itself. In my opinion, the correlation of such data is crucial for diagnosis and prognosis.

Psychoanalytic experience to date nevertheless enables us to assert that the principal source of information is that which derives from the interview itself, that is, from that which the patient provides spontaneously, with his whole person, to this relationship. The rest of the data, the biographical and psychopathological, will need to be contrasted with this data in order to gauge the importance and intensity of these. For example, a person might claim to have had a happy childhood or, conversely, an unhappy one, and yet provide in the interview, by the attitude he adopts at the time of giving such information, elements which would suggest otherwise. This is because what guides us on the psychic value of such data are not the facts he describes to us, but at what point in the interview they arise, what degree of anxiety is experienced, and what type, what the accompanying emotions conveyed are, and so on.

It is for this reason that I consider the value of the data provided by the patient *within the setting of the relationship* between the two participants of the interview as a priority. I will not give an exhaustive account of the data provided from the other two areas. First, as plenty of literature already exists on the topic, in some cases excellent, to which we may refer. But the fundamental reason resides in my wish to highlight the significance of this component as an essential tool in diagnostic evaluation, as well as seeking to warn of the risks involved in underestimating it, where the diagnosis is made based exclusively on psychopathological and biographical data. There are both technical and ethical reasons that justify such an approach and that, at first glance, might not be evident. To begin with, let us examine the technical reasons.

There is a longstanding tradition regarding the best way to obtain the diagnosis of an illness, whatever its nature (somatic or mental), and that is according to the medical model of the clinical history. The adjectives used in medicine allude not only to the nature of the object of study—the body—but also to the nature of the method used to achieve the diagnosis. Traditionally, this consists of a part where the symptoms are listed, which the clinician compiles and correlates as data, serving to provide a nosological "understanding". He will then take into account the physical examination, in which the somatic correlate of the symptoms subjectively described by the patient is sought, as well as other possible findings not previously detected by the patient.

Running parallel to this is the idea that the greater the amount of data compiled, the greater assurance there will be of diagnostic accuracy. This has given rise to the elaboration of very detailed and extensive medical records that seek to include all possible pathological manifestations. Fortunately, on this issue at least, the huge workload in the field of public healthcare makes unfeasible what is, for many, a serious aspiration: the systematic application of such medical records by all healthcare professionals. Proponents of this position argue on the grounds of the progress of scientific research, whether to broaden our knowledge of pathology or to further our epidemiological studies. Undoubtedly, these are arguments we must consider. But what I am trying to demonstrate here is that the elaboration of such comprehensive clinical histories is not, strictly speaking, essential to the understanding and diagnosis of the pathology and the possible therapeutic referral for a given patient. And, therefore, the upshot of this could be certain ethical considerations that might make the use of such medical records inadvisable. I shall return to this point below. Clearly, this question raises a problem for scientific development, which imposes the pursuit of different solutions.

There has been an attempt to extrapolate this eagerness for scientific rigour to the field of mental health, which might have certain beneficial consequences. But, arguably because of the fact that we are dealing with disciplines branded as "unscientific"—owing to various historical and social reasons, as well as to the nature of mental illness and the relative infancy of these disciplines in comparison with the other sciences—this seems to be forcing compliance with certain scientific demands that are inapposite to our field, which has been to its detriment. Furthermore, there is the paradox that, precisely because it is a discipline (one which deals with mental health) that is still young, the excessive accumulation of data hinders its use towards establishing a better understanding of (mental) reality, which it aims to deepen.

From a *technical standpoint*, the compilation of a comprehensive clinical history that seeks to collect the maximum possible data from the patient entails a number of disadvantages and can be detrimental. Let us take a look at some of them.

1. *It provides a "de-individualised" image of the patient.* Whenever there is a primary concern to complete each of the sections of a supposedly complete medical record, there is a risk of putting this before

anything else, in seeking to make the patient "fit the boxes" at all costs. The result is that the profile we obtain from the patient might be quite flat or one-dimensional; at most, not much deeper than the profile offered when we talk about the characteristics of "any" depressed or anxious patient, or of the "depressive personality" faced with certain circumstances, or the "anxious personality" faced with others. But ultimately, however desirable it might be to establish distinguishing characteristics common to a group of patients in order to determine a personality or psychopathological profile, this will never be able to reflect the identity of the actual patient sitting in front of us. Obviously, this type of diagnosis could be useful in terms of other therapeutic outlooks, but not from the psychodynamic perspective.

2. *It causes the patient to adopt a passive role in the relationship.* When we rigidly follow a set of predetermined questions according to the appropriate protocol, be they in sight or out of sight, but even more so if the patient is able to see them (this also raises another technical issue, discussed in the previous chapter, relating to the inadvisability of making written notes during the interview), this can induce a type of relationship where spontaneous manifestations in the patient become inhibited, as everything appears to be directed and controlled by the professional. This then stimulates a kind of passive and dependent relationship in the patient.

3. *It stimulates phantasies of an omnipotent therapist.* The image of assurance provided by knowing which questions to ask suggests a false image to the patient of a professional who will know everything about him; it is simply a matter of following the therapist's indications, which will result in a complete knowledge of his character. Nothing could be further from the task of a psychodynamic interview, in as much as it is a joint labour of discovery between patient and therapist, and requires the efforts of both.

4. *It activates psychopathological attitudes.* This process subjects the patient to a painful experience that might be unnecessary. To talk about one's personal matters, especially if they are unacceptable, is always painful. We must, therefore, establish which data we consider strictly necessary for a better diagnostic understanding of the patient and that justify their investigation. It might be that the patient feels a certain pleasure in exploring the intimate details of his life, in which case psychopathological

mechanisms could be operating, such as an exhibitionist attitude towards pain, or otherwise a relationship with sadomasochistic components.

5. *It increases the risk of the "evacuatory" interview.* The excessive contribution of data can lead to the interview becoming an evacuatory activity, during which the patient has "emptied" himself. While it is inevitable that this tendency to get rid of what is unpleasant will always be present to some extent, the problem we are discussing here is when the professional himself stimulates such defences. This results in several possible consequences, as set out in the following points.

6. *It stimulates the projection of the patient's anxieties into the therapist.* The patient hopes that the professional will take charge of all the anguish he has deposited in him. What is more, he hopes that it is the therapist, to whom he attributes the quality of omnipotence, who will return to him the resolution and relief from all his emotional suffering, without any great involvement in such a task on his part.

    In fact, when an interview has been too comprehensive or "exhaustive", owing to the therapist's demands, with the consequent emotional stress to the patient, it would make sense if the patient then said, "Well, I've done my part, now it's up to you to give me the solution to my problems." In a way, we can consider this a fair claim: that the therapist should recognise, should value, and should compensate the patient's efforts by returning a proportionally equivalent effort. Because if, after such a painful diagnostic process, because of its exhaustive nature, the professional simply responds that what the patient needs is psychotherapy, he might think, at best, "Why did I bother?", or he could even react with anger or indignation, feeling unjustly treated.

7. *It can encourage paranoid anxieties.* Another possible consequence of the exhaustive interview consists of the fact that, upon making "public", albeit within a professional relationship, many painful and, at times, shameful, half-hidden pieces of information, which have probably never been told to anyone until now, the patient might experience persecutory anxieties. "What will the professional do now with everything I have told him? Will he disclose it? Will he (in cases where there is material that might compromise the patient) tell my family?" and so on.

In any case, this may mobilise anxieties of a different type, such as intense depressive anxieties, or feelings of guilt, and so on. This is because the very fact of verbalising difficult and conflictive emotional and psychological content often gives rise to these feelings. The person who speaks in detail of the ill treatment he has inflicted on another might expect the therapist to give him an easy answer, which immediately exonerates him from blame and soothes him with words negating his guilt. Not only will this clearly have a short-term effect, but will also undermine the professional who duped him, or who could not contain the patient's guilt. Or, otherwise, he might be expecting punishment, simply via the professional's comments, which somehow make him think that he really has been a bad person, or by means of a silence on the part of the therapist which might be experienced as disapproval, through the actions of a rigid superego projected into the professional.

8.   An interview that is too exhaustive can also have damaging effects on the subsequent course of a possible therapeutic relationship. If it is the same professional who has conducted the diagnostic interviews who will undertake the psychotherapy, the therapy will begin already determined by the patient's own expectations and fears, but which were stimulated by that interview procedure. Either he will expect everything to come from the therapist, by maintaining a passive attitude, or will feel accused, or will aspire to be comforted completely. If a different therapist is to undertake treatment, the problem of going back and conducting new diagnostic interviews to confirm the indication for psychotherapy with the therapist assigned to the patient is particularly painful. Although this circumstance is unavoidable, if the first diagnostic interviews have not been excessively tiring, through being exhaustive, the transition from one to the other will be less painful and conflictive. In such referral cases, a comprehensive diagnostic examination would be much less justified.

In terms of the *ethical standpoint*, to subject a somatic patient to unnecessary examination in order to make a diagnosis of his pathological state clearly violates his basic rights; all the more so the more aggressive the examination. What in the field of general practice might seem quite obvious—although perhaps not as much as one would hope—is harder to recognise in the field of mental health, because the harmful effects of verbal interventions are not always perceptible.

Here, we support the position that to carry out an approximate diagnosis that is able to refer a patient to the therapeutic resources best suited to his needs, there is no need for an exhaustive and detailed study of the person and their psychopathology. Neither is there any basis, from a psychodynamic perspective, in the view that the more complete the clinical history, the more accurate the diagnosis, according to the principle of "the more, the better". On the contrary, these can result in damage being done, as I have shown. On the basis of this premise, we can say that in the psychopathological examination and the preparation of the clinical history in psychology and psychiatry, *the professional has a responsibility to try to achieve an adequate diagnostic assessment with the minimum possible data.*

The psychodynamic "clinical history"

There seems to be some confusion with regard to the purpose of the clinical history in mental health. If we think of its use in public healthcare, as a document retained by the institution to which the professional who compiles it belongs, we lose sight of something so obvious and elemental: that, depending on the patient and only in a very secondary way, it is a tool at the service of the justification for clinical treatment or for hypothetical subsequent use in psychopathological or epidemiological investigations. The institution, through its professionals, is merely the agent that ensures its proper use, that is, to assist professionals to reflect upon the best treatment referral for the patient or to review the patient's progress.

But, furthermore, and I think arguably most importantly, the granting of such primacy to the clinical history has the disadvantage of being strongly conditioned by a particular understanding of the traditional medical model, although it is worth noting that in terms of the clinical history itself, this classical conception is under review, in so far as even here it is necessary to consider "the psychological components of any medical practice", as we have known for years owing to the contributions of Michael and Enid Balint.

Therefore, we first need to rid ourselves of the prejudices of a particular medicalised model of illness and of the patient, which is inadequate even for patient care in the strictly organic sense. Very briefly, I will say that such a conception suggests an understanding of illness as the expression of a malfunction of the organism in one or more of its apparatuses and systems, and that the treatment will derive from the restoration of the previous state, all of which is removed and decontextualised from the immediate surroundings and from the doctor–patient relationship. Such a view corresponds to an idealised image of health, according to the now ancient principle of equating it to the absence of illness; a principle that has its roots in infecto-contagious disease, in which it is possible to detect an aetiopathogenic germ, the transmission routes and the set of symptoms or syndrome to which it often gives rise, with the corresponding effective treatment against the germ. This simplistic scheme has been entirely invalidated when it comes to dealing with any non-infectious pathology. Today, we think of illness as the result of a number of factors that interact and converge, including constitutional, immediate environmental, psychological, and social factors.

However, I fear that this latter conception of illness has no suitable correlate in healthcare and welfare practice. I believe that one of the principal reasons for this, among others, is that this simplistic understanding of illness is often much more reassuring for the professional. The multi-causal, interacting conception of illness is more difficult to tolerate. This is the case precisely because, owing to the existence of a set of causative and determining factors, the diagnostic conclusion cannot be as categorical and dogmatic as originally intended, as there is always a margin of ignorance and uncertainty, which we struggle to tolerate. On the other hand, it is precisely that opening to the unknown, that margin of ignorance, which offers the possibility of acquiring new knowledge.

Whatever we have said about organic disease, we may assume that this will be more complex in the case of mental health disorders (although such a clear difference between organic and mental illness is not in keeping with the model of illness/health that we are putting forward here, and we are simply mentioning it for the purposes of expository clarity). Therefore, if we attempt to devise some kind of model clinical history to serve as a reference, the first task this presents is to leave aside the traditional medical model. But this does not suffice, as it is essential to also take into account the specificity of mental phenomena and how best to deal with them. This implies a particular way of collecting data, in the sense of the interviewer alternating between two attitudes: one being that of floating attention or listening, and the other, that of making interventions in order to explore some aspect of what is communicated by the patient or to request something that is missing, or to introduce or open up new avenues of investigation. This is the attitude of the participant observer that I have already described, and has the characteristic of being able to achieve the most spontaneous manifestations possible from the patient, as little determined or contaminated by the professional's questions as they can be. In this way, there will be more likelihood of the unconscious aspects of mental life emerging, that is, those that are truest and most authentic to the patient. (It is assumed that this attitude of benevolent listening is equally valid and necessary in any helping relationship, but I wish to emphasise that when dealing with mental issues and conflicts requiring subsequent psychotherapeutic help, such an attitude needs to be maintained in a very particular way, which is no easy task.) Hence also, incidentally, the need for continuing professional development that goes beyond the academic, by means of what we call "supervisions", among other activities.

On the basis of the above, I have put the expression "clinical history", in the field of mental health, in inverted commas. As I have already said in the previous chapter, although in any first interview we expect that it is the patient himself who expresses his requests as spontaneously as he can, albeit with the appropriate professional assistance to facilitate the progress of the interview for him, the professional does, however, require a minimum of data in order to carry out a diagnostic assessment, which will probably need to be completed by making the necessary enquiries in subsequent interviews, as we have already seen.

Below, I mention some of the data, in my opinion the most significant, from the three areas that should be explored: the psychopathological, the biographical, and the interview itself with the professional.

Psychopathological data

As with any data we seek to gather from the patient, we do so first by listening to what complaint he has or what symptom he is "bringing" to us, and then we attempt to investigate it. It can, however, be detrimental to the course of the interview to insist too much upon certain aspects of a symptom if it is not something that ties up with the material provided by the patient. For instance, the patient is telling us that he is depressed. It is a mistake to think that both professional and patient understand "depression" to mean the same state of emotional discomfort, as it would also be to seek to then question him about those symptoms which, according to psychopathological treatise, tally with depression in order to then try to enquire into the possible causes that have engendered it. At that point, we would be acting according to the *medical* model, concerned about detecting symptoms and possible causes.

Furthermore, the fact of assuming that patient and therapist immediately understand what the former means at the mere mention of a particular label—depression, for example—none the less constitutes a defensive stance on the part of both. On the part of the patient, because this saves the indispensable effort required to communicate his experience of emotional suffering in an approximate way, when he comes to talk about his depression. But, moreover, he thereby plays down the substantial initial problem of any therapeutic encounter: that of establishing that the professional is someone who knows nothing of the patient, who is not inside the patient's mind, but is external to it, which stands in the way of communication, or, rather, makes manifest something that is intrinsic to the very nature of communication between people, that is, how difficult it is. But in so far as this type of communication is accepted by the interviewer, it also constitutes a defence on his part, who is claiming to "get the message", thus knowing the patient's emotional state, when really he hardly knows him at all. On the other hand, the professional's insistence on questioning about specific psychopathological aspects can lead to the patient interpreting that the professional is particularly interested in this and, therefore, he will endeavour to provide material to that effect, perhaps at the expense of sacrificing other issues that were closer to his consciousness and he felt more of a need to communicate. So, too, might the patient feel that the professional's interest in certain symptoms lies in the fact that these are the most significant ones, or are the ones that are the most severe.

Therefore, it is imperative that it is the patient himself who specifies what he means when he speaks of depression, and, in any case, the professional will restrict himself to seeking clarification on issues that are not clear. Even if a further explanation by the patient fails to clarify them, it will be useless to stress the point, as there must be some underlying unconscious difficulty, for which reason it is preferable, for the time being, to leave the matter to one side and continue the interview. Insistence would be detrimental, as the patient could potentially feel accused of not being able to explain himself well enough and not satisfying the professional.

Data from the patient's biography and internal world

From a psychodynamic perspective, biographical data hold special value. We do not simply seek to enquire into the patient's history for potential indications of pathology: we are not concerned with searching for the pathological elements of his medical history, we need some knowledge of how the patient's history has developed, his relational history in particular. According to the conception of the mind that we set out in Chapter One, the emergence of psychopathological manifestations is the product of a particular dynamic of the patient's personality, which has been constructed and structured throughout his history, resulting in a unique way of relating to himself and to others. This is a history that has likewise contributed to his growth and to the development of personal aptitudes and abilities, which we must also take into account for prospective psychological treatment.

But here we must once more insist upon the error in thinking that the more detailed the patient's biography, the better we will understand him. There is no psychodynamic basis to support such a hypothesis. Quite to the contrary, psychoanalysis has brought into sharp relief the tendency to repeat certain forms of conduct and of relating in the individual. Therefore, it will be sufficient to take a few samples of such experiential and relational patterns that, in my opinion, we can basically relate to the patient's current situation and childhood. If the patient speaks of other moments of his life because of lived experience that he considers to be of concern, we will obviously take these on board. The account that the patient gives of his adolescence is also significant; this is another crucial moment in people's lives.

In any case, it is my view that exhaustively trawling through each stage of the individual's development, from breast-feeding through to early childhood, latency and school issues, pre-puberty, adolescence, and, within this, the onset and subsequent stages until adulthood, places the professional in a role similar to that of an official, at very least, if not a police officer, which can have detrimental consequences for the relationship with the patient. In the first instance, it will stimulate the patient's affective dissociation of the relationship and the emotional content, because, in those interviews during which, despite the therapist's administrative attitude, the patient becomes emotional upon evoking a stage in his life where some particularly significant and painful fact is touched upon, the professional will hardly be able to participate—not even from his position and his respective distance. In addition, the patient's experience in relation to the professional who is questioning him in a civil service/police style will clearly translate into persecutory fears of being accused of something, and so on.

As we have said, an exhaustive gathering of data on the patient's life not only will not give us any more of an understanding as a result of having amassed a greater amount of information, but, on the contrary, it can be harmful in the sense that we have already commented on. So, it seems to me to be essential to make an effort to keep necessary data to a minimum. I, for my part, consider the most pertinent data to approximate some understanding of the patient's internal world and relationship patterns are those that are encompassed in the following sections: current relationships (family, work, leisure); early childhood (relationships in family of origin); dreams and sex life.

Current relationships

This is an area of the patient's life that will probably be relatively close to consciousness. First, it will include his family relationships (this is the order I usually grant these aspects, according to their greater emotional significance, which might not coincide with their order of appearance during the course of the interview, as this will depend on the order chosen by the patient himself). Then, the spontaneous description he gives at various points of the people in his family, the relationships they sustain with him, and vice versa, the type of functioning of the family dynamic and the role the patient fills within it.

As I have often insisted, I believe it is important to follow the course of the patient's associations. Thus, when the patient talks a lot about his relationship with his wife and tells us nothing about his children, this itself provides a piece of information to take into account that has significant emotional value, in that it points towards certain hypotheses. Does the patient have a dependent, or conflictive, relationship with his wife, so much so that there is little space in the mind of the patient to accommodate the link with his children? Is his role as a father therefore undermined or not fulfilled? If the therapist is impatient and pushes forward in order to ask "bureaucratically" about the composition of the family, to be sure he will obtain the family genogram data, being able to then draw the corresponding graph, with circles and squares indicating gender differentiation and successive lines linking up its members. But all of this will be at the expense of losing tremendously valuable psychodynamic data. If we wait for the patient to speak unprompted, it might be that he does not even make any reference whatsoever to his family, which will constitute, clearly, an extremely important piece of information. What happens in the patient's relationship with his family so as to cancel it, at first, from his mental life? This suggests the existence of some significant conflict.

But if he does talk about his family, where did he start? Does he refer first to his mother, enlarging considerably upon that theme, as if only she existed? Or does he talk about his mother, his father, and himself as if there were no one else, and only later, at the request of a question our own, do we learn that a brother does indeed "exist"? Can we then infer from this that, in the patient's psychic life, that little-present other family member has been "actively" excluded? In short, depending on this spontaneously provided information, the psychodynamic genogram we can mentally draw will be very different from that obtained if we ask outright about parents, siblings, and other family members and their respective ages. For example, in a person who is highly dependent on his mother figure, a graphic is likely to emerge in which one would see only the patient and the mother, as this is what, in his internal and relational world, carries real significance.

Sometimes, an adult comes to the interview accompanied by a relative, which is a telling piece of information. It demonstrates, from the outset, an inability in the patient to tolerate the anxiety of the first encounter with the professional alone. If his pathology is not very serious, it will soon become clear during the course of the interview that the patient has to continue it alone. But even when the patient comes to the interview alone, we will take into account to what extent his family members are present in his mind, if his request is determined by the advice of any one of them, or if, when he talks about a personal matter, he immediately refers to said family member's opinion on the subject without actually putting forward his own. Upon talking about domestic living arrangements, the description the patient gives will help us to approach some kind of configuration of the type of relationships he establishes. Does he speak in an idealised way about the other family members, or does he complain about them? When he gives an opinion, does he speak for himself, or is it some other familial image, perhaps more specifically paternal, who, as if installed in his internal world, holds the opinion for him? What is the kind or quality of the emotions present in these relationships: love, hate, resentment, guilt, affection, or tenderness?

As I have already said in relation to psychopathological data, I believe it is important to gather the information provided by the patient just as it is, that is to say, according to his own language. The terms he utilises to describe a family member express how he experiences that family member internally. For example, it is not the same thing to say that his father is an authoritarian as to call him a dictator. If the patient chooses the this latter noun, even though the information he gives us at other moments of the interview in relation to his father, in different contexts, does not evoke the image of a dictator, but perhaps that of a person who is resolute in his decisions, it is evident that the image he holds of that father who exists in his mind—the internal object that represents him, in other words—is that of a dictator, and, consequently, his relationship with him will be determined by that internal reality.

As for the aforementioned, included in clinical histories, in my opinion it is equivalent to the graphic expression of that bureaucratic trait of a certain type of interview, which I have been pointing out. As we know, this consists of a graph with a series of symbols and connections between members of the family (of origin and current, if any), indicating the position in the family of the person making the consultation. The male members, represented by a square, and the female, by a circle, are joined together by solid lines, depending on the type of union: father and mother are bound by a line and, descending from this, the patient and any siblings there may be, each of these with their respective ties with other little circles or squares, if they are married, and so on. Once the chart has been drawn up, this might give the professional the impression of knowing the patient's family background. But, clearly, and I repeat, nothing could be further from the patient's internal reality. And this is because the result is what appears to be links of entirely equal intensity between each of these family members in the patient's life, as if each one held the same significance. Thus, from a psychodynamic standpoint, the traditional genogram not only tells us very little, but can, to some extent, distort our perception, as we grasp it, of the patient's family relationships in his internal world.

Occasionally, during some of my supervisions with colleagues with little clinical experience, and who as part of their presentation of the patient illustrate his family composition with the genogram, I have proposed to them that they try to redraw the chart from the perspective of the "psychodynamic" data they had obtained. For example, we might represent those family members who have only been mentioned later on in the interview, and perhaps at the request of the interviewer, with the same characteristic symbols but with broken lines, thereby expressing that weak presence in the life of the patient. Similarly, the line that connects the patient with any of these members should also be broken, according to the lesser intensity of the relationship between them. In contrast, bold lines would indicate those relationships with greater content in his emotional life. Naturally, this is a slightly convoluted task that, granted, I do not usually undertake in my notes, and the proposal to colleagues is for didactic purposes, to show that perhaps it is preferable not to make any genogram at all and stick rather to what we have constructed mentally.

In another vein, I consider the sphere of work to be significant within the patient's current relational life. And it interests me in a number of respects. On the one hand, it provides information on how the patient relates to people in that sphere, which can then be contrasted with what has been established in the family environment. Thus, it might be that the same pattern of relationship is repeated in both areas, or, conversely, whereas in the family sphere we might find a dictator father, at work the patient's relationship with his boss is idealised, thereby expressing a splitting of the relationship with the father figure. In the same way, peer relationships might denote competition, or feelings of envy, and so on. The other valuable piece of information provided by the patient's working life includes knowing the type of relationship the individual establishes with work itself, which acquires the status of an object: to what extent is it something creative, despised, or valued, and so on? Is it a source of gratification or frustration, a road to reparation (or sublimation) or, conversely, to atonement?

Data from childhood

The value accorded our origins is a classic subject for the psycho-analytic approach. But, today, we are not so concerned by its objecti-fication, in terms of attempting to verify the credibility of that which is communicated to us by the patient in external reality, in order to determine the traumatic situation. On the contrary, what takes prece-dence is the subjective account, the particular version the individual offers us of his origins—as with any other piece of information he provides. But, here, it arguably holds more significance, in so far as it is a version that is highly influenced by the patient's phantasies. In fact, memories of those early years are extremely scarce, and those that do exist are distorted, elaborated from fragments of information that the patient has gathered together later on, which has enabled him to reconstruct that particular version of the beginnings of his personal history. For that reason, it is valuable information, again, not only because the content of the "real" facts or circumstances will serve to provide a dynamic understanding of the patient, but because it relates a story to us that is tinged with, and determined by, his internal world, above all by the most primitive levels of the individual.

However, it is important to clarify that I am not suggesting that I would do away entirely with the information the patient provides on the circumstances of the external reality that surrounded his early years of life. I do, of course, take them into account, but they alone do not help me to understand the development of the patient's personal-ity. Most importantly, with these data alone I will not be able to effect changes in his internal world. They will, however, help me to under-stand his strong resistance to change, despite the insights obtained in the course of the potential treatment. Thus, as a therapist, I shall under-stand that the patient needs to test the goodness, the consistency or inconsistency, the badness, or the strength of the therapist many times over against certain internal objects that he has constructed in his inter-nal world, which is also determined by the specific characteristics (weakness, rejection, badness, etc.) of his primary external objects.

If, during the second interview, the patient has not yet made reference to his childhood, I usually ask him about it, although in a very generic way. I am attentive to any potential information regarding certain questions that I believe are revealing and significant, such as *food or feeding* and *illnesses*, or situations that might well have engendered some kind of *traumatic experience*. I also ask if the patient has any idea about the kind of baby he was, through information provided to him at home. Generally speaking, the exploration of this area of the patient's life often provides us with comparatively very little information in relation to other periods of his life. But, notwithstanding its scarcity, it occasionally amounts to a very significant piece of information, bearing in mind that it can be of great help in understanding a part of the patient's mental dynamic. Such data could be accompanied by an image or scene, depending on the patient's account (as we shall see later on when we discuss the indicators), which is invaluable to the therapist in specifying a dynamic and relational profile.

As we know, data from *childhood organic illnesses* are important for various reasons. Although it depends upon the severity of the illness, for the child this has meant coming into contact with the experience of impending death and the concomitant anxieties. If the disease has required hospitalisation, with the consequent separation from the early external objects, this will also be significant. I also value as an equally significant factor whether any of the people who looked after the patient as an infant have suffered from an illness (physical or mental), especially the mother, and if this has resulted in physical separation (through confinement or separation from the infant's care) or, indeed, an emotional distancing, which might almost be worse. This latter situation can be more damaging because, whereas in traumatic situations of physical separation from the infant through the mother's illness, there might be some surrogate "mother" who performs the maternal functions, in the case of emotional absence or distance, the infant's needs are apparently met, as all of his physical needs are attended to, in which case the idea of emotional trauma does not have the acute character of physical absence, yet none the less constitutes a real or "authentic" trauma of which the consequences will be worse as a result of its persistent nature. It is also important to know at what age, as a child or infant, the patient became ill, or what age he was when his mother or parent became ill, or even when he suffered the definitive loss of one or other of them, with the attendant repercussions not only for the child orphaned by the death of one of his parents, but also for the surviving parent, with depression to work through and the commensurate impact on the infant's care depending on how the depression is resolved. Furthermore, if the patient was very young at the time, I am interested to know what version he has held on to, in terms of what he has remembered or heard, in relation to the consequences caused by his illness for the rest of the family, as this can indicate the degree of containment of the illness, at least from the patient's perspective, that is to say, the degree of containment of his internal objects. The physical location of the injury or illness might also provide some psychodynamic information, in as much as that site of the body and the function associated with it could also have been "injured" psychologically. What I mean by this is that this site becomes disproportionately large in terms of the interest it arouses in the patient, in the sense that conflictive aspects converge upon it, and there might be a libidinisation of the site, or, conversely, it might be charged with destructiveness. In any case, it often becomes a *locus minoris resistentiae* that conveys the emotional conflicts. For example, a woman with problems of oral greed explained that as a child she had suffered an illness relating to her mouth because "pus pockets" had formed under her teeth.

Other data from childhood, such as the chronology relating to the start of teething, walking, toilet training, and speech, I do not consider so relevant as to ask about them directly. It is to be hoped, in cases where there has been some serious anomaly (for example, not having full bowel control until a late age, or some delay in starting to talk), that the patient will make reference to it unprompted.

Dreams and sexuality

If there has been no spontaneous contribution by the patient relating to either of these two areas, I consider them to be important enough to point out that perhaps we could investigate them. But again, I will formulate the suggestion in a non-specific and generic way: for example, "And how about your sex life?", or "And how about your sexuality?" If the answer I get is, "Everything's fine, well, normal . . . there are no problems," the most I will ever stress the point is with a succinct, "Normal?" implying that perhaps for the patient the expression "normal" has a particular meaning. If he refused to go into detail, iterating that "normal" is exactly what anybody might consider as such, I consider the enquiry into this field closed, accepting, for the time being, the patient's resistance, unless other interview data has provided indications which evince the existence of certain difficulties or pathological aspects in this area. If this is the case, and if the contradiction is flagrant to the extreme of making it evident that the patient is openly lying, I will simply point out this contradiction, and move on, having raised the matter, as there must be some hidden reason why the patient has felt the need to be dishonest, but I do not stress the point further.

Of course, I should not need to stress that investigation into the patient's sexual life beyond what he is willing to disclose at the time of the interview becomes a completely unacceptable source of excitation in the patient–therapist relationship, if not a police matter. Questions about the frequency of sexual relations, or orgasm, or masturbation and respective fantasies clearly should be avoided. It is another matter when the patient refers unprompted to the subject as a matter of concern, in which case we shall have to observe to what use he is putting such information: is it to show himself off or "expose himself"; to create a climate of excitement involving the therapist, and so on; or, conversely, to collaborate by providing significant information.

In short, the patient's sex life is an important area to know, while, however, taking great care and tact in exploring it, never going beyond what he is willing to show. It is surprising that, a hundred years after Freud's early works on sexuality, there still remains a certain reserve, a certain hesitation when it comes to dealing with such matters, in spite of the fact that sexuality has become such a public, such a "known", subject. Perhaps we are less prudish nowadays, but it continues to be no simple matter, except for when it is trivialised or perverted, of course.

We should re-examine that which we call speaking "naturally" about sex, above all when this is done with a professional. We should say, rather, speaking *somewhat* naturally. Sexuality is something that is fundamentally a lived experience. For that reason, the "natural" thing is not to talk about it, but to experience it, and when we seek to relate this experience we will always do so in an approximate or inadequate way, unless it is talked about as if it were being experienced, to some extent, which would constitute an *acting out*, by means of a form of perversion. It falls within those areas of life which are most intimate and, therefore, most difficult to convey in terms of verbal communication. Hence, the extreme sensitivity and tact with which, I believe, the professional should deal with the issue, if and when it is entirely necessary to broach it. Incidentally, speaking naturally about sexuality should not be mistakenly presumed to mean doing so in a technical manner, that is to say, by stripping the subject of any emotional connotation (shame, fear, even some degree of arousal, etc.). Such a posture would provide rather one-dimensional information of little significance about this aspect of the patient's life.

With regard to dreams, no less surprising is how, over a century since Freud's *The Interpretation of Dreams* (1900a) was first published, the study of dreams remains as relevant today as a means to access the individual's internal world. The question, as always, will be generic and "natural" (it is surely natural to consider that there is something that we call dreams, which form part of the individual's mental life and can thus provide data about it).

Without seeking to accord them conclusive value, dreams, particularly those that the patient communicates during the early interviews, in my opinion do rank rather highly in importance. And this value is accorded because they may offer a dramatised image or representation of some of the patient's central conflicts which are often very helpful in guiding the therapist, both during the remainder of the diagnostic interviews and probably in the subsequent therapeutic process as well.

Data from the interview itself

This area of data comprises two fields. One refers to the patient's relationship with the therapist; the other refers to the relationship that the patient establishes with the material he brings to the interview.

Relationship with the therapist

From the first encounter with the therapist, the patient adopts an attitude and a form of behaviour that provide us with information about himself and his mode of relating. During the telephone call with the therapist or, in the case of a public institutional setting, with another member of the team, he is already conveying a form of relationship that might or might not tally with the manifestations described to us in different areas of his life or those which are expressed within the purview of the psychopathology. His style of communicating in the interview itself is also representative: how he asks for help; what he expects of the therapist; whether he is passive or proactive; his response to the therapist's indications; his extraverbal behaviour and tone of voice. Everything that "comes out" of the patient is subject to observation, which I then try to contextualise in terms of his relationship with the therapist. I will not elaborate on this here, as I have already done so in Chapter Two.

Relationship with the material he provides

How does the patient treat what he says? When he talks to us about his symptoms, does he do so by taking a certain pleasure in it, as if the material were syntonic or, on the contrary, alien to himself? Does he do so urgently or tolerantly, and so on? If we listen to the symptoms the patient complains of as if he were speaking about someone with whom he has a relationship, if we anthropomorphise the symptom or, rather, if we "objectify" it, as if we were an internal object, this may shed some light on certain aspects of the type of object relationship he usually establishes. They will show the dark side of that relationship, the conflictive side that is harder to recognise and accept as something that forms part of himself. If he is telling us about the people in his life, how he does or does not do so will be very significant. This is equally true of when he makes explicit reference to the therapist or other therapists whom he has previously consulted.

Psychodynamic focus and diagnosis

To reach some understanding of what we have come to consider a psychodynamic diagnosis, on the basis of the three areas described above, presupposes that we obtain a profile of the patient's mental functioning, which will always be partial, given that two or three meetings will not have been sufficient to know or understand the enormous complexity of a personality. In this sense, then, we may make the assertion that any psychodynamic diagnosis is always partial, or, if we prefer, has to be focal. I prefer this designation, because once the therapist has been able to maintain an attitude that is open and receptive to the patient's presentation and to the account he gives in the interviews, he will need to make an effort to synthesise, to articulate some of the most significant data, in conjunction with his experience of the patient. This is, logically, equivalent to choosing some data over others. But this focus for the diagnosis should not be confused with the focus for treatment. I think they are two different things. Once we have acquired a certain idea of the patient's mental functioning, everything will depend upon the type of treatment chosen. Whether the choice goes to a particular psychotherapy in which certain conflictive aspects of the patient will be examined as a priority, that is to say, as a focus, or whether a treatment is chosen which resolves to address all of the patient's conflicts and transferences, through psychoanalytic psychotherapy or psychoanalysis.

Interview for formulation and return of the indication

The fact that we are discussing this subject separately does not necessarily mean that a meeting should be convened with the sole purpose of informing the patient of the professional's opinion, after previous meetings with him. This could form part of a last interview that has also served to fill in certain gaps in the data, or to achieve a more accurate assessment of the patient.

The fundamental aim of the interview is to establish a psychodynamic diagnosis, as we have said, which enables us to assess the suitability of the patient for psychological help. But if that knowledge or understanding is not shared, in some measure, by the patient, it will be of little use to us. Therefore, a vital and integral part of the aim is that the professional is able to communicate to the patient that the matter for which he is seeking consultation, of which all the salient elements are gathered together so the patient sees that he has been understood, requires psychological help.

But this transmission should not be exclusively contingent upon the final moment of the interview(s), as if it were a medical diagnosis enclosed in the label, "You need psychological treatment." So that the patient can have some understanding of what is being "returned" to him and participate in it, during the entire course of the interview(s), that is to say, during the diagnostic process, as far as possible and where sufficient data is held, the therapist demonstrates how the psychological approach to emotional problems works. This involves the therapist adopting a particular attitude, together with making certain interventions that, without being interpretative, attempt to approach the problem, to observe it, and investigate it, though without always obtaining an immediate result. That is to say, returning the recommendation of psychotherapeutic help to the patient will be possible only if he has been shown during the course of the interview what is involved in the method of psychological approach to emotional problems, which we have already discussed in the previous chapter.

As Michael and Enid Balint (1961) maintain, the termination of the diagnostic process is, at the same time, the beginning of treatment. To summarise, in my opinion, the diagnostic interviews should attempt to reflect three questions:

- a psychodynamic understanding of some of the most significant conflictive aspects of the patient's life with regard to the reason for the consultation
- a psychodynamic or psychoanalytic method of approach for such problems; such that the patient has the opportunity to learn something from this method
- an explanation of the type of help that is considered appropriate on the basis of the understanding given to him of his conflicts; that is to say, to make the indication for the type of psychotherapeutic or psychoanalytic help that appears to be the most suitable, explaining the particular characteristics of the setting.

Nevertheless, patients unfamiliar with the psychoanalytic and psychotherapeutic fields, who do not have any information about it, will require some explanations for guidance. I do not think such information should be given ahead of time, but should be supplied by request of the patient, in addition to what we might consider essential for the setting in motion of treatment.

The other question that I think is important to clarify is whether the type of treatment the patient needs is psychotherapy or psychoanalysis. Many patients think that talking about themselves, especially if they make references to childhood, and even more so if the therapist has asked them about their dreams, is already a form of psychoanalysis. They have simply taken the literal translation of the term: "analysis of the psyche". And psychotherapy is taken to mean the same thing. Therefore, when we talk to the patient about the possibilities of indications for help, by mentioning psychotherapy and psychoanalysis as different procedures, the patient who is uninformed in this area will ask for clarification. Each professional needs to find their own clear and concise way of explaining the differences. Of course, this will depend on whatever stance the therapist takes on this matter. It might be that for one there is no net difference between one and the other.

For my part, it is my view that psychoanalytic psychotherapy is a method of applying the principles of the theory of psychoanalytic technique, but that it may be clearly differentiated from psychoanalysis in terms of a therapeutic practice. Therefore, I think it is advisable to clarify the differences to the patient, when they are not already clear to him. I tell him that both the aims and the technique used differ from one to the other. In psychoanalysis, we seek certain aims that require us to access deeper levels of mental life, and this requires a greater frequency of sessions, four or five per week, as well as the use of the couch. In psychotherapy, however, the relationship is face to face, the frequency is once or twice a week, and intervention accesses other levels of the patient's mental and relational life. I then add that in his particular case what he needs is psychotherapy, and I explain the reasons why I think this treatment will be enough. We must take into account, I tell him, that analysis is an experience that demands a lot of time, emotional and financial efforts, and, therefore, is only justified when the aims covered by psychotherapy are not sufficient. Or I propose an indication for psychoanalysis, if I consider this to be the most appropriate option, and then I check with the patient to see whether this is financially feasible for him, along with any resistances that might arise. Of course, in order to supply this information, the therapist must clearly support such a distinction, as I have said. As this is a controversial matter, I devote an entire chapter (Chapter Eight) to this subject, in which I discuss the specificity of the psychoanalytic method along with that of psychoanalytic psychotherapy.

Once the indication is established, the patient must give his response. It is always difficult to know whether we should offer him more time to think about it, or whether we accept whatever immediate response he provides. In my experience, there are cases where the patient's response comes fluidly and coherently as a result of how the interviews have progressed. That is to say, it is clear to both therapist and patient that the proposed treatment offers him a feasible opportunity for help, and that there is no need to delay in starting it. In certain other cases, where the patient's affirmative response to the indication I have offered has been very acritical and submissive, I suggest to him that he defers the decision for a week or two and arrange to meet again after that, emphasising those difficult aspects of the therapeutic experience that, based on my impression, might have been avoided by the patient.

CHAPTER FOUR

Therapeutic factors in the interview*

Virtually all of the authors who have dealt with the subject of the diagnostic interview, as cited throughout this work, have highlighted its therapeutic components. Even at the risk of overestimating the beneficial aspect of the interview, of which the primary aim—we cannot forget—is evaluative, in the sense of establishing a diagnosis and then deducing the most appropriate type of help, we must, however, recognise the existence of this therapeutic effect. To cite some of those who have dealt with this aspect, we are reminded of Balint and Balint (1961) who said that, "whenever a doctor listens to a patient's story in a professional setting and with some therapeutic skill, treatment will start even if it is his intention only to make a diagnosis" (p. 150). Based on the experiences of these British psychoanalysts at the Tavistock Clinic, Thomä and

---

*A shorter version of this text was presented at the Tenth Congress of Psychiatry organised by Spanish Psychiatric Society. Although I have expanded and corrected the text for the purposes of this chapter, I have kept in some references and specific sections, which were written for an audience of psychiatrists rather than psychoanalysts. For this reason, some of the themes, which have already been discussed in previous chapters, appear to be repeated here.

Kachele (1985) expand upon the need for the interview go beyond the diagnostic aim, arguing that, during the initial interviews, the patient must experience some indication of what treatment might come to mean for him, and that this is already in itself a therapeutic experience.

Clearly, the fact that a person should have the opportunity to talk about their suffering with someone who, by their professional status, inspires respect and trust, has a "cathartic" therapeutic effect, comprising momentary relief and the raising of expectations about the resolution of his problems. On occasion, the handful of interviews brought about by the request might even be sufficient to resolve whatever it was that motivated it. This, however, is an unusual situation, contingent upon there being a precise reason for the consultation, which does not implicate other significant aspects of the patient's personality or life. And even then, once the patient has established a good relationship with the therapist and has had a positive experience, being reasonably realistic, I believe that a certain idealisation of the situation certainly will have contributed to any benefits obtained during these first meetings. The patient will have conferred a certain magical component on the therapist and the interview, or, in short, an omnipotent component, so, accordingly, there is a danger that any therapeutic results obtained will be insubstantial.

Notwithstanding these caveats, I would like to look at a particular case of the question we are studying, one that occurs infrequently, at least in my practice. And it is when the diagnostic interview can become a psychotherapeutic one, because the patient's therapeutic aims outweigh the evaluative ones, owing to a certain urgency in the request and the feasibility of the conditions. I am interested to examine this not so much to encourage its practice for therapeutic purposes, but in order to highlight that therapeutic component— although without losing sight of the main purpose of the interview— as a precursor to a deeper therapeutic experience. This will enable us to examine those factors in the interview that might determine the therapeutic component. To this end, I shall set out what I consider to be common to the "diagnostic" relationship (in the diagnostic process) and the therapeutic relationship (in the psychotherapeutic process) in terms of patient and therapist.

Knowledge: basis for the diagnostic and therapeutic processes

As we saw in the previous chapter, the diagnostic process has certain precise aims. It seeks to define, describe, and synthesise certain psychopathological manifestations, which can then be encompassed within a concise terminology: that which is traditionally known as "diagnostic", which has been defined—and more or less agreed upon—by various specialists based on their experience with a number of patients. The DSM (*Diagnostic and Statistical Manual*) of the American Psychiatric Association, in its various versions, or the WHO classifications, serve as examples of this. From a psychodynamic point of view, the diagnosis does not have such precise limits, although we must not discount the need for sufficient rigour in establishing it according to its own particular parameters: the predominant type of object relation, anxieties, and defences.

On the other hand, the aims of the therapeutic process consist of encouraging some modification in the patient that will relieve their suffering. One way of achieving such aims is based on the empirical correlation between the psychopathological manifestations and its equivalent diagnosis, on the one hand, and the specific therapeutic intervention by means of drugs to attain said benefit, on the other. In this case, the therapeutic "process" derives from the biochemical changes taking place in various parts of the central nervous system. Another way to achieve the therapeutic aims includes the verbalisation, by the patient, of the emotional experience tied to their suffering as well as the circumstances, direct or indirect, that have contributed to it. The (psycho)therapeutic process is based, then, on the changes effected in the patient's personality as a result of becoming aware of lived experiences that are also articulated.

While it is clear, from a psychodynamic point of view, that the aims of the diagnostic process differ from those of the therapeutic, they do, however, have something in common: the acquisition of knowledge. My intention in this chapter is to demonstrate that some of the therapeutic factors operating in the therapeutic process do likewise in the diagnostic process. I shall attempt to explain that the basic elements of the diagnostic interview are present in the therapeutic session, and vice versa, that the main substance of the latter is also a valuable component of the former. Hence, we might deduce that any interview for diagnostic purposes will have some therapeutic function.

The natural corollary of this would be to establish a modality of psychotherapeutic intervention, where conditions are conducive, which I suggest should be called the "psychotherapeutic interview"— an idea I have already developed elsewhere (Pérez-Sánchez, 1996a).

Of the various therapeutic factors involved in a psychotherapeutic process, I would highlight the following: verbalisation (catharsis, evacuation, and expression in words); containment (provided by the therapeutic framework or *setting*), and the understanding or knowledge of the meaning of what is verbalised (along with any psychomotor or emotional accompaniments), as well as the working through of this knowledge (through repeated experiences of understanding obtained throughout the psychotherapeutic process).

Of these factors, the first three are present, to some extent, in the diagnostic interview. But I will focus on the factor of knowledge, as, from a psychodynamic perspective, it is the most specific one. The aim of any psychoanalytically orientated psychotherapy is for the professional to continually acquire a certain *knowledge* and understanding of aspects of the patient's mental functioning which determine his relationships with himself and with others, which are also manifest in his symptoms. We endeavour to share that knowledge with the patient, by means of *interpretation*, in order to achieve certain changes in his personality or aspects of it, from which symptomatic relief may be derived. Moreover, psychotherapy brings about an experience in which the patient is able to learn the fundamentals of a *method of facing up to reality*, the method that has enabled us to attain such knowledge. Enabling the patient to assume an increasingly large degree of responsibility in that process of (acquiring) knowledge is one of the hurdles that we must overcome in the therapeutic process. The patient's ambivalence with regard to his knowledge of himself operates continually, at times collaborating with the therapist and at others hampering the task for both. Therefore, the essential factors of the psychotherapeutic process derive from knowing the patient's psychic reality, by means of a method of observation, and enabling the patient to be involved in it through interpretation.

In terms of the diagnostic interview, it is easy to see that here also we are engaged in a process of acquiring knowledge. From a psychodynamic approach, is not enough simply to collect together a list of symptoms and establish the appropriate diagnostic label. As I have said many times over, to diagnose psychodynamically involves knowing or understanding something, if not of the psychopathology (which cannot always be understood from data from the first meetings), then at least of some areas or aspects of the functioning of the mind, of the personality that "produces" such symptoms and of his relational life. The diagnostic interview, as I said in the previous chapter, also shares in a method of observation that comprises three areas: psychopathological data, biographical data, and those provided by the interview itself, regarding the patient's relationship with the professional.

In the same way as in the diagnostic interview, in the psychotherapeutic session we attempt to know the patient by means of observation, as much of the emotional slice of life made manifest in the account he gives us of his lived experience and the acts of his current existence as of his manifestations in the here and now, before the therapist. Such data enable a *microdiagnosis* to be established, in the psychotherapeutic session, of his mode of relating and defence.

Consequently, *one might consider the diagnosis and the therapeutic act proper as two moments of the same process*. To be able to "cure" it is necessary to know; and knowledge paves the way to the "cure". Clearly, the understanding generated by the diagnostic interview essentially takes place in the therapist, and, moreover, it is a knowledge preferably concentrated on establishing the appropriate therapeutic indication. In contrast, in the psychotherapeutic session, the patient needs to share in that knowledge, by means of the therapist's interpretation. However, the guidelines established for diagnostic knowledge in interviews for that purpose, as we have seen, are similar to the method provided to the patient in the psychotherapeutic session, which gives him the opportunity to learn something from it.

Obviously, between the diagnostic interview and the therapeutic interview, be it in the psychotherapy session or in the planned interview conducted for therapeutic purposes, there are other differences in terms of technique and the degree of therapeutic aims achieved. It is not my intention to overlook such questions, as this would be akin to attributing therapeutic power to the diagnostic interview beyond any realistic potentialities and would be rather typical of the omnipotent expectations that, as I said, the patient occasionally deposits in the professional. One of the most significant differences between the diagnostic and therapeutic situations lies in the greater presence of working through in the second. As we shall have the opportunity to see in more detail (in Chapter Eight), the patient's resistance to psychic change means that it does not suffice merely to have knowledge of that which he discovers about himself, not even when this is at once a cognitive and emotional knowledge, that is to say, when it is a true *insight*. It is, furthermore, necessary that that experience should occur again and again, with subtle differences, thus enabling integration of this new knowledge. This is what we call working through, something that is not possible in the space of a few interviews except in very small measure.

So, in terms of aim, the diagnostic interview aspires to grant sufficient knowledge of the psychopathological clinical work inserted in the patient's personality in order to deduce the most appropriate type of treatment. In terms of technique, the interview for diagnostic purposes will demand, first, the collection of clinical data on the basis of the patient's spontaneous manifestations and, with the professional's help, the investigation of the pertinent questions in order to complete this data. From a psychodynamic perspective, however, it is not advisable to have a very structured interview—particularly at the first meeting, as discussed in Chapter Two—as it is precisely those things that the patient conceals and forgets which are significant. In the therapeutic session, however, the therapist will adopt a more passive attitude, although, according to the type of psychotherapeutic procedure providing the setting, there will be more or less verbal activity on his part. In any case, there will be greater openness to the patient's spontaneous manifestations than in the diagnostic interview. Likewise, in the therapeutic session, the professional will usually make interventions in the form of interpretations, which are absent from the diagnostic interview except for so-called test interpretations, where an indication for psychotherapy is being assessed.

In short, both the interview for diagnostic purposes and the therapeutic session share a process of knowledge acquisition within the framework of an observational method, taking into account, however, the respective technical differences. This process of knowledge acquisition is crucial to illustrate the idea that implicit within any diagnostic process is the therapeutic factor. Below, I shall weigh up other elements that serve to reinforce this factor. I shall do this by making a distinction between the patient's perspective and that of the therapist.

The interview from the perspective of the patient

In terms of expectations

Any person who seeks help from a psychiatric professional will have certain expectations or fantasies about it. The prevailing expectation is that the professional will make some kind of intervention that will be useful to them. But the nature of this expectation varies along a *continuum* that ranges from the most realistic vision, in terms of finding a professional with the expertise, experience, and skill to provide help, even though this requires time and the collaboration of the patient himself, to the magical expectation that deposits certain omnipotent gifts or qualities in the figure of the professional, which will result in the prescription of a miracle drug, or otherwise conclusive indications or advice in order to resolve his discomfort and fix his life.

Under normal conditions, that is, when the patient's expectations have not been too magical or the professional's responses too unfortunate or inadequate, the patient will experience a certain sense of relief owing to the fact of having felt cared for by an authority figure in whom he has placed his trust. In psychoanalytic terms, we say that the patient has developed a predominantly positive transference. This is not to say that negative elements do not exist, but they are dissociated and do not interfere with the establishment of a good initial relationship with the professional.

Based on the so-called cathartic effect

The patient who "vents" his pain or distress to the professional will gain momentary relief. What is the dynamic underlying this phenomenon? In psychoanalysis, we know that in any relationship where there is one person in need and another who attempts to answer such needs, a linking is established that has certain unique features. As mentioned above, the container–contained model as described by Bion provides us with an explanatory foundation for this. The patient presents his complaints and his troubles, hoping to find in the professional a certain disposition and receptivity which will enable him to listen and to tolerate what he hears, without responding immediately with accusatory responses or false reassurance. We can say, then, that the psychiatrist acts as a container for the patient's anguish. This is a step that is always required in any diagnostic interview, even when it is not an interview for the purpose of assessing the patient's suitability for psychotherapy, but is a psychiatric interview in the strictest sense of the term, in which it is likely that the therapeutic prescription will be that of a psychotropic drug. When a professional of a psychodynamic orientation observes that the patient has anxiety, he is also attentive to the account the patient makes of the conditions under which it arises. He does not respond immediately by prescribing an anxiolytic without letting the patient talk about what he needs to specify, even if it is something unrelated to the description of his symptoms. Certainly, the more or less favourable attitude of the professional in listening and tolerating the anxiety of the patient, together with institutional conditions of varying workloads, will determine the degree of containment that he will be able to exercise by means of that position as listener.

Depending upon this element, the therapeutic effect might have varying results. So, sometimes the patient vents in the sense that we call "evacuatory". That is to say, he expels from himself that emotional discomfort that was unbearable to him as if he were vomiting it up; as if it were something he cannot digest and wants to rid himself of completely. The result will be momentary relief, but if the patient does not attempt to delve deeper into the problem, the therapeutic effect will be but fleeting. In other cases, the patient needs to vent before someone who listens, shares his discomfort, and might understand some of what he is going through. Here, the therapeutic effect might be longer lasting, because implicit to the patient's attitude is a certain capacity to take responsibility for his psychic reality, which will make him stronger, and because he will be more able to collaborate with any treatment plan proposed to him.

The interview from the perspective of the therapist

Making oneself available as a suitable container

According to the container–contained model, faced with the patient's need to communicate his anguish, the therapist correspondingly presents himself as a suitable "container", making himself available to receive it. To be a suitable container involves listening to the patient without letting ourselves become confused by the anxieties he communicates to us, but, at the same time, without distancing ourselves so much from them that we lose contact with them, by taking a rather cold stance that would not make the patient feel understood, or, rather, contained. Furthermore, as I have mentioned, only the professional who is able to tolerate that situation without rushing to give an immediate response, be it drugs or advice, be a suitable container.

Providing a method of observation of psychic reality

The therapist sees the patient within the setting of certain conditions for therapy, and adopts an attitude in the sense we have noted: that of carrying out a containment function. All of this first offers the patient a certain confidence and trust that there is a method to address his discomfort. Second, although, of course, that method is the prerogative of the practitioner, the patient is able to grasp or intuit that he is able to learn something from that experience. This constitutes another element that contributes to his wellbeing.

The transformation of a diagnostic interview into a psychotherapeutic interview: clinical material 1

Using clinical material as an illustration, I shall attempt to demonstrate the potential for transformation of certain diagnostic interviews into therapeutic help in its own right. I have spoken about this form of help elsewhere, which I have called the "psychotherapeutic interview" (Pérez-Sanchez, 1996a).

The patient is a man in his thirties who came to the first interview with some urgency, having deliberately ingested anxiolytic drugs. There was no clear idea of committing suicide, he said, but, rather, to "sleep to get away from work and family problems" that were overwhelming him and that he did not feel able to cope with. He had been unemployed for several months. Some days prior to this, he had had an argument with his wife and, that night, had swallowed four tablets of the drug she was taking. The next day, he took another four. He insisted on the fact that he did not intend to kill himself; rather, to cause his wife concern. Indeed, this disturbed his wife so much that she urged him to seek help at our Mental Health Centre.

The patient's concern was immediately orientated towards his uncertainty regarding whether the suicide attempt reflected a mental state over which he had no control, and which could, therefore, happen again, despite his wish for this not to happen. So, straight away, we see that behind this concern there is another: that of whether he really is mentally ill, that is to say, a person unable to cope with life's difficulties without risk to his (mental) integrity, who might lose control of himself even to the point of committing suicide. When we enquired into these fears, he explained his history. At the age of eighteen, he was admitted to a psychiatric hospital where he stayed for two months and underwent electroconvulsive treatment (two per week). Once discharged, he continued to be administered this therapy for a period of approximately two years, but at a progressively lower frequency, from a weekly session to one session every month or every two months.

The patient did not know the reason for his admission to psychiatric hospital, as it was not explained to him what illness he was suffering from, and all of his attempts to clarify and to demand the diagnosis from the psychiatrist were useless. Since then, throughout his life, he has been dogged by the worry of whether or not he could be mentally ill. In part, he says, he hoped that today's consultation would answer that question. The therapist tried to help him to verbalise what he remembered of his breakdown as a teenager. The man explained that at his place of work he felt mistreated by his boss, but was not able to voice his protest. For a time he endured the situation, but, at the same time, continued to feel depressed, until one day he lost his temper. He broke some objects in the workshop, mounted a colleague's bike, and headed towards a nearby river with the idea of throwing himself into the water. He recognised the absurdity of this supposed suicide attempt, as he knew how to swim. He maintained that this was the reason he was committed. As for the fact that he underwent electroconvulsive treatment, he hypothesised that it must have been owing to the fact that, at the time, and in his province, they did not know how to treat "these things" any differently. Years later, he consulted another psychiatrist to clear up any doubts that remained in his mind over whether or not he was mentally ill, and was told he did not need shock therapy or any other treatment. And this was how his relationship with psychiatrists had been interrupted, many years previously . . . until today, although since then, with varying intensity, he had continued to be gripped by the idea of being mentally ill and that, consequently, he could suffer another breakdown at any time, just as had happened now.

Following on from this, the patient explained his history of a lack of stability in his working life. He did not often remain for very long in any job, as he would soon lose interest and leave. Currently unemployed, he was doing odd jobs. He had a young son. He acknowledged that his wife had helped him a great deal, and that it was he who caused the majority of the conflict in the relationship, as he was always making mountains out of molehills. While he did not have any fixed employment, he thought that he should help out more at home, as his wife was working. He was also concerned that this whole situation could be harmful for his son.

He was not able to study, he went on to say, because his father, who was uneducated himself, thought that what he needed was a job. He had always liked books and was interested in expanding his cultural horizons. As an adult, he tried to study, but could not keep up the pace required. He was an only child from a lower-middle class family. His parents had become very concerned about his mental health after the episode during which he was committed, although he admitted that he had previously been a cause for concern to them as he had been a difficult child. His father had died several months previously. He had been suffering from an incurable chronic illness; however, the end had come quickly. His mother had not wanted to come to live with him, as he had offered to her, as she preferred to be alone. He spoke about his parents in a respectful and affectionate tone. His only complaint about his father was his authoritarianism and the fact that he had not given him any incentives to devote his life to more ambitious endeavours.

At the end of this first interview, the patient asks if he should be worried about ingesting the pills. He adds that his wife had become very frightened, to the extent that she would not let him be alone for fear that he might do "something stupid". As a response, the therapist introduces an interpretative intervention. He suggests that perhaps his concern and doubts over whether he might be mentally ill are a way of avoiding responsibility for his own feelings and actions, which would then be a product of the mental illness. That is to say, they would be something outside of him, and the consequences of them would fall to his wife, for not watching him adequately. He seems to understand and agree with this comment. He wants to continue to discuss this in a forthcoming interview, so we arrange to meet again two weeks later.

The impression the patient gives, after the data he provides and the type of relationship he establishes in the interview, is that of a person who is quite dependent, with a great need for the other and very much afraid that the relationship could be damaged through his own fault, but, at the same time, expecting the other to make the effort to preserve it. I believe that the patient uses the psychiatric history (being committed to hospital and the indication of electroconvulsive treatment) as an excuse to live off the menacing shadow of mental illness and not assume responsibility for frustrating or painful situations, which leads him to emphasise his dependence on the people around him, in particular his wife. In the interview, he comes across as collaborative, capable of self-observation and communication of his psychic life, although with little tolerance for containing emotional pain. This is very evident when, after he had told the therapist that he does not want to commit suicide, he asks at the end of the interview if he should be worried about this matter. That is to say, he hopes that the therapist, with his authority, will assume responsibility for his wishes not to kill himself. It seems clear that the fact of trying to "hurt himself" with the same pills his wife takes is a way of blaming her and forcing her to pour everything into him, by putting more effort into the success of the relationship. But, at the same time, this does not satisfy him, hence his need to make the consultation, although this is only half true, I must say, as it was his wife who pushed him to make the request. However, he did manage to come alone.

We must also highlight the primary importance of the diagnostic request. The patient would like to know, while at the same time fearing, his psychiatric diagnosis. Is he mentally ill? If he is, he will be able to delegate the responsibilities of his life to others, since he, being "mentally ill", cannot take them on and shall be under the protection of someone close: his wife, the doctors, and so on. But, at the same time, if this is so, if he is diagnosed as "mentally ill", he will live with the threat of acting without control at any moment, that is to say, in a self-destructive way, which might even lead him to commit suicide, as there is no protection that can ensure complete control. Here we notice a curious situation, and one that is very relevant to the topic we are discussing: the patient hopes that the therapeutic intervention that is made will involve providing him with a diagnosis, although, of course, in a very different sense from that which we are attempting to give it in this chapter. The patient is ambivalent towards his request to be given a diagnosis. On the one hand, he would like it—the diagnosis of "mental illness"—as it would, thereby, have resolved his attitude towards life in terms of delegating all responsibility to his wife, not only in terms of his work commitments and those as a husband and father, but even the responsibility of preserving his own existence. But, on the other hand, it scares him to be in such a painful and dependent condition, unable to exercise any control over himself and his life, especially if we consider that this is someone who maintains his cognitive and instrumental ego capacities well preserved. I have placed the expression "mentally ill" in inverted commas because, for the patient, it has a very precise meaning, which is not the otherwise broad and generic literal sense of the term. He gives this definition to anyone who loses control over his person and who might commit a self-destructive act.

Uncertainty remained over the nature of the aggressive episode in adolescence that led not only to him being committed, but to the application of electroconvulsive treatment. The possibility of a psychotic breakdown did not seem plausible, given the intervening years and subsequent development without any new episode having occurred. Rather, we might consider a personality disorder with impaired impulse control and a low tolerance threshold for frustration, characteristics that in adolescence became particularly intense. I felt it was very important to wait for the second interview to observe the evolution in relation to the first, in order to make a more accurate assessment.

In the *second interview,* the patient had experienced clinical improvement in terms of anxiety, depression, and fear of the risk of uncontrolled suicide. However, he immediately asks if what has happened to him is because he has had endogenous depression. (This was the diagnosis given to him in adolescence, he recalls now. Not being satisfied with this label, he wanted more of an explanation; hence his complaint when this was not forthcoming). The therapist once again points out his tendency to deflect his discomfort in terms of the label, and in addition to the "unknown" one, according to his idea of the expression "endogenous". Also, that he was hoping, once again, for the therapist to assume responsibility for that.

On the basis of this intervention, the interview experiences a significant shift. The patient makes reference to something that was a cause of conflict and concern. It is in relation to his son. When the child was one year old, he was also unemployed, while his wife had returned to work. As such, it was he who took care of the child, and derived satisfaction from this. But now, for some time, certain compulsive ideas of aggression towards the child were arising in him. The therapist explains to him, in another interpretation, by way of a test, that perhaps this was a jealous reaction to the child. He was an only child, as he had been the only one with his wife until the birth of his son, and during the period in which he took care of him he was able to establish an exclusive relationship with him, the wife being the one who was excluded. Now, however, he has to share the child with his wife, feeling that it might be he himself who is excluded from the relationship with his wife. The patient listens carefully and takes the comments of the therapist on board, which seems to calm him. At the end of the interview, the therapist proposes another meeting three weeks later, adding that, depending on how things go, this would probably conclude the help for the time being.

We shall note that the third interview is offered three weeks later, which in my experience is too long a period of time if one is carrying out a diagnostic process. However, the decision is taken alongside the prospect of terminating the help. And it is precisely because this latter element was introduced that it seemed appropriate to give a long enough time period to see how the patient responded. The reasons that led the professional to take such a decision were, first, the favourable clinical response after the first interview. Second, the fact that the patient agreed to leave the issue of the "mentally ill" diagnosis to one side in order to proceed to talk about relational concerns and conflicts. And third, by giving him this "trial period", it afforded him the confidence in the fact that he had the potentialities to exercise some "control" over his destructive tendencies, which, in the therapist's view, did not entail any risk whatsoever. With regard to the therapist determining that the help would, in all likelihood, be terminated at the next meeting, this decision he based on the following. The interviews had been able to transform the patient's request for diagnosis into the manifestation of a focalised conflict which he had been able to talk about: the triangular situation mobilised by the birth of his son. Another factor was the attitude of the patient in asking for an immediate response to his question, which he knew was not possible, but which arose from his tendency to settle into a dependent relationship with the other, another reason why it did not seem appropriate to run the risk of encouraging this tendency.

In the *third and last interview*, the clinical improvement is sustained. The patient has returned to occasional work, where there was a minor incident with the person in charge, which had made him feel impotent as he had to control the ensuing violent reaction. But he is happy, because previously he would have lost his temper, and would have left the job, as his wife has suggested to him in the face of his continual complaints. He values the fact that he did not wish to react in such a way because it would mean once again being without a job and being dependent upon his wife's income. He then remarks that it was good for him, in the previous interview, to realise that behind the ideas of aggression towards his son were feelings of jealousy. He has been able to talk this through with his wife, and this has helped him. He adds that it has also been useful to him, despite his insistence on the psychiatric diagnosis during the first interview, that we had put this aside to talk about other things. And when it seemed that there was no longer anything else to look at, but there was still time left in the interview, he associates the memory of his father's death and, by evoking his image, relativises the failures that he had always criticised him for, such as not helping him to study or being very demanding, to conclude that he probably did what he could. After that, he even expresses feelings of guilt towards his father, as he perhaps did not give him all the attention he should have when he was unwell.

In the same interview, I decide to revisit the idea of his request for psychiatric diagnosis as an alibi used by the patient so as not to recognise certain painful experiences, such as those tied to the feelings of jealousy towards his son which we were looking at the other day, or now, perhaps, the feelings of guilt regarding the death of his father. The patient replies that, every morning, upon waking, he feels as if a wall had been raised, separating off that time in the past in which he was or felt he could be mentally ill, in order to be able to face the day with vim and vigour. The patient himself, sensing that the interview time is running out and recalling the last session's proposal, says, "So we can consider it concluded, then" (the help). Then he himself asks about the possibility of returning at a later date if necessary, which, obviously, remains open.

Observations on the third interview

I think the last interview confirms some of the therapist's expectations. The patient was able to use his own potentialities to contain and curb any possible violent reaction, which "previously, would have exploded". The delay in the third interview and the proposal of terminating the help appear to have acted as a shock to the patient, activating his own self-confidence. In other words, given that the therapist does not accept the projective identification of the potentialities that belonged to the patient, it is the patient who, as far as possible, has taken them up again. It should also be said that by having dismissed, for the time being, any other possibility of help once the diagnostic process is concluded, this avoided the patient depositing the assumption of responsibility in the treatment and in the therapist, especially the one that so concerned him: the responsibility for the control of his impulses.

But this question of not having responded to the patient's dependent tendency by offering him a therapist on whom he can depend, and referring him instead to his own potentialities, had other consequences. Indeed, one of the reasons that he continued at work, after the confrontation with his boss, was to avoid being made unemployed and, as a result, being more dependent on his wife. Here, we note a possible therapeutic effect of his experience in the interviews, which began with a diagnostic purpose. The experience of an object (the therapist) who does not accept the projections of his potentialities (those of the patient)—and, consequently, his dependent relationship—is something that he has been able to introject and transfer to the relationship with his wife, to act in a more healthy way.

Moreover, this experience has offered him a new perspective on how to face up to his conflicts. The patient, showing signs that he benefited from the previous interview, recalls the comments made by the therapist on the situation with his son and his wife, which has led him to reflect upon it and, this is what I think is significant, has prompted him to talk to his wife. Voicing concerns as a means to confront them is the new approach that the patient seems to have incorporated. We must emphasise that he seems to find great support in his partner, who has agreed to work with him.

The patient does not "forget" the issue that brought him to make the consultation, which was that of a request for a psychiatric diagnosis. And there is recognition on his part that the method followed in the interview, of setting aside this request in order to address the issues that were concerning him, has had beneficial results. It is true that the image the patient presents, of the wall he has raised regarding his fears about being "mentally ill" as something that has been relegated to the past, suggests a radical defence, a splitting, and, therefore, would imply a poorly integrated concept in his mental life, in terms of not being sufficiently resolved. Similarly, there is no guarantee that the achievements we have spoken about as a result of the interviews will continue to be consistent. It is likely that if they are to be maintained, this will depend upon healthy collaboration between him and his wife. I am not, however, seeking to grant these interviews a therapeutic potential that would simply not be possible in such a limited experience. As I have said, one of the keys to potential psychic change lies in the possibility of working through everything that has been made conscious, which, of course, requires time. My intention in this chapter has been simply to emphasise the therapeutic factors of diagnostic interviews, not only because through them the patient is able to derive some benefit, but also, above all, the therapeutic potential of the psychotherapeutic process proper can be demonstrated, in cases where it is suitable.

One might wonder why this patient was not given an indication for a more intensive psychotherapy. In my opinion, however, for all the reasons given, this would have meant taking an iatrogenic position. We do not dismiss the possibility that he might need it later, but for now, it seemed prudent not to respond immediately to such a proposal, as it would have encouraged the patient's dependence by not trusting in his own potentialities. The patient wished to place the therapist in the dilemma of either giving him a psychiatric diagnosis, or telling him that there was nothing wrong with him. This was in spite of the fact that each of these alternatives corresponded to the two psychiatric experiences he had already had, both proving unsatisfactory. However, he tended to repeat them because they were equivalent to evading the experience in several aspects: in his current family life, both in his relationship with his wife and with his son, and also towards death of his father, which were the themes emerging in the interviews as burning issues.

Conclusions

Therefore, in my opinion, some of the factors that contribute towards a diagnostic interview having therapeutic effects can be said to be: the development of a predominantly positive transference, the cathartic effect, the professional's function of containment, the implicit proposal of a method of knowledge apprehension and approach to psychic reality, and a realistic therapeutic response or proposal.

The interest in considering the therapeutic factors in diagnostic interviews lies in the fact that it helps to encourage an attitude of greater involvement in the therapist, by seeking that the interview, from the very first moment, should be beneficial to the patient. Of course, in seeking this, any omnipotent tendencies should be avoided, as I have iterated many times over. But, in addition, in some cases, to be open to the therapeutic potentialities of the interview enables a meeting which is begun for the purpose of diagnosis to become a therapeutic interview, such as did occur in the clinical example set out above.

Note

1. Part of this material has been used in another publication by the author (Pérez-Sánchez, 1996a), although for different purposes. Furthermore, here the content has been modified and adapted to the subject we are dealing with.

CHAPTER FIVE

Interview analysis: the mother with difficulties in her feeding function (clinical material 2)

I shall dedicate this chapter to setting out in detail a number of diagnostic interviews, analysed from a psychodynamic perspective. The material has been taken from a group of psychotherapists with whom I collaborated as a supervisor for several years. The purpose of this clinical illustration is to closely follow the cognitive and emotional movements of the relationship between patient and therapist, thereby enabling us to demonstrate a number of things. First, the patient's (and the therapist's) anxieties and defences during the course of the interview, and second, the patient's suitability for psychological help; that is, for brief psychoanalytic psychotherapy. I have endeavoured to reproduce the notes exactly as they were presented by the therapist during the supervision, although with the necessary modifications regarding external data in order not to compromise patient confidentiality. Occasionally, I will interrupt the narrative in order to introduce a comment or two of my own in analysis of the interview. At times, I have also added comments that were suggested during the supervision itself.

Diagnostic interviews

Observations on the first interview

The patient was referred by her GP for psychological help. The patient comes to the interview alone. She is simply but neatly dressed. Her attitude is collaborative throughout the interview. She speaks with ease, scarcely even pausing. She cries throughout almost the entire interview.

These brief introductory remarks made by the therapist demonstrate several things. First, they illustrate his skill for observation and synthesis of that which has drawn his attention in the interview. From the outset, the fact that the patient does not come to the interview accompanied by someone indicates an adult capacity to deal with the interview, and that her anxiety and pathology are not so pressing that they require the external support of another. The observation about the "simple but neat" way of dressing suggests that the pathology is not so intense that it has taken its toll on the care she takes over herself. These "adult aspects", moreover, will aid collaboration, which is also revealed by the fluidity of her account. Nevertheless, the patient shows her discomfort by crying throughout almost the entire interview, although not so much that it interferes with communication.

> *Patient (P)*: Well, I feel a little better [since she requested the appointment one week ago, at the Centre]. Around three months ago, I suffered from a depression that lasted around a month, where I didn't really feel like eating. I lost weight. I was treated for it and felt better; but now I'm not feeling very well again and I am afraid of falling (ill again), as it has already happened to me before.

The patient directly relates her discomfort (the depression), as well as her doubts over the long-term effectiveness of the previous treatment (which was pharmacological), as, although she recognises that it worked well, its effects have not lasted long. Implicitly, she is introducing the possibility of another form of help, the psychological kind, since the pharmacological one has not been enough.

> *P*: The problem is that I have a depressive personality, because this has already happened to me before. But this time I've come down with it a lot worse . . . It seems as though it made me weaker and anaemic, with low

[blood] pressure and no desire to do anything, and I was in a really bad way . . .

One would say that, with her insistence upon her having a depressive personality, her intention is to give a clear message to the therapist. Is it that, by doing this, she will better convey the intensity of her predicament? She emphasises this when she makes it clear that her depression has lately been more severe, perhaps owing to her poor physical condition. With this, it seems as though she is talking about an illness that is contracted because of some external pathogen and which, depending on the condition of the body, one can combat more or less effectively. Might what she is communicating point towards a theory of her "illness" being of a fundamentally somatic nature, in contradiction to the psychological perspective which, implicitly, she had just insinuated might be feasible?

P: I have two small children who make me very anxious. And if you're not well . . . then, it's all the worse. For the last few months, my son hasn't been feeding well, and that makes me anxious . . .

With this information, the patient modifies this last impression. There is an external reality, certainly, but now she indicates that it is of the relational kind; that problems in the care of her children might be at the root of her discomfort. Furthermore, her maternal function is further upset when it comes to dealing with her youngest son's feeding difficulties. These data bring us away from the idea that the patient is proposing a biological theory and point, on the contrary, to the hypothesis that her depressive discomfort is related to difficulties in tolerating the problems which arise from the care and the feeding of her children.

P: What's more, my husband works a night shift, so I felt really alone [she cries]. But many people are alone and this doesn't happen to them. Seeing me like this [depressed] my husband . . . even changed shifts [to be able to be with her] . . . The fact is I don't know what can be causing all of this. I haven't had any major problems, just these little things [the children eating badly]; as I have no problems with my husband. Nobody close to me has died . . . (She pauses). When I was fourteen years old my mother died and yes, it was a very bad time for me, but I wasn't like this. A while ago, my husband was made redundant, but now he is working. So, my husband has his job, we have two children who are fine . . . What reason do I have to be depressed?

First, she adduces the fact of feeling alone as a circumstance which might have contributed to exacerbating her discomfort. However, subsequent information about how her husband reorganised his work timetable to be with her would indicate that this is not a loneliness related to her partner's neglect, so the patient asks herself what it is that causes such states of depression. Our interpretation is that it is an inner loneliness. She does not understand this, and shows an interest in finding out more about it. There is a curiosity to get to know herself, which reinforces our last idea that we are moving away from the somatic theory of the illness to instead come closer to a psychological position. A brief review of her current life would give her no reason to feel bad. In order to do this, she has had to relativise and minimise the problems she articulates at the beginning relating to the feeding of her children: "They are little things." On the other hand, and, curiously, one of the facts cited by the patient that might account for someone being depressed is the death of a person close to them. Yet she states that she has not suffered any loss recently. But she goes on to revive the memory of her mother's death, when she was a teenager, in order to specify that not even then did she feel as bad as she does now. Therefore, there are no apparent motives for her to be depressed. "Why am I, then?" she seems to be asking the therapist.

> *Therapist (T)*: But it seems as though these little things are, in fact, making you feel bad.

The therapist simply establishes certain facts: the "little" things she talks about are making her feel bad. By doing this, he does not give a direct reply, as perhaps the patient would have wanted him to; neither is he acting omnipotently, and nor does he trivialise her discomfort. So, with this good indication, the patient has no choice but to continue the interview in search of new pieces of information.

> *P*: The thing is I had no enthusiasm for anything. And luckily, because of the children, I had to get up every morning . . . Today I was anxious about having to come here [she starts to cry again]. The month when I felt the worst, I went for acupuncture, but I didn't notice much improvement. I went through a period of not sleeping. And the problem was that I was

thinking about sad things, without meaning to. People would tell me not to think about it. [She pauses]

Faced with the therapist's response, the patient also accepts the reality of her discomfort. And she takes a step forward in the course of the interview by showing a piece of information relating to the "here and now": the anxiety she felt over coming to the interview, which she also exteriorises with weeping. She recalls that she has received other treatment that was not effective (acupuncture). Upon seeing that the therapist accepts her discomfort, in spite of it being caused by these "little" things, she elaborates upon the description of other symptoms, such as insomnia and thinking melancholy thoughts. But at home they tell her not to think about it. "What will the therapist say to that?" the patient might be pondering.

T: You thought about sad things?

Quite correctly, the therapist enquires about the sad things the patient was thinking about. With this, he is giving her the clear indication that the therapeutic space is different to that of familial or social relationships. Here, it is possible to look at the sad thoughts, and this implies that the conditions are in place to tolerate them.

P: Yes. For example, I thought about how something might happen to my husband on the road, or with the machinery at his work. Just yesterday, one of his colleagues had an accident, and apparently his guts spilled out. Afterwards, he (the husband) said that he shouldn't have told me … I have an eleven-year-old girl and a boy of two. So, when I was feeling worse, I was also afraid for them, because if something happened to me, what would become of my children? Who would look after them?

T: If something happened to you?

Little by little the patient is able to verbalise her unhappy thoughts. If she thinks that something bad might happen to her loved ones, she must feel that she herself is "bad". Thus, there is a certain relief that comes from being able to express these thoughts. We soon see where all this is going. When she vaguely alludes to her fear that something might happen to her, and indirectly to her children, who would then be deprived of their mother's care, the therapist helps her along the same lines as before, by encouraging her to express any "bad" thoughts she might have, simply by gathering together her concerns in the form of a question.

> P: If I were to lose my mind and not be able to look after them. As I was not well, it was very hard for me to get things done, and they weren't eating. The children realised [something was wrong] and they weren't as carefree, they were miserable. My husband said that it wasn't like that, but I knew that they were all over me more than usual, to get my attention, precisely because I was not looking after them. It's just that my brain was dulled . . .

Once again, we see a reappearance of the patient's worry that she is not in a fit state to carry out her maternal functions. When she was unwell, she does not know why, she feared that the discomfort would go even further, to the point of her "losing her mind" and not being able to look after her children. Here, also, the patient demonstrates a certain capacity for insight by observing that the children's being miserable and not wanting to eat was related to her emotional detachment.

> P: My husband and my sister helped me a lot. And it upset me to find out that a girl I know started out with depression and has now lost her mind. I became obsessed with the idea that the same thing could happen to me. I would wake up at night thinking about that girl. Now that I'm feeling a bit better, I don't think about her so much. But I was afraid to run into her. Before, that girl took care of herself, but now she has put on weight. Sometimes I tell myself, "Of course you can do it." My father always used to say, "You'll get through this—you'll see." Because I have been through a few things in my life, like my husband's [surgical] operations on his knee, a slipped disc . . . And I have always managed . . . But maybe the problem is that things keep building up, until there comes a day when you just can't cope any more. Although I have never been very upbeat; I have always been pessimistic. I have always been a quiet, reserved kind of person, although not unusually so, and not like now, when I couldn't even talk to my own family, whereas my sister has always been a bit livelier . . . Coming here has been very difficult for me.

> T: You say this has happened to you before.

The patient is able to recognise the help she has received, both from her husband and from her sister. The fact that she admits to being helped by others is information to bear in mind, faced with the prospect of psychological help. Later, she once again raises her doubts about her own abilities to tolerate life's challenges. At times, she has been able to overcome particular adversities, and she remembers the encouragement her father gave to her—another piece of information to retain; that of the father figure as someone who has been able to give her something good: an encouraging piece of advice. But she continues to enquire into the reason for her current state: could it be that things have been building up? She also shows a degree of self-awareness in recognising that she is reserved and not very talkative. Suddenly, she is very open with the therapist, and tells him that it has been difficult for her to come to the session. At that point, I believe that the therapist missed an opportunity to enquire into those fears, by inducing her, instead, to explore other depressive episodes.

> P: Well, I have had other bouts where I've been like that, although without actually becoming deeply depressed. When I got depressed, I would take D [commercial name of an antidepressant]. Actually, the problem started when my son [the second child] was six months old. Until then, the boy fed well, but he became unwell with a bad case of gastroenteritis, which really scared us. Since then I get scared whenever he gets a little unwell. And the fact is that I had a lot of problems with food with my daughter as well. I was told she had a narrow stomach or something like that, but that it would get better by itself. So, when my son had gastroenteritis, I thought the same thing that had happened to my daughter was happening to him. But now she is actually rather chubby [she smiles]. She was ill until she was three or four years old. And with the boy, what happens is that he throws up [vomits] his food, well, the little he does eat. And I get so upset. It makes me anxious. I don't know if it's because he is dirty or if he has some problem with his stomach which makes this happen . . .

The patient responds to the therapist's intervention by again speaking about her depression, but immediately associates it to her principal concerns: her children's problems with food. Although she reports that the difficulties with her first child, her daughter, have been overcome, to the extent that she can say with some relief (smiling) that she is now chubby, this does not help to alleviate her anxiety towards her son's feeding problems. We are struck by the reaction she describes when her son "throws up" her food—that is to say, he rejects it—and this is what upsets her. What can such a somatic manifestation mean? Does she get angry at seeing her son being so "dirty"? Or is her upset caused by feelings of shame or guilt, for being a mother who is not able to adequately perform her nutritional function? Nevertheless, the patient also admits the possibility that there might be a problem with his stomach that "causes this to happen", perhaps as though it were a bad object that, from inside the child, makes him throw up the food. This seems, once more, to evince her ambivalence towards the possible aetiology of her illnesses and those of her son. At times, they are supported by a biological theory, and at others, a psychological one.

The patient continues,

> I am afraid of taking medication for my nerves as it might become habit-forming. Although I've been told that it won't . . . But I am also afraid that if I come off the medication, I will go back to feeling bad. I would like to have the complete assurance that neither of these things will happen. Now I'm taking D again, one tablet in the morning and another at midday.

The therapist goes on to ask her about other aspects of her life, such as work.

It is likely that, here, the patient is expressing her fear of excessive dependence, whether this be to drugs or to a therapeutic relationship. She answers her own question, admitting the possibility that, in spite of dependence, it seems as though it is possible to come off treatment. The therapist validates the answer the patient supplies to herself, and goes on to look at other aspects of her life.

She works as a cleaner in several houses. During the months when she was at her worst she could not do it, as she did not even look after her own house. She works three days a week. "It is also good to get out of the house," she says. She only goes for three hours at a time, as she has to get back to the day nursery to pick up her son, who eats lunch at home, as does her daughter. As her husband is working at that time, she gets bored being alone. She is not one to go to the gym, or anything like that.

She adds that she has never been a very upbeat person, or full of life, although neither did she ever have to go to the doctor. "When that happened to my mother [her death]," she continues, I had a hard time. But I got over it. My father has married again. I think he proposed straight away to an aunt of ours, who said no. And then he proposed to another woman, whom he married six months after [the death of her mother]. And it wasn't that he wasn't looked after, because I was at home and I took care of whatever he needed, but he had a thing about getting married."

The therapist asks her about the rest of the family.

She is the youngest of several brothers and sisters. And she thinks that, being the last, she probably arrived "as a bit of a fluke". Her mother died from stomach cancer in her fifties. Her sister got married the year after her mother died. She was fourteen years old and was the only single one. She had no idea about how to run a home, as she had devoted herself to her studies.

For this last part of the interview it would appear that she has a somewhat more "bureaucratic" or rule-bound character. The patient restricts herself to simply answering the therapist's questions, despite the fact that they are very general, but with a somewhat defensive attitude. When she talks of her arrival being, "a bit of a fluke", she does not accompanying this with any comment, or any discernible display of emotion. The same thing occurs when she comes to touch once again upon the theme of the death of her mother, which she focuses on her father's difficulties in doing the work of mourning, thereby projecting into him her own inability to do that work. She also talks about the burden of responsibility that she had to bear as a teenager, as if to account for why she could not do the work of mourning either, as her external conditions were too burdensome.

As the interview is coming to an end, the patient says, "The sign outside shocked me somewhat [Primary Psychiatric Healthcare and Mental Health Centre]. It's just that when they sent me here for psychological help, I thought it was a centre for psychology, and when I saw the bit about psychiatry, I was shocked. And it made me feel quite anxious, as I have never spoken about these things. But, on the other hand, I wanted to come and talk to someone, because at home I mention certain things and I am told not to think about it. So, with someone who is impartial, a specialist, well, I think that gives you confidence . . . not to cheer you up straight away, but they can tell you, 'this means this, and that's it.' It was good for my cousin."

At the beginning, it appears that the anxiety she relates to is caused by coming to a centre for psychiatry, that is to say, for mad people. But then she refers to her concern ("the anxiety") that she has never spoken about these things to anyone else. Here the patient is being honest in expressing the difficulty involved for her in talking about personal matters that are worrying her. But, on the other hand, once she has overcome this anxiety, she declares her wish to talk to a professional who, contrary to what takes place at home, enables her to express what she is thinking. Likewise, the patient declares what she understands by "psychological help". She dismisses the quick-fix meaning, of "cheering you up straight away", and accepts the idea that this is instead a centre where people tell you things exactly as they are, where "This means this, and that's it."

T: Would you like to talk about anything else?

P: Well, the things that are worrying me are everything I've said to you. My husband says that if necessary, he'll come too.

The therapist suggests that for the time being it is sufficient for her to come alone, and they arrange to meet a week later, before specifying the type of help.

The patient states that she has already spoken about the significant things that worry her and the things that she is able to recount, but does so as if she did not trust herself to continue talking in the next interview by her own resources; hence, the question about whether the presence of her husband might be necessary That is, whether the therapist, after the experience had with her in this encounter, considers her fit to go ahead without the intervention of a third person.

I have transcribed below the notes taken during the *supervision* that followed the presentation of this first interview to the working group.

"Already, in her early statements, the patient explains in quite a direct way what is concerning her. The material she provides 'brings' or conveys the conflict. She is seen as a sincere patient. She relates her depression to her lack of desire to eat and then associates it to the children's feeding problems. On the other hand, she says that she does not understand what is happening to her, because her depressive reaction is out of proportion to the accumulation of 'little things' that are happening to her. She admits that her children are a source of conflict, but at the same time they give her an incentive: 'Thank goodness they would get me up [out of bed].' She recognises that it is important to come and 'talk with someone'. She is able to relate to the therapist's interventions. She takes in what is said to her and collaborates, always making some comment in relation to the indications made to her. While her problem is related to food, during the interview she is instead quite receptive: she is able to accept what the therapist provides her. That is to say, there is no rejection of the 'food for thought' (explanations, comments, and suggestions) that the therapist provides her. She does not 'throw it back (up)' [vomit], but quite the reverse; she accepts it and even collaborates by expanding on the information. Therefore, in the interview dynamic, we can see that the patient does not present problems with 'ingesting' the 'nourishment' that the therapist is bringing her. She is, essentially, receptive."

Second interview (one week later) with comments

The therapist suggests they continue where they left off in the last interview, to see how she can be helped, and asks if she wishes to add anything relating to what she said previously.

> P: Just like that . . . Well, I always need to be with someone, if I am on my own I have to keep busy for fear that I will fall [into a depression] again. The other day . . . I explained quite a few things to you.

The patient expresses her tendency to form dependent relationships, the need she has of others for fear of "falling" if she is alone. This raises the question of what happens when she is alone, why does she have to keep herself busy, which are the thoughts that might assail her and cause her to sink. Recalling the end of the first interview, when she sought the therapist's opinion on the advisability of continuing the interviews alone or accompanied by her husband, I think that the beginning of the second interview shows her difficulty in coping alone. However, she has made the effort to come alone. And she is prepared to continue.

> T: The other day you explained the situation that is worrying you. Today I would like it if you could give me some more information about your life, perhaps starting with your childhood, pregnancy, birth, and so on; whatever you remember.

The therapist suggests possible areas for investigation to the patient. Just as in the first interview his technical approach was that of conducting a "free interview", now he attempts to direct the patient towards issues that need exploring.

P: As my mother died so early, (!) I don't have much information. I have never heard anything about my birth being difficult or that anything unusual happened. I spent my childhood at home, in the village, the usual things. All my brothers and sisters are much older than I am. I always say that I came along "as a fluke", although maybe they did plan to have me. I don't know. I lived in the village until I was three years old, then we moved to another town until I took my first communion, and I moved to Barcelona a year before I got married. It was good because I was the youngest. My brothers and sisters went off to work straight away. I was the only one who studied. When I lost my mother, I was left alone. My father wanted to get married straight away, but I didn't stay and live with them [the father and his partner]. I must have been sixteen or seventeen years old. I wasn't at all keen on seeing them throwing out my mother's things . . . because his new wife wanted to bring in her own things. So I went to live with my sister. [She pauses]

It is significant that the first idea the patient introduces when asked about her childhood is the death of her mother; who "died so early", even though she was already fourteen years old. It is as if this fact had erased any other information acquired in relation to her experiences during the first fourteen years of her life. Immediately afterwards, she once again contributes the information that she let slip at the end of the previous interview, that perhaps her birth was not planned. Now, however, she admits to having some doubt over this: "Perhaps they did plan to have me." Shortly afterwards, she refers once more to the death of her mother in order to show that after losing her she was left alone, as she did not want to live with a father who would "throw out her mother's things." That is to say, the past is dominated by this fact, by the death of the mother. She then talks about her father as someone who was unable to do the work of mourning, by parting so easily with the mother's things. But it seems as though she, too, has problems in this regard, as she hardly remembers anything of her childhood, as if she also had "thrown out" her lived experiences with her mother.

T: Is there anything else you remember from your childhood?

P: When I was little, I would get gifts. That is, I did well, compared to my brothers and sisters.

T: Breastfeeding?

P: No idea! . . . I started nursery school when I was three or four years old, when most children start at six. I wasn't an outstanding student. I was average. We loved the teachers. I don't remember any of them ever hitting me or telling me off. I wasn't a naughty child. [Silence]

Also very significant, in the sense we have just been discussing, is her answer to the question about breastfeeding, "No idea!" Such a blunt reply expresses that she has had to "throw out" of her mind many of the items relating to her lived experiences with her mother or the phantasies she has reconstructed around these experiences. At this point, the patient does not seem very "sincere". She says that she did well as she received more gifts than her brothers or sisters, but she has "no idea" about breastfeeding, and she was sent to nursery school before other children, that is to say, removing her sooner from her mother.

T: Were you close to your brothers and sisters?

P: Not really, because there was such an age difference between us. With one sister, yes, but only until I was two years old, as she started working when she was twelve. She tells me that she used to take me out in a big pram with another boy, and that I would get jealous. But I didn't play with them. Whenever we have returned to the village on holiday, with one of my brothers or sisters, they show me certain places where we had been or played, but I don't remember. I do remember the other house, in X, when I took my first communion dressed like a nun. So pompous! That's not for me. I didn't even get married in a bridal gown; I was too embarrassed. My daughter, on the other hand, is the complete opposite, because now she is taking her first communion and, if she could, she would do it in a polka-dot dress . . . I worry about not being in good spiits by then.

T: And about your mother? What more can you tell me?

Once again, this forgetting is made evident, this "throwing out" of her childhood memories; memories that would, in any case, refer to experiences of solitude, as we can gather from the fact that, being much younger, she did not play with her brothers or sisters. She is also able to recognise feelings of jealousy, although in passing. She then seems removed over the matter of her daughter's first communion and her concerns about not feeling well by then. Here, the therapist takes the opportunity to redirect the interview towards an important subject that the patient has difficulty dealing with: that of her mother.

> P: She was ill for a year or so, without knowing what was wrong with her. At the beginning they thought it was gastritis, but as she continued to lose weight she was referred to another doctor, and then we found out what was wrong with her. She didn't know, so you had to pretend, especially if you felt like you were going to cry. She died during the operation [surgery]. And as they didn't let us take her out of hospital so she could be at home, we had to act as if she were still alive, which is another reason why we weren't able to cry. For a time, I couldn't pass by the room she was in while she was at home. Through the glass it looked to me like the candles were lit, or, rather, I felt afraid.

This fragment reveals several things. The site of the mother's illness is in her stomach, precisely the organ that was the cause for concern on her part in connection with her daughter, as well as what concerns her in relation to her son. She then attributes her failure to grieve for her mother to external circumstances. Here, she seems to be exhibiting signs of mourning that is still not worked through, or, at least, not sufficiently.

> T: What was your mother like?

The patient evidently has difficulties in approaching the maternal figure, as she gives an account referring to the external circumstances surrounding her mother's death. She mentions very little about the kind of person she was, which might cause her to connect with her true feelings towards her loss. It is for this reason that the therapist decides to help her by asking her directly about what her mother was like.

> P: They say that she was very happy while she was in the village. But then, when she went to the town, she was miserable. I always knew her as someone who was unhappy.

In other words, she was never fortunate enough to enjoy a happy mother, as her brothers and sisters did. We are coming to better understand that expression, "No idea!" with which she replied to the question about breastfeeding. This experience might be one of the elements that have complicated the work of mourning the death of her mother. Might resentment—over having been born by accident, having had a sad mother, having been removed from her side early by being sent to nursery school—have acted, standing in the way of her experiencing the loss of her mother in a more complete way?

T: And your father?

P: He's very serious, he isn't affectionate or loving. He hardly ever takes his grandchildren in his arms or kisses them. He is a cold man. My parents-in-law are affectionate and loving, like my husband; he loves children [she pauses)]. My husband is a quiet man but he's more upbeat and optimistic than I am; he's stronger. I go to pieces more easily.

Neither did her father show any affection towards her, although she is obliged give the example of the relationship with his grand-children, as if she were unable to refer directly to his relationship with her. In any case, we can take it as read that neither did he take her in his arms or kiss her. But it seems as though it would be more painful to say it like that, openly. Nevertheless, she introduces other subjects who are capable of giving affection, such as her parents-in-law and her husband. That is to say, despite the fact that her report of her parental figures, up to this point, has not been very satisfactory, the patient indicates to us that in her life there have been, and continue to be, "good" relationships. For example, she warmly appreciates her husband for his optimism and strength.

T: Have there been any other relationships apart from with your husband?

P: When I was little, I used to play with boys and girls. There was a boy I liked the most, but we never got to go out. I started going out with my husband when I was sixteen, and he was seventeen. We got married when I was twenty. Now he is perhaps a little less affectionate. He doesn't go out of his way to help you, you have to ask him. It's also true that he's getting wearier. He tells me I'm very soft with the children, that I give in to them too much. But, the truth is, I haven't enjoyed having the children as much as he has [weeps], although perhaps I do enjoy them more now. It's just that before I didn't have any patience. I didn't know what to do with them, like playing. But since I had my younger son, I think I enjoy them more [she continues to cry]. I'm just a cry-baby. I cry over every-thing, whether it's sad or happy.

It is important to note that, although the patient is following the suggestions of the therapist in terms of collaborating with the questions he raises, she does not merely answer "bureaucratically" or "meekly: rather, she always adds something. So, at first she describes her husband, but afterwards she continues talking about how she sees herself: as a person who cries very easily and who had little patience with the children. This is not only indicative of her collaborative attitude and sincerity, by showing herself just as she sees herself, but it also highlights her capacity for self-observation. Moreover, this points towards a certain aptitude for change: now she has more patience with the children, unlike before. The patient goes on to say:

> There is quite a large age difference between the children. And of course, there's too much of a gap for them to play amongst themselves. I would have liked to have had the second one earlier, but my husband was made redundant. The little one goes to nursery . . . [she pauses] They have taken an X-ray of his stomach. I don't yet know the result, but I'm not worried, because he's a little better; now he is vomiting less. He isn't a big boy; I think he's rather slight, although the doctor says he is average. As he's always on the go, I can't spend all day playing with him, so he gets bored. So, it's good for him to go to nursery. There they tell me that he's very difficult: he's a little terror.

By talking about her children, she shows her limitations as a mother. She harbours doubts over whether her son is too small, which might support the idea that she has not fed him well enough, and so the doctor has to reassure her that this is not the case. She also has to justify him going to nursery; the truth of the matter is that she has difficulties in playing with him.

T: Any illnesses?

P: Tonsillitis, a vaginal cyst . . ."

T: When did you have your first period?

P: When I was twelve. They had already explained it to us at school . . . And it was fine. My mother never talked to me about any of that, although when she died I was fourteen. My sister did get a fright, because she didn't go to school. When she got hers, she went running for my mother.

T: How about food?

P: During the bad time I didn't have any appetite. But, the truth is, I've never been one to eat lots. Now I eat everything, but when I was little, I ate very badly. My sister tells me, 'I don't know why you complain about your children, because you, when you were little, you only wanted your biscuits and all that fussy nonsense.' Now, the children eat first, and then I eat alone; so, because I'm alone, I don't really feel much like it. It seems that when there are more people around I feel more at ease and I eat better.

Of these last pieces of information, obviously those referring to her own difficulties with food during childhood are significant, which appear to be linked to her lack of appetite as an adult, when she is alone. That is to say, that receiving food depends upon whether or not there is a good relationship accompanying it. *Mutatis mutandis*, she must not feel that she is very good company for her children, since they have feeding problems, even when she is there. She once again recalls her age when her mother died, as if with this she would like to point out—albeit unconsciously—the significance of this fact, in case the therapist had not sufficiently grasped this.

T: And what about dreams; do you remember any?

P: I dream very little. And when I do, they are not generally nightmares or anything unusual.

T: What about work?

P: When I finished studying, I worked in a dressmaking factory. Then I worked in a few large department stores, which I didn't like because there was a lot of competitiveness among the sales assistants to see who was the best-dressed.

T: What idea do you have in terms of what we can offer you here?

P: Today, I thought that I wouldn't know what to say, but just look at how many things I've said. A cousin of mine came here for a period, to talk a few times, as she was getting depressed, and it seems as though it was good for her. She said to me, 'Maybe you'll feel better talking to some-one.' But in truth, I don't know what you do here. I do know that I'm depressed, but I don't know much else . . . I don't know why I'm getting depressed. I don't know if it's something in my personality.

T: And how do you see yourself?

P: People tell me that I'm not one for talking very much . . . I never thought I was that unhappy, but I'm scared that it's going to happen to me again.

In fact, the patient does have a certain idea of the help she might receive at the Centre. First, as a result of the favourable information provided by her cousin, but, above all, because she has had the experience of these interviews, during which she, "thought she wouldn't know what to say . . . but just look." Although she goes on to emphasise that she does not know what goes on here, that is to say, how help of this kind works. This is true in part, but, on the other hand, it is as if she would like to ignore what she has just said as a result of her own experience. In this way she would delegate to the therapist, and thus save herself the work of recognising and coming to terms with what she has experienced herself.

Remarks on the supervision of the second interview

The patient presents an apparently contradictory version of her familial relationships. On the one hand, one would say that she has been the child who has received the most, as she has had her studies, gifts, and so on. Yet, she harbours doubts about whether her birth was "a fluke". When she eats alone with her children she has little appetite. We might suppose that when she eats with her children, she identifies so much with them that it becomes a conflictive situation. Instead, she eats better if she is in the company of adults. It is likely that this has happened in the interview with the therapist, that when she feels that she is with an adult who acts like one, by showing a professionalism that she herself recognises, she is then able to take and to receive what he is providing her.

On the other hand, she says that she has received many things from her parents: studies, more gifts than her brothers or sisters; but, as for breastfeeding, "No idea!" This is because her studies do not serve to "feed her" emotionally as having received maternal nourishment would have, with all of the concomitant emotional care. In any case, her studies were a substitute for her mother's milk. So, the patient has not been able to identify with a mother who offers the "breast". Consequently, she feels like an inadequate mother when it comes to feeding her own children, for which reason they have to "return" what she offers them.

As a point of focus, it is suggested during the supervision to broach this question of her difficulties as a mother in feeding her children, as she does not manage to do it as well as she would wish. And to put it to her as well—as a second level or background point of focus—that perhaps this is related to the fact that she has not been able to grieve at all for her dead mother; that is to say, she has not been able to do the work of mourning for her.

Third interview (one week later) with comments

P: I feel better. And I came here thinking that I didn't know what I would talk about today, because I've already told you everything.

T: Something similar also happened in the previous interview, and then you were surprised about what you did in fact talk abou

P: Well, yes. That's what I thought, and then . . . look at what we did talk about.

The patient offers light resistance, which easily gives way before the therapist's brief intervention, reminding her of the similar experience she had in the previous interview. The therapist slightly modifies the interview technique. Although he will continue trying to enquire into certain aspects which he considers necessary to explore, now, in addition, he will gather together some of the data already gained from previous interviews in order to make the proposal of the indication for psychotherapy.

T: In the last interview, you were explaining to me that there was a number of "little things" that made you feel bad, and that when you felt bad it was harder to care for your children in the way you would like to, especially since there were problems with feeding them. But we did not talk about whether you breastfed them.

In order to orientate the focus for treatment, the therapist once again takes up the theme of the feeding of the children, in order to place it in the foreground and to explore further aspects of child-rearing.

P: At first we offered my daughter the breast, but she didn't latch on very well; so I had to express the milk, warm it and give it to her like that for two or three months. After that, she only took the bottle. My son fed well from the breast during the first three months, but after that I didn't have enough milk so we had to supplement the breast with the bottle. He fed well until he was six months old. Since then it often takes me two hours to feed him, because if we go any quicker, he throws it up. Before we even begin I am already wondering if he will feed well. And if I'm feeling all right, then it's just a case of starting and then seeing how it goes. When my daughter was four, she went to the other extreme, she ate too much . . . In any case, my little boy is a real handful. He's very much like this [she clenches her fist tightly] with me. Just now, when I was coming here, I left him with my sister, and he had a tantrum . . . Sometimes he doesn't even want to go with my husband. He [the husband] says that he leads me on a merry dance. I have always liked boys more than girls. When my daughter was born . . . I was a bit fazed by it, I didn't react. Whereas, when I had my son, I was beside myself! As soon as I had my daughter, they hadn't even finished stitching me up and I was already thinking that we would have to start trying for a boy.

T: By what we have been seeing in these interviews, it seems clear that the subject of the children is very important to you. It is as if you do not seem to feel satisfied with how you are looking after them, that you do not do it as well as you would like to. That is why a treatment in which we might be able to continue to talk about these concerns you have as a mother would be appropriate. You could talk about anything that concerns or interests you, too, but we would principally address this issue of how you experience the care of your children. Treatment would be once a week, for a year, and we would try to make it at the same time each week. If you cannot make it on a certain day, just let us know.

Indeed, faced with the therapist's indication about the care of her children, the patient opens up and contributes more information on the vicissitudes of breastfeeding them, which confirms the therapist's hypothesis. Here, the patient introduces another piece of information, and this is her preference for boys over girls. It is likely that her disappointment with her first child, a girl, had something to do with her fear of identifying too much with the little girl, as she was the same sex as her, as this would lead to confusion which would not enable her to adequately differentiate her functions as a mother. But, to her surprise, these problems were also repeated with her son. In any case, now the therapist is able to make the indication for psychotherapy, outlining, but not being limited solely to the treatment focus, thus leaving the possibility open for her to contribute anything else that might be worrying her. He also makes the conditions of the external setting clear to her. The therapist has not made any mention of the secondary or background focus that was talked about during the supervision, that is, the unelaborated mourning for her mother. It did not seem appropriate at the time to share this with the patient, as she might perceive it as somewhat too forced. It was preferable to wait for psychotherapy to progress in order to introduce it at the appropriate juncture.

> P: A year! That's a long time . . . Of course, a year actually goes by very quickly, because these interviews have gone by very quickly for me.

The patient's reaction is significant. Initially, it is one of resistance, in the same way as when coming to the interview she thought that she would have nothing to talk about, but then had plenty to say. Straight away, however, she is able to refer back to this experience and realise that, just as the interviews have gone quickly, so a year is not such a very long time.

> T: In one of the interviews you told me that at home they told you it was better not to think too much [about things]. Here, you have the opportunity to talk about whatever is on your mind; whatever you experience or dream, as we have seen is possible to do during these interviews.

The therapist sets out another reason to support the indication for psychotherapy. He offers the patient a containing framework where it is possible to tolerate the "bad" (sad) thoughts, as she has been able to appreciate in previous interviews, unlike the attitude taken at home. He also uses this to introduce some suggestions about possible material to provide which will facilitate the investigation into her internal world: what she thinks about, experiences, and dreams.

> P: Yes, because I was always thinking about sad things and I just could-n't seem to be happy. My medication worries me, whether, if I stop taking it, the depression will come back, or if it's habit-forming. Sometimes I think it is like taking drugs . . . And actually now, in my life, I'm fine. You could say that the better I am (given the external conditions) the worse I feel. I don't know why I have to be like this [she cries]. There's no illness, or anything serious like that at home. If anything like some of the things you hear about ever happened to me, I don't know how I would be. I don't have a mongoloid child, or anything like that [she starts to cry again]. So I don't know why I get like this. And today I actually came here

in a good mood! I talk to my husband about this and I don't cry. And now, look at me. Maybe it's good to let it all out. [Rather long silence.]

This week is full. On Wednesday it's my daughter's X-ray appointment. On Thursday we have an appointment with my daughter's teacher at her school, the same as every year, although it's a little earlier than last year's. The other day, while my daughter was getting something from the wardrobe she found my old school reports. 'Mum, you got such good marks!' she said. Well, there's a real mixture, sixes and sevens. And then she saw a photo of when I was twelve years old and said how beautiful I was. She went to her father and asked him who was more beautiful, her or her mother in the photo. Her father answered, 'Your mother.' And she replied, 'But I'm beautiful too, aren't I?' Then she asked her father about his marks at school, but he told her he had nothing like that, as he hadn't liked studying. But me, on the other hand, I did like school. But when I was left without a mother . . . My father discouraged me, 'Women should not study,' he said. I would have liked to have studied medicine. I don't know, though, because seeing blood and hearing about certain things upsets me. A niece of mine went to do some voluntary work at Cotolengo (a residence for the poor) the other day. I couldn't go. I wouldn't be able to look after those people.

In the first part of the intervention, the patient recognises that she has sad thoughts and, once again, expresses her ignorance of the reason this happens to her. Contained within that question is her need for professional help in order to attempt to answer it, as she alone cannot. If she goes over her external living conditions, there is no cause for her to be depressed. Therefore, one might deduce from this that the reasons are within her. Furthermore, pharmacological treatment does not seem to be an adequate solution to her. Perhaps there is an underlying unconscious idea that if the hidden reasons are not made clear, there will always be a need for medication, which would explain her fear of addiction. Hence, this causes a silence, which the therapist tolerates. We might consider this as a "test silence", for the purpose of seeing the patient's tolerance faced with that situation. Once the need for psychological treatment has been made clear, the therapist allows a few moments' waiting time in case the patient wishes to contribute anything else spontaneously. In this case, we see that the reaction is favourable, as the predominant attitude is one of collaboration, in talking about what is on her mind. It is as if, with this, she is showing signs of wanting to begin psychotherapy immediately. She also refers to "having the week full" because of the children. That is to say, with this she confirms that the subject of the children is, in fact, the central issue of her concerns. But she moves on, by explaining an Oedipal scene that is very tender and at the same time realistic: father prefers mother. It should be emphasised that the episode takes place, according to the patient's version—the one that interests us—in an undramatised atmosphere, where the father figure revalues the mother figure in the eyes of the daughter, but with no intention of humiliating her. With this, the patient is showing a good acceptance of the triangular Oedipal situation, in which she now occupies the place of mother partnering with father without this having to mean a hostile exclusion for the daughter. But immediately afterwards, albeit in a collateral way, the issue of the lack of the mother emerges: as she was left without a mother, she says that she could not continue at school. Hence, the patient would seem to be suggesting that, although the subject of the children's care, especially their feeding, is important, there is another which should not be overlooked: the death of the mother. Her next contribution is rather surprising: she would have liked to have studied medicine. It might be useful to understand this as an attempt at identification with the therapist. But as her mother was not there— she stresses once again—she was not able to realise her desire, although she adduces further reasons that thwarted such a realisation. And the fact is that she would not feel able to "listen to the (painful) things that happen to others", as they would upset her too much. She might also be implicitly recognising this capacity in the therapist. At the same time, she accepts her insufficient working through of experiences of loss, particularly that of her mother.

> T: Perhaps you have now reached a time when you need to look after yourself and be looked after, in order to be able to care for others.

> P: The other day I was told about a baby who was mistreated, who was shaken. I just don't understand.

The interview ends.

This last intervention by the patient, in light of the therapist's suggestion that she needs to look after herself—implicitly making her aware of his capacity to "look after her"—is still not clear. It might, perhaps, be related to her concerns about not looking after her children properly. In her case we are not dealing with physical mistreatment or neglect, but there are doubts (in her mind) over whether or not she is caring for them well enough. And for her this might be tantamount to harm on a large scale, almost as if she were "shaking them".

The therapist and the patient agree on the time for the weekly session and begin psychotherapy.

Summary of the evolution of the psychotherapy and confirmation of the indication for psychotherapy

The fact that a patient shows certain indicators that might suggest their suitability for a certain type of psychotherapy should be confirmed throughout the subsequent course of treatment, in order for our suppositions for the purposes of diagnosis and indication to continue to hold validity. Given that the case to which this transcribed material corresponds was subject to supervision not only during these diagnostic interviews, but throughout the entire psychotherapeutic process—forty-four sessions, to be precise—a brief glance at its progress will allow us to confirm many of the hypotheses established at the beginning.

Indeed, predominant during the first stage of treatment was the subject of the feeding of the younger son, a focal topic, together with a feeling of a certain uncontainable sadness that resulted in weeping during almost every session. There was also repeated reference made to the death of the mother, in the form of complaints directed at a father who "did not mourn", as he remarried so soon. Later, the subject of the dead mother gains more urgency, which the therapist includes as the secondary focus for treatment, even though this was not explicitly stated at the beginning of psychotherapy. However, as we have said, this subject is closely associated with her problem of maternal difficulties in her nutritional function. In one session, after over half the session time had elapsed, the patient manifests her envy towards those of her friends who have a mother, *because when her mother died, if she wanted to eat, she had to make the food herself.* In this one statement, the two issues that we have considered to be central to the problems underlying this patient's depression are brought together. She has recovered photos of her mother and has shown them to her children, which was gratifying for her. Until now she had not been able to do this; we might consider that this was owing to her

anger towards a mother who, according to her experience, was unhappy throughout her childhood and who then died, leaving her
alone. In addition, in one of the photos she appears as a child. Or,
rather, now the patient is indeed able to show to her children that she
was also a daughter and that she had a mother, and to show them
who that mother is. At the end of the treatment, during the last
session, she says, "When the psychotherapy started, I thought that a
year would be a long time, but it has flown by." She recalls that during
the early months she cried at every session, which is something that
has not happened to her for a while. "It must be because I am stronger
now", she adds.

In the course of the year following the termination of psychotherapy, the patient undertakes three *follow-up interviews*, an option
that was made known to her during the last stage of treatment as part
of the setting. The first interview takes place three months after
completion of therapy. She says, joking, that she's now "got some
nerve", because if she is told painful things about other people,
whereas before she would be devastated by it, now she is of the view
that everyone "has their hardships to bear". She had many things to
talk about while she was coming to the interview, but she seems to
have lost them on the way. She feels better; she feels more able to
endure any challenging situations that arise. Previously, she would
cry over nothing; now the issue of her son's food does not worry her
to the same extent. At the end of the interview, she gives the therapist
some sweets from her village as a gift. The patient recognises the
improvement she has experienced. The gift is very significant, not
only as an expression of thanks for the help she has received, but also
because it alludes to the specific content of the problem that has been
treated: food. I do not think that such a fact can be interpreted as an
attempt to take the place of the therapist, in a negation of her dependence on him, in that it is now she who is administering some kind of
food to the professional. First, because her recognition of the help
received has been made explicit; second, because she is bringing him
a souvenir specifically from her village. That is to say, the gift is something linked to her origins, which were related to her problems, to the
dead mother: something she had not been able to verbalise or work
through before coming here.

In the *second follow-up interview*, eight months after the termination
of treatment, she says that she continues to feel well, despite the death

of a neighbour and friend, who left two children. Her stepmother has also died, whom she was not close to, but neither do feelings of resentment emerge from this. Rather, she is critical of the fact that her father has once more insinuated that he will perhaps get married again. She realises that she is explaining many things, and she adds, joking, that perhaps she might need to come more often. That is to say, she has experienced the deaths of people who were relatively close to her; deaths that previously would have activated her unresolved mourning for her mother, and yet she has been able to tolerate this well. She still has more to say, so much, in fact, that she even jokes about the idea of coming more frequently. Or rather, there is recognition of the help she receives from the therapist, of the "food" that he provides her, but she accepts that if she is feeling better then it is right to end treatment.

In a *third follow-up interview*, the last, held one year after the termination of treatment, she remembers that when she first started the psychotherapy it was a real effort for her to come, but that afterwards she liked it. Her son no longer presents any problems with food. She continues to be able to deal with daily life in a different way: her daughter is jealous of her brother; her husband faces an uncertain future at work; and so on. The stuff of life and its challenges continue, but now the patient is equipped to deal with them.

CHAPTER SIX

Psychodynamic indicators

Introduction: overview of indication criteria in psychotherapy and psychoanalysis

I think that several factors should be borne in mind when establishing the indications for a psychodynamically orientated therapeutic technique (psychotherapy or psychoanalysis, for example): the patient's psycho(patho)logy, the therapeutic aims, and the technique employed. To this must be added the therapist's experience and the institutional context. As can be gathered from what has been said in previous chapters, it should be clear that, when I mention psychopathology, I am not simply referring to a clinical or syndromic picture of psychiatric nosology, but I also include the unconscious dynamisms that underlie it: in other words, the psychodynamic diagnosis. That is to say, I am attempting "to discern the type of object relations, anxieties and phantasies which predominate in the patient's internal world and which . . . configure his forms of adaptation and external behaviour" (Coderch, 1987, p. 151, translated for this edition). Such elements enable us to establish a profile of the patient from which we will deduce his suitability for psychotherapy.

Broadly speaking, Enid and Michael Balint assert that it is "the patient's potentialities for forming [and developing] human relationships which is decisive to whether psychotherapy can take place" (Balint & Balint, 1961, p. 185). Of course, this statement must be qualified. This position is in line with the accepted psychoanalytic thought in the 1954 Symposium held by the International Psychoanalytical Association, on "Extending the Reach of Psychoanalysis", where emphasis was shifted away from nosological diagnostic criteria towards criteria of patient "suitability", as it may be said that ". . . the indication for psychoanalysis [and psychotherapy, I am adding for my part] can only rarely, if ever, be derived from the nature of the illness" (Thomä & Kachele, 1985, p. 185). Indeed, this is a position that is consistent with the theoretical and technical foundations of psychoanalysis. The fact is that, a hundred years ago now, Freud himself was already moving in this direction when he said, "The nature of the psycho-analytic method involves indications and contra-indications with respect to *the person* to be treated as well as with respect to the *clinical picture*" (1904a, p. 253, my italics). Shortly afterwards, he stresses the theme in another work: "One should look beyond the patient's *illness* and form an estimate of his *whole personality*." (1905a, p. 263, my italics).

The psychoanalytic understanding of the personality presupposes that it is a whole, comprising various different—at times even contradictory—aspects in its dynamic and its objectives. These aspects are interrelated, thus configuring an organisation of the personality that guarantees a certain degree of mental equilibrium, independently of whether the consequences of such a state of organisation are harmful to the individual's very health, in which case we would talk about a "pathological organisation", or, conversely, if the outcome is predominantly healthy, this would then constitute a "non-pathological organisation". So, in order to establish the patient's diagnosis from a psychoanalytic viewpoint, it is necessary to include his capabilities along with the pathological dimension. There is another reason, of a technical nature, why we might consider the clinical psychiatric diagnosis to be inadequate from a psychodynamic perspective. In order to carry out a psychoanalytically based treatment, we require the patient's collaboration. And this is impossible if we only consider the pathological part of his character, without taking into account his potentialities and capabilities, which are necessary if they are to be put in the service of a therapeutic alliance with the therapist.

I shall make a distinction between two routes for approach to assess the indication for psychoanalytic psychotherapy in general, which, far from being mutually exclusive, I believe complement each other. First, I shall briefly set out the fundamental criteria that have been identified in establishing the indication for psychoanalytic psychotherapy according to an approach that I will call "classical". Second, I will describe another means of approach, via what I will call the "psychodynamic indicators", in order to establish the patient's suitability, or otherwise, for psychoanalytic psychotherapy or psychoanalysis. This I shall define as the *psychodynamic indicators* approach.

Classical approach

I have assembled here a number of criteria that have been considered by various authors to be basic or fundamental to formulating the indication for psychoanalytic psychotherapy and for psychoanalysis (Coderch, 1987; Etchegoyen, 1999; Mitjavila, 1994; Paz, 1980; Thomä & Kachele, 1985). Of the possible list of criteria that point towards the indication for psychoanalytically based therapy—such as I understand them based on my reading of these authors and according to my professional practice—I will enumerate those I consider to be the most notable.

1. *Motivation for change.* The need for change must be driven by the experience of some type of discomfort or personal suffering from which there is a desire to be free. The person who seeks psychoanalytic treatment, of any type, because he merely wishes to know himself is exhibiting an inauthentic or false motivation. There is no possibility for change if there is no anxiety generated by the concomitant discomfort. Anxiety is the necessary prime mover, as we have already seen in Chapter Two, and is indicative of certain aspects of life in peril. But it is not enough to seek to reach a different state to the one currently experienced, since, as Bion points out, while one tendency might be the evasion of pain, that is, avoiding the reality (both external and internal) that generates it, it is quite another to attempt to change this reality.

In this respect, united within the motivation for psychological treatment is the desire to end the suffering, along with the wish to establish certain connections between the discomfort experienced and the individual's own particular psychological or relational functioning. That motivation will be further consolidated in the patient whenever there is also some degree of curiosity about his psychological world: that is, to know why things are as they are in the functioning of his personality; why certain decisions were taken in his life that were damaging, despite him knowing the risk of this being the case, and then repeating them in similar situations; or why certain inappropriate behaviours are repeated towards those people who represent parental figures.

2.   *Capacity for self-observation and insight.* The patient is somewhat curious to know himself and the world around him. That curiosity is linked to a capacity for self-observation, to observe as much his own behaviour and feelings as those of the people with whom he relates. His capacity for insight is also something to be valued, involving becoming aware of what is observed, accompanied by a certain degree of tolerance to that self-recognition, even when it is painful.

In my view, *motivation and the capacity for self-observation and insight* constitute the two factors that take key priority over all the others when it comes to assessing the suitability of a person for any kind of psychoanalytic psychotherapy in general. For this reason, the fact that they appear first on the list is entirely intentional. We must also add *tolerance to and management of mental pain*, but this is a very wide criterion, which, in fact, would amount to a summary of several of the individual's capacities, though I shall expand upon this when I go on to talk about the psychodynamic indicators.

3.   *Other criteria.* In addition to the aforementioned, there are other criteria that are often cited in the assessment of the suitability of a person for psychoanalytically based help: intact areas of the personality; the patient's capacity to circumscribe relational conflicts; favourable therapeutic expectations for working together, based on mutual trust between patient and therapist; not very rigid psychic defences, to which we could add a not very serious psychopathology. In Table 6.1 these criteria are cited according to the classical approach.

Table 6.1.   Classical approach.

1. *Motivation for change*
    – Need to modify the suffering
    – Desire to understand in order to change

2. *Capacity for self-observation and insight*   – Recognition of the psychological basis for the discomfort

3. *Other criteria*
    – Intact areas of the personality
    – Patient's capacity to circumscribe relational conflicts
    – Favourable therapeutic expectations for working together, based on
      mutual trust between patient and therapist
    – Not very rigid defences
    – Not very serious psychopathology, in the sense of no predominant
      self-destructive or hetero-destructive tendencies

The *intact areas of the personality,* in the spheres of work and relationships, for example, are those where the ego capacities are evinced,
as well as the value accorded to the internal objects. The *capacity of the
patient to circumscribe relational conflicts* is where the individual has
some idea of the existence of his own psychic problems, which he is
able to recognise externalised in relationships that are significant to
him. In terms of the *favourable therapeutic expectations* for a potential
treatment, these must be grounded in the mutual trust between therapist and patient in the respective potentialities of each to successfully
carry out treatment. Since each time we are dealing with a new experience, for which there are no guarantees, even when conditions are
most favourable both in the patient and the therapist, perhaps it
would be more apt to use the term *faith* (as indicated by Bion, 1970) to
describe the state required to initiate the psychotherapeutic experience; this is not a blind faith, but, rather, one based on the data
obtained during the interviews. It is also to be hoped that there should
not be a predominance of primitive or very rigid defences. To avoid
listing them here, I would say, to simplify, that the defences utilised
are not overly determined by the trait of omnipotence. Last, that there
should not be a very serious psychopathology is a factor to take into
account, which I would define, simply, as there being no absolute
predominance of hetero-destructive and self-destructive tendencies
over those which are life-generating and tend towards integration.

The problem with indications for the psychoanalytic psychothera-pies and psychoanalysis is that, whatever diagnostic—even psycho-dynamic—criteria might be established, these are always too broad to be adapted to any particular patient. Such criteria are useful in a vaguely orientative sense. But, in my opinion, they do not tell us enough about the prospects for the feasibility of psychotherapy or psychoanalysis in any one specific patient.

In order to specify the suitability of a patient for psychoanalytic treatment, it is necessary to construct a profile for that person, using the relevant data with a view to establishing the indication. In order to do this, as we have already seen, I consider it useful to contrast the data collected in the three areas we have studied at the time of obtain-ing the diagnosis: the psychopathology, the biography, and the inter-view itself. In this correlation matrix there might be *agreement*, *complementarity*, or *discord* between one or more areas. I grant priority to the data observed in the patient's relationship with the therapist during the interview. In other words, the data provided by the "here and now" of the relationship constitutes a basic point of reference, to which all the other data can be contrasted. Or, rather, the *vertex* (in the Bionian sense) of the "here and now" makes possible an understand-ing of the data from the other areas and, as such, an understanding of the patient's wider personality.

In fact, every therapist will draw on his or her knowledge and experience in order to stipulate whether, for example, a particular depressive patient who shows signs of a schizoid personality with a tendency to form dependent relationships, but with a capacity for insight and motivation for treatment, and who, finally, has sustained a good relationship with the therapist, will be capable of the indica-tion for psychotherapy or psychoanalysis, that is, whether he supports the reasonable hypothesis of his feasibility for treatment. But they will arrive at such conclusions on the basis of the series of data resulting from what is obtained in the three areas mentioned previously. I shall attempt to systematise a few of those many elements that are indica-tive of the functioning of a person's mental life, so that this categori-sation might help us to configure a profile of the patient which will be useful in evaluating his suitability or otherwise with a view to psychotherapeutic or psychoanalytic help.

So numerous are the signs we could observe in the behaviour of a person that there are, in fact, entire treatises dedicated to giving a full and exhaustive account of them. But, in view of so much compilation of data, there is the risk that we can lose track and fail to delineate a basic configuration or sketch of the mental and relational functioning of the actual specific individual in front of us. As such, I believe the therapist–observer requires an attitude where his observation of the patient (his look and his listening) comprises that rare skill of maintaining a constant to-and-fro motion: first coming close and examining certain aspects (the "trees") of his personality in detail, then moving away, keeping his distance and taking in the broad strokes (the "forest"), to afterwards return to the particular detail, and then once more to the context of the personality within which they are framed, and so on, until an image is gradually configured; one which is as close as possible to the patient's reality.

Psychodynamic indicators approach: definition and summary

On the basis of the above, in addition to establishing certain criteria to delimit the psychodynamic profile of the patients with sufficient potentialities for an indication for psychotherapy or psychoanalysis, I think it might be useful at this point to describe the *indicators*. As I have already said, this should not be regarded as an alternative to the classical proposals, but as a complement to them, and, in some cases, a reformulation of what has been discussed within the classical approach. I have named "psychodynamic indicators" those elements I am able to extract from the conjugation of data obtained in the three previously mentioned areas (the biographical, the psychopathological, and that of the interview) and which I consider significant when it comes to specifying the degree of patient suitability for psychotherapy or psychoanalysis. In some ways, this idea might be said to be close to Liberman's proposal (1980), in terms of the items it describes; however, its conceptualisation and respective outcomes are quite different.

I use the word *indicator* in the sense of "[a] sign that indicates something" (Moliner, 1979, translated for this edition); a sign or signal that serves to point in the direction where we will find something we are looking for; in our case, this is an indicator signal that orientates us on the feasibility of psychotherapeutic or psychoanalytic help. The meaning is equally valid in the English language, in the sense of

"[A] device providing specific information on the state or condition of something." (*New Oxford English Dictionary*, 1988). But there is a further meaning of the word *indicator*, common to both Spanish and English, and it is relevant for our purposes. It is that which belongs to the field of chemistry: "a chemical compound which changes colour at a specific pH value or in the presence of a particular substance, and can be used to monitor a chemical change" (*Oxford English Dictionary*, 1995). Applied in such a way, this term may be used to describe those signs in the patient's personality which are displayed and revealed to us in the "medium" of the patient–therapist relationship, at the time of the interview, as markers for the feasibility, or otherwise, of this couple being able to undertake psychotherapeutic or psychoanalytic treatment.

In order to establish the indicators, I propose that we be guided by the psychoanalytic principles of ambivalence in emotional life and the duality of the impulses or basic drives, those of life and death. It is for this reason that for each indicator I shall also refer to its opposite. It is the balance of both which determines the predominant tendency. So, although we might have made reference to just one of the component elements of the pair in each of the indicators, turning our attention exclusively to the sole outcome of such an assessment, I believe it is preferable to conserve the duality of its components, since this offers a greater wealth of variation and contrast when it comes to carrying out a conclusive evaluation of the patient in order to weigh up a potential indication for psychotherapy or psychoanalysis.

I must make a few clarifications with regard to *terminology*. Psychoanalysis, in the sense that it deals with the individual's emotional life by considering his unconscious foundations, has necessitated the creation of a specific nomenclature. What is more, in its origins, many psychoanalysts' efforts, beginning with Freud himself, were directed at psychoanalysis attaining the status of a discipline to be included within the field of the natural sciences. For this reason, a specific, "technical" language had to be created, which is often one of the guarantees of scientific presentation in any discipline. Furthermore, given that psychoanalysis studied new phenomena, this required the relevant terminology. Nowadays, the development of psychoanalysis and the consolidation of its theoretical and technical approaches have enabled it to be less concerned with the formal aspect—that of its language—as its identity is no longer dependent to the same extent on the use of a new, at times even cryptic, terminology. Rather, this has enabled psychoanalysis to establish a relationship with freer and more enriching language. While we might still need to coin new terms when the usual ones no longer encompass new meanings, the task of incorporating elements of our everyday language, when they truly fit what we are trying to describe as a psychoanalytic object of study, is always a worthwhile one. Bion has perhaps been the psychoanalyst who has most expanded upon that tendency with considerable broadmindedness. Although we find in this author some entirely novel terms (*alpha-elements, beta-elements,* those referring to the *Grid,* etc.), we also find an incredibly wide use of words taken from everyday language (*love, hate, knowledge, learning from experience, truth, lies, reverie,* etc.). Clearly, from a psychoanalytic perspective, these words hold a content that differs somewhat from that which is commonly recognised. But we are not, in fact, trying to give new meaning to these terms. What we are seeking to do is to delve deeper into them, so that psychoanalysis might provide those layers of meaning which are also present in everyday life, but which can only be observed, analysed, and studied from the viewpoint of the specialist. In accord with this Bionian stance, the vocabulary I have used to designate the indicators is taken from expressions similar to day-to-day language, with many of the terms, as we shall see, taken from Bion himself.

I shall present a list of *indicators* that I have chosen on the basis of my own experience. I am sure that it would be possible to elaborate other lists, based on different premises, or similar lists, formulated in a different way. Here, it has been elaborated on the basis of a certain conception of the mind and of psychopathology, which may be inferred from what has been set out in previous chapters, as well as the fact that it adheres very closely to clinical practice.

One might notice that the indicators, taken as a whole, reflect a certain profile or view of the personality state in which as much the potential for, as well as the limitations to, its growth are taken into account; as much its potentialities as its pathology, in accord, as I have already said, with the prevailing tendency in psychoanalysis. Consequently, the psychodynamic indicators might be of use in evaluating the ongoing degree of progress during the course of the therapeutic process. But this is a question that exceeds the scope of this book.

I shall differentiate between certain basic or fundamental indicators and other complementary ones, expounding them briefly at first, to then describe each one in more detail further on. I will intersperse this with clinical material, although the place of inclusion does not necessarily allude exclusively to that indicator; rather, it is the one that is best reflected by the material, although we might notice other indicators which are also present. Clearly, it is not always possible to detect in every patient all of the indicators summarised here, but it is to be hoped that several of those we consider to be fundamental will be present. These I have listed below.

(a) *Sick aspects/sane aspects.* Here, we are dealing with the degree of recognition of suffering in the patient, of "the part that is sick" within him. It is worth considering this "part that is sick" in a double sense: first, in that he is experiencing a painful affective state, which makes him feel unwell, which makes him suffer, and second, in that his mental and relational functioning adhere to pathological patterns, that is to say, they are harmful to him. The other side of the bipolarity of this indicator relates to the sane resources of his personality, those that, moreover, allow him to take cognisance of this functioning.

(b) *Infantile aspects/adult aspects.* In this indicator, I have attempted to apprehend the infantile aspects and the adult aspects of the patient's personality, as well as the linking between each of these. With regard to the infantile aspects, we should differentiate between "regressive" and "progressive" dimensions of them. The first involves the tendency to return to patterns of mental functioning typical of the infantile structures, of which the most fundamental characteristic is that of omnipotence, where the other is recognised only as a part of oneself, giving rise to unhealthy dependence to the detriment of growth. However, there are certain individuals with more serious psychopathologies in whom there is not so much a regression as a very precarious progression and development of the infantile aspects, which has continued to preside over and to dominate their entire personality. The progressive infantile aspect, on the other hand, comprises the dimension in which the patient recognises the need for, and dependency on, the adult-other in order to receive from him or her that which, through that relationship, contributes to and enables his learning and growth.

The opposite pole of this indicator is the adult aspect of the personality, which concerns the capacity for responsibility and participation in dealing with reality (both external and psychic) in a gratifying way, using one's own resources.

(c)   *Degree of sincerity/insincerity (lying)*. As we know, the ability to recognise one's own (psychic) reality and reality in general, without distorting it, is not always easy. For this reason sincerity, in view of this recognition, is a question of degree. The same is true of the tendency to create a distorted version of this reality, or insincerity, which can vary in intensity.

(d)   *Love/hatred of the truth*. Although it might seem as though this indicator could have come under the previous paragraph, I believe we can legitimately distinguish it from the above. Here, we are dealing with a tendency towards the search for something we need to know, moved by curiosity, in so far as we are not content with the prevailing state of things, that is, of our mental functioning. This demands a capacity for observation, and for self-observation, of the reality that surrounds us and that we experience. Contrary to this, when that search, which is always difficult, becomes very painful for us, or we feel that any potential discoveries might be painful, an attitude emerges that I call "hatred" because it deals with an emotional state of intense aversion, such as could only be akin to hatred, directed against that possible search for the truth about oneself.

(e)   *Degree of tolerance to pain/pleasure*. All of the indicators mentioned up until now take the degree of tolerance to mental pain as their main point of reference. Or, in other words, the degree of tolerance to frustration, if we take the meaning of frustration in a very broad sense: as all those facets of reality that are unsatisfactory to us. But the opposite pole is also significant, to assess the degree of tolerance to wellbeing, to enjoyment, or to pleasure. In fact, this indicator defines the degree of tolerance in the patient to various feelings that he is given to experience in his contact with reality, whatever kind they might be: love, hate, blame, envy, gratitude, pleasure, and so on.

(f)   *Tolerance to separation/linking anxieties*. It is well known that tolerance to experiences of separation is a decisive factor for growth. Otherwise, we would not be able to separate from the object, from the people upon whom we depend; hence, it would be impossible to construct our very identity. Absence from the object is necessary, in so far as it is tolerated, but for this to be so, one previously needs to tolerate and accept the link with the people we need in order to grow.

(g) *Capacity of, and tolerance for, the masculine/the feminine.* Although this is seldom taken into account, I believe this is an indicator to be considered, given that it alludes to problems of identification with each of the parental figures, principally the maternal and the paternal. Depending on the patient's gender, this indicator assesses the degree of acceptance of the respective characteristics of one's own gender, as well as those of the opposite gender. This works on the Freudian idea of psychological bisexuality. It also takes into consideration the integration necessary between these two aspects, which refer to the type of introjection that has occurred in relation to parental linking.

The following indicators I shall catalogue as *complementary*, in so far as, while their presence is not decisive (or, rather, we might say that they carry less specific weight, given that no one indicator is a determining factor *per se*—not even the fundamental ones, in exclusivity), they might, however, be of use in the decision-making process. They are as follows:

(h) *Responses to the therapist's interventions during the interviews.* Although the patient's reactions to the therapist's specific interventions, such as his interpretations of the material provided in the interview, are of particular use, I think that, in fact, reactions to *any* type of intervention may be considered valuable, as they show us a mode of positioning oneself in relation the professional: with acceptance, rejection, indifference; if he is valued, idealised, and so on.

(i) *Capacity for containment in the patient's immediate social/family environment.* The psychotherapeutic or psychoanalytic experience brings about changes in the patient that will have repercussions in his relationship patterns, especially with the people in his immediate environment. Therefore, if this environment is excessively intolerant to the changes taking place in the patient— changes that will not always be favourable to the people within it—this could threaten the course of treatment.

(j) *The psychotherapist.* By this I am referring to training, experience, and ability to syntonise with the psychopathology and personality of a particular patient, as well as his impression, both conscious and unconscious, of the patient's potentialities in terms of undertaking therapy with him.

Before going on to study each of the indicators in more depth, please refer to Table 6.2 for the complete list.

Sick aspects/sane aspects

The person who seeks help recognises that he is suffering some affliction and, to a greater or lesser degree, he links this with some or other inadequate psychological functioning, although he does not have any precise knowledge of it. So, there is a sufficient degree of mental health in order to recognise this, to mobilise himself, and to make the request for help. By sick aspects, I mean any aspect which brings about a particular disturbance in the patient's psychic functioning, as well as its consequences in terms of suffering, where the individual himself is unable to find the means to overcome it in a "sane" way.

It is assumed that in any individual who seeks help, as serious as their mental disturbance might be, both aspects will always be

Table 6.2. Psychodynamic indicators.

Basic indicators

Sick aspects/sane aspects

Infantile aspects/adult aspects

Degree of sincerity/insincerity (lying)

Love/hatred of the psychic truth

Tolerance of emotional pain/pleasure

Tolerance of separation/linking anxieties

Capacity for tolerance to the masculine/feminine

Complementary indicators

Responses to the therapist's interventions

Capacity for containment in the social/family environment

The psychotherapist

---

present, the sick and the sane. In order to assess this indicator, how-ever, we should bear in mind the degree of imbalance between both of these facets. Thus, the patient who comes to request help accompa-nied by a family member is expressing little sane capacity to recognise the part of himself that is sick (as in the case of the psychotic patient), or, rather, he does not trust in his capacity to deal with the new situation entailing coming face to face with an unknown person (the therapist) who might treat problems which are also unknown to him (as is the case of some adolescents or phobic patients). In these latter cases, the positive assessment of the indication for individual psycho-therapy will depend on other indicators.

But, even if the individual does come alone, it is not always so clear that he is truly coming to the interview with "that part (of himself) which is sick". Quite the opposite might occur, that is to say, that the person (and here we are not referring to the psychotic patient, but to one who is presenting problems of a neurotic or character pathology kind) comes because "it was recommended to him" and who, while recognising the presence of some discomfort or emotional failure, minimises it, or otherwise considers that the approach of specific professional help is incommensurate with his problem. And, likewise, we will encounter the person who apparently recognises his need for psychotherapeutic help but who, in the interview, does not show any trace of anxiety, or talk about any emotional suffering which might be troubling enough to require help. In such a case, this would probably be a patient with narcissistic defences, at best, or a basically narcissistic personality structure who is unable to bear the "wound" of being psychically ill; far less the deeper wound caused by the existence of another person who might be able to give him that which he himself has not been able to provide.

In contrast, I am also interested to observe the sane aspects, as much in the patient's life, activities, and relationships as in the way he behaves in the relationship with the therapist, his collabora-tion in providing material, and helping him (the therapist) to achieve the aim of the interview: to arrive at an approximate "diagnosis" that is not only clinical, but of his mental functioning. The patient's sane capacity is also apparent in his tolerance to the inevitable deg-ree of frustration that the interview always involves, when it does not provide immediate satisfaction, in terms of mitigating his discomfort.

Infantile aspects/adult aspects

From a psychoanalytic perspective, and in accord with Meltzer (1967), therapeutic achievements derive from the adult part of the personality acquiring control over the infantile structures, so that these can then surrender omnipotence. That is to say, to make possible the integration of the infantile aspects, as much in their "regressive" as in their "progressive" dimension, according to the distinction made earlier. Therefore, in order to assess the availability of a person to help of this kind, his degree of recognition of his infantile aspects is significant.

This does not mean that the patient who is able to talk about his childhood is necessarily demonstrating a positive capacity in terms of this indicator. It is possible to narrate the early years of life in a totally defensive way and, in consequence, to be very removed from the infantile aspects of the personality which are present now. This happens when the patient talks about the child he was, at a certain place and time, in order to distance himself from the child who still exists inside him and who it is difficult for him to recognise. It is true, none the less, that when a person retains memories from his childhood, even in a somewhat dissociated way, he is closer to his infantile aspects than the person who has completely erased them, or who idealises them in such a way that there is scarcely anything else to say about them apart from how good everything was.

In order to assess this indicator, I am guided by all of the data and indications that, throughout the interview, directly or indirectly link the patient to the infantile aspects of himself. I consider unprompted reference to childhood itself, or otherwise upon the suggestion of the interviewer, to be positive, but where the patient connects easily with his memories, as if these were experiences that are more recent than the twenty or thirty years since their occurrence, would have us think. Sometimes, it is a surprise to the patient himself to see how easily these memories, which seemed forgotten, come to mind. Here, I think it is important to evaluate to what extent these evocations are "sincere"; that is to say, whether they are accompanied by the appropriate emotions of joy, sadness, anger, affection, and so on, which might be triggered.

Sometimes, indications present themselves in an indirect way. For example, in the relationship that the patient says he has with children, whether this is through his own children, if he has them, or others who are relatively close to his sphere of living. Conversely, we might find ourselves faced with the surprise of a mother who does not make any mention of her children, giving the therapist the impression that she does not have any, until the misunderstanding is finally cleared up, well into the interview, which she justifies under the pretext that her motives for making the consultation lie instead in her work or relationship difficulties. Evidently, such an omission is significant, not only in terms of the type of relationship she sustains with this hypothetical child/ren, but in terms of the neglect or denial of the infantile levels in her own internal world.

When this data arises, not only does it indicate to us the presence of infantile aspects, but also provides us with information about the nature of the relationship established with the infantile parts of the self in the sense of care, affection, tenderness, and so on; or, conversely, indifference, intolerance, or active rejection.

Socially, there continues to be a certain devaluation of the recognition of the infantile parts or aspects of an adult person, even when this is the "progressive" infantile part, that is, which is able to recognise the need to depend on others. Such a prejudice would be in line with a conception of adulthood as being a state of full autonomy, of self-sufficiency, in some way close to omnipotence and, therefore, paradoxically, closer to the infantile, in its insane and regressive dimension, than to that which is authentically adult. Instead, it might perhaps be more acceptable, in our culture, for women to recognise dependence when they need it without this being to the detriment of their prestige or status, as occurs in the case of men. But, regardless of these social factors and gender differences, each individual, man or woman, will show a certain closeness or distance in relation to the infantile parts of themselves, although the mode in which this is expressed might be different, or more or less eloquent and expressive.

At the interviewer's invitation for the patient to talk about his childhood, the responses are extremely varied. We find the person who does not remember anything about it at all, considering it to be a closed chapter of which he holds no significant experiences, as if it were something now over and dealt with, and could almost be said to form no part of his life. Or the person who, conversely, holds his childhood memories so close that we could almost say that, in fact, he is not able to accept that it is over and that it is still so present that it basically determines his decisions and his behaviour, as occurs with certain teenagers or adults with adolescent personality structures. Others will situate this stage spontaneously in later childhood and even in adolescence. There are also those who speak directly about their first years of life by means of what has been explained to them at home and of vague recollections they have, or those that they have reconstructed from such pieces of information. Sometimes, too, the patient who previously had not questioned his early years, upon this being pointed out to him by the interviewer, comes to the next interview with information he has obtained by asking family members, thus indicating his capacity for contact with his infantile aspects.

But, while we assess the presence or absence of the infantile, we also need to assess the degree to which the adult part of the personality is present, as may be gathered from what has already been said. The "child", above all at his most primitive and needy levels, requires an "adult" to "bring him" to the interview with the professional, in order to collaborate in its realisation and to establish a therapeutic involvement, as well as to sustain this involvement, with the therapist.

At first glance, it might seem that adult aspects and sane aspects, on the one hand, and infantile aspects (in adult patients) and sick aspects, on the other, might be analogous. Certainly, adulthood is the state in which the individual is expected to achieve a reunification of the various aspects of his personality that belong to him, accepting and assuming them in order to face up to and cope with reality (both external and internal). But the infantile, in the adult, is not always tied to regressive tendencies to evade reality, as I have already said. Quite the opposite, as at certain moments it is necessary for the adult to recognise the child he carries within him in two fundamental senses: in order to continue to desire growth, and to accept dependency on certain people who are necessary to this end—even more so if also present are physical illness or adverse external circumstances which impose that dependency on others. Therefore, it is necessary to recognise the sane infantile aspects. Just as, the other way round, we should not overlook when the *adult* part is manifesting a less than sane functioning, when he claims to be able to look after himself, in a self-sufficient way, in situations where he needs others. In such a case, we might think of a narcissistic, pseudo-adult or pseudo-mature personality (the so-called "as if" personalities). From the indicators we have reviewed up to now, we can assert, then, that the result of the conjunction between the infantile, sane, and adult aspects constitutes a good basis for psychotherapeutic and psychoanalytic treatment, provided there is a certain curiosity in the patient to know what has caused his suffering, he possesses certain ego resources, and is willing to assume responsibility for collaborating in the interview and enabling it to advance in order largely to achieve his aims with the help of the therapist.

So, bearing in mind the two indicators given above, the first, and often useful, questions I ask myself as an interviewer are, "In this person who has made the consultation, where is the 'patient' who is suffering and who needs help?" And, "Where is the 'child'?" Put another way; is this person before me exhibiting the suffering for which he says he needs to see a doctor, that is, is he bringing the sick person, the sufferer, with him? Or is the sick person not present? For example, in the case of the patient who comes because it has been indicated for him, the "sick person"—the sick part of him—has been left in the person who indicated this referral, and it is likely that, during the course of the interview, he will have deposited this part in the therapist, too. In the same way, in relation to the infantile aspects, it is worth asking oneself the following: "Is this person bringing the child who exists within him, with his fears, his wishes, his expectations, his needs, and so on, or has he also left him somewhere else, dissociated and projected?" To summarise, in the task of reconstructing a personality profile for the individual who is seeking help, I try to imagine whether I find myself before an "adult" who is bringing a "patient" and a "child" to the consultation. Obviously, the structure of the self is not composed of these three characters alone, which have been simplified and outlined here in terms of the *infantile* aspect that recognises dependence, the *patient* aspect that manifests the suffering, and the *adult* aspect that provides the capacity to assume responsibility. There are other facets of the self that encompass different nuances within the previously mentioned aspects, such as the regressive-infantile and the pseudo-adult parts, as well as others: the adolescent, even the "old" parts within each of us; the masculine or the feminine—which I shall discuss in the following section—and so on. To simplify, however, *I find it useful to stage a kind of dramatisation in my conscious (or unconscious) fantasy, taking into consideration the proportions that the "adult", "patient", and "child" acquire.* Later, I shall go on to deal with this question of the therapist's unconscious aspects to complete this dramatisation. It is possible that, during the course of the interview(s), the patient will continue to provide many more figures, which will go to populate the mind of the therapist with varying degrees of intensity, according to the degree of projective identification that takes place. But I believe it is important to gauge the presence of the infantile self, the sick self, and the adult self in relation to the rest of the personality.

I remember receiving an urgent visit from a relatively young adult who was experiencing a florid manic–psychotic episode, which had gone on for several days, and had driven him to a state of extraordinary hyperactivity, wandering ceaselessly for several days and nights. He came accompanied by a woman, to whom outwardly I did not pay much attention, as I was completely immersed in the verbal diarrhoea of the patient's megalomaniacal delusions. The patient was telling me that he was Frank Sinatra himself, though the doctor might find that surprising; so, in order to lessen that surprise, he offered long-winded and confused arguments, which seemed perfectly consistent to him. Suddenly, the patient stopped, looked at the woman who had sat down next to him, and said to the professional, "This is my mum," with an expression of satisfaction and in the same euphoric tone, reflecting the maniacal state with which he was presenting. The mother took the opportunity of this introduction to go on to inform the psychiatrist of her version of events. The patient added, "Yes, yes, explain to him. Explain to the doctor." No more than two minutes had elapsed since the woman had begun her story when, upon looking over at the patient, both she and I realised with some surprise that he had fallen into a deep sleep. Of course, this was not an interview to assess the indication for psychological help, but that image of the patient, asleep after having introduced his mother to the "doctor", has remained fixed in my professional experience. Sometimes, before certain patients, I have the impression of seeing repeated a similar situation to the one I have just described, even when I find myself before a patient who is capable of asking for psychological help by himself. In these cases, the "mother" is an internal object who has rapidly been projected into the therapist, to the extent that, once the patient has explained some of his difficulties, he then delegates any mental activity to the professional. That is to say, to a certain extent he remains distanced from contact with the problems that affect him, as if he had emotionally "fallen asleep", just like the patient above achieved by actually falling asleep.

Sincerity/insincerity (lying)

In any person's unconscious conflicts, there are some of which little is known, as there has been no opportunity to have the kind of experience which might give rise to it. But there are others that are more accessible to consciousness. We can say, then, that the patient "knows" that such conflicts or disagreeable facets of his personality exist. However, in order to avoid the painful implications of recognising them, he tends to feign—although not in a fully conscious way—that he "does not know". It is in this sense that I speak of "lying".

Of course, the capacity for sincerity and mental health must have some kind of direct relationship, and one is the function of the other. The ability to recognise all that one might know about oneself also contains a painful component, so it follows that self-deception (the *defences*, in psychoanalytic terminology) should emerge to conceal that recognition. Consequently, some degree of insincerity and lying always exists. An equivalent to my use here of the word "lying" might perhaps be that of Money-Kyrle's "misunderstanding" (1968).

I am not referring here to someone who lies consciously, in which case this would be someone afflicted by a specific psychopathology, consisting of the tendency to use lies in order to fight against a difficult reality. This being something he is aware of, he can, therefore, condemn it at any time, from the sane aspects of his personality. This was the case with a girl who came for help because she was a "liar", by her own admission, both in the sense of distorting or inventing the facts that she would tell her family, as in the form of concealing facts from her partner. Her interest in protecting this relationship, which she felt was basically loving, from this dishonest functioning, was what urged her to seek help. It was very significant that, in order to explain what was wrong, she needed to bring a written list of troubles and worries to the first interview, implying that she did not trust herself, owing to her wavering faithfulness to the "facts" (real or psychic), and that faced with the anxiety of that first encounter, she might twist or distort and/or hide the truth about her discomfort and her difficulties. In this case, then, we may see that there is a degree of sincerity to be taken into account, despite the symptom being, in point of fact, lying.

I consider lying to be an inevitable universal phenomenon, as I have already said, to deal with painful reality. As such, we may establish a direct relationship between the degree of lying (or, rather, of the functioning of the mind which is based on lying) and mental pathology. From this viewpoint, we would say that the patient who lies the most is the psychotic, which is exemplified by the case we have just seen, where the patient stated that he was Frank Sinatra, as well as those who have a pathological personality organisation, where lying constitutes an essential factor, as is the case with perversions and paranoid personality types. Or, in less serious pathologies, the patient who tells us that all, or almost all, of his problems stem from the ill treatment he has received and continues to receive at the hands of others; everyone else being the ones responsible for his misfortunes.

By the term sincerity, or authenticity of a person, I am also referring to the correlation and coherence that exists between what is spoken and what is felt. We might say that the degree of sincerity/insincerity depends on the degree of dissociation existing between affect, or emotions, on the one hand, and verbal content and behaviour (including non-verbal language) on the other.

In order to assess this aspect, it is also useful to bear in mind the emotional (countertransferential) reactions the patient engenders in the interviewer; reactions which are not always made evident in a clear and unequivocal way, but are repeatedly experienced throughout the course of the interview in a partial, dispersed, and disorganised way, up until the point where those reactions regroup and organise themselves in the therapist's mind, finally becoming concrete or fixed in certain feelings which cause him to make contact, or tune into what the patient is saying. With other patients, on the other hand, that emotional process does not take place in the therapist while the patient is speaking. That is to say, with certain patients, the professional might experience close communication, which stirs up anxiety, worry, or interest, while others convey or transmit little emotional intensity, provoking a minimal reaction, if not outright disinterest or boredom. This countertransferential component—as long as it is not one of the therapist' own defences—enables our impression to become established in relation to the patient's degree of sincerity. Such countertransferential reactions, which have been engendered in a dispersed way, as I was saying, often become more concrete once the interview has ended, when the therapist is left alone with what the patient has tried to communicate (or not). It is only then that all those feelings gain more clarity, which shall then be accompanied by significant content when we come to relate them to the rest of the data from the interview. I shall return to this point again later on.

There are patients who talk a lot and provide a large amount of material about their life and relationships during the course of the interviews. However, all of these data are based so clearly on external facts that we can scarcely gain the slightest idea of what is happening inside themselves. Or it might happen that these pieces of information do not match up with the way he behaves in the relationship established with the therapist in the interview. This impression might be said to be somewhat similar to that experienced by contrasting the knowledge we have acquired by observing how a certain person comes across to us in the "here and now" and the version the patient gives us of that same individual upon relating the vicissitudes of his life, and realising with some surprise that there is little correlation. Hence, we would say that, to a certain extent, he is lying to us.

I think that the idea of sincerity can be linked to the idea of psychic depth in a patient. That is to say, the sincere patient provides a fair amount of information about everything relating to his internal world within the scope of his abilities at that point in time. This allows us to "enter" into, or access, certain depths of that world, in so doing transmitting to us the impression of cutting deep into his psyche, in contrast to the less genuine patient, who leaves us with a sensation of having encountered a superficial person.

Likewise, I find it useful to observe the patient's emotional mobility throughout the course of the interview. Most commonly, this is produced spontaneously by the content of the account he is giving, when he touches upon matters that are particularly painful, or otherwise satisfying, to him, and the accompanying emotional tone is consistent with the subject matter. But this emotional mobility must also be observed within the context of the interview itself, that is to say, the attitude the patient adopts in relation to the therapist: the way he communicates with him and how he receives the indications given to him. We also need to address whether, between the beginning and the end of the interview, we experience any change in the emotional climate. This kind of emotional contact and flexibility will indicate the degree of sincerity, authenticity, or dishonesty of the patient.

I have encountered some patients who, while exhibiting some sincerity during the first interviews, limited information about certain details of their lives, which they did not speak about until treatment had begun, owing to the feelings of shame they experienced. Only when they had already been accepted by the therapist did they feel confident enough to reveal such information, in the hope that, in spite of the poor impression such a thing might give, this would not be cause for rejection on the part of the therapist.

Love/hatred of the truth (psychic reality)

This indicator is, in fact, closely linked to the previous one; however, it is useful to differentiate between them. In the sincerity/lying indicator, we highlight the capacity to accept the emotional and cognitive recognition of what one knows or could know (as it is quite near to consciousness) about oneself. With the love/hate for the truth indicator, I am seeking to emphasise an *attitude of searching* for that which is needed in order to represent one in one's identity, in so far as the current representation is not enough. The opposite attitude is one of hatred towards that search or towards what might be encountered were such a search to take place, thus directing all one's efforts towards obstructing or destroying this undertaking. Bion's work is marked by the emphasis he places on that search for the truth, which adds a further dimension to the Freudian maxim that the central aim of psychoanalysis is the search for the truth (Freud, 1937), be this the historical truth as occurred in the life of the patient, that which corresponds to his psychic reality constructed from certain fantasies, or both at the same time. In various passages of his work, Bion refers to the importance of truth for mental life, to the point where its growth seems to depend as much on truth as living organisms depend on food; and, if it is lacking, this causes either a deficiency in the personality, or is damaging to the mind. For example, "Psycho-analytic procedure pre-supposes that the welfare of the patient demands a constant supply of truth as inevitably as his physical survival demands food" (Bion, 1992, p. 99).

Thus, by the expression "love/hatred of the truth" I mean the desire and, at the same time, the rejection that exists in the individual when he comes to know the reality of his psychic life and the relationships in which he finds himself immersed. The desire for knowledge is expressed whenever a patient shows curiosity to know about himself and questions the reason behind certain ways of functioning, or to know about others (his external objects), particularly those with whom he has a significant relationship. At the opposite extreme, we see the patient who rarely questions either himself or others. In the case of the latter, any attempt to ask him open questions usually produces the response of a terse and assuring, "I don't know", or a brief pre-prepared answer.

In the interview, the patient in whom "love" for the truth predominates will relate to us that he has spent time questioning himself about personal matters that he does not understand, and that he has turned to other people, family members and friends, with whom he has tried to clear up his doubts, taking into account what has been said to him. Finally, faced with these efforts coming up short, he has found it necessary to consult a professional in order to follow that line of enquiry about himself and his surroundings.

I include the capacity for self-observation and hetero-observation in this section. Any desire to know leads to the development of the capacity for self-observation and observation of others. The latter does not always need to be considered an expression of projective or intrusive tendencies, or tendencies to control the other, as the fact of seeing and knowing through one's fellow man can be the first step in the approach to thinking about something that, at first, would be too painful in one's own self.

Degree of tolerance of emotional pain/pleasure

This involves to what degree one has the capacity to tolerate and to recognise various feelings and emotions: hate, guilt, anxiety, sorrow, aggression, and, in short, emotional pain in the broad sense of anything which is experienced as displeasure. Of the displeasurable feelings, I emphasise pain as a paradigm for all the others. The reason for this is that, in accord with Segal (1993), I consider it to be the expression of the life aspects faced with the threat of annihilation of the very self (real or phantasised); it is the point of emergence at which the life aspects react in the face of such a threat. I think that the analogy of somatic pain might be very illustrative. But I also include the other pole as part of this indicator, that of the capacity to tolerate feelings of quite another kind, or, rather, those that are associated with pleasurable states: love, gratitude, generosity, joy, and so on. In any case, I wish to emphasise that with this indicator I am assessing a patient's tolerance threshold to *the intensity of the feelings experienced*, of whatever type they might be.

Certainly, we may consider, although in a very schematic way, that any psychopathology is but a form of mental organisation structured to evade psychic pain, faced with the difficulty of modifying it (Bion, 1962). The relationship between pleasure and pain poses psychopathological problems in the area of the perversions, for example (particularly regarding the sadomasochistic components), but now is not the time to address these. Neither may we study here the nature of pain—another interesting subject—which, broadly speaking, in the clinical setting enables us to clearly differentiate sadomasochistic pain, let's say, from depressive pain resulting from the loss of the object. In other words, it enables us to distinguish between the pain necessary for growth and that which is not. In a general sense, however, one might say that the question lies in distinguishing between the pain that is in the service of life or, conversely, that which is subordinated to the destructive tendencies.

But also significant is the patient's capacity to feel pleasure, that is, to experience situations that are gratifying to him. As we consider the patient to be seeking help because he is experiencing some degree of suffering, perhaps we do not give sufficient consideration to his need and his capacity for enjoyment and gratification. While the manner of providing relief to the patient entails helping him to face up to, to tolerate, and to modify pain, instead of evading it, no less important is the experience of a "good" relationship with the therapist. And this gratification includes the therapist having accompanied him through that painful process of the recognition of reality, as well as that which, at certain moments, provides him with immediate relief owing to the conditions of containment and support of the setting, by the therapist making himself available as a stable object. The problem is that it is not always easy to accept such experiences, given that they often generate complex emotional reactions. One of these might be, for example, the fear of losing the object that is the source of gratification, which could lead to a precipitous rejection of it; or the fear of the patient's emotional needs not being met, or envy being aroused by not being the source of gratification itself, or feelings of guilt, or masochistic tendencies, and so on. Hence, we may talk about capacity and "tolerance" for pleasure in the broad sense of the gratification provided by a good relationship with one's objects (external and internal).

In the material set out below, we might notice how the incapacity to tolerate pain owing to a specific feeling, that of guilt, leads to the organisation of a pathology of which the predominant symptom is of the conversive type, and, furthermore, particularly expressive in its emotional and relational significance.

Clinical material 3: pathological mourning and conversive symptoms[1]

I have respected the order the account followed in the interview, according to the therapist's transcript. I have not set out the material with the same detail as in the case of the previous chapter for the reason that—just as there my concern was to show the emotional and cognitive movements in the relationship between patient and therapist in order to analyse the interview, in addition to those aspects which might point towards the suitability for psychotherapy—here I shall simply gather together these latter aspects, according to what we have said so far about the psychodynamic indicators. As in the afore-mentioned account, I will intersperse my comments with those contributed in the supervision group.

> In the *first interview*, after introducing herself, the therapist invites the patient to speak. The patient says that this will be very difficult for her because she almost has no voice, and that this is her problem. Indeed, it is a great effort for her to speak. She asks whether she can bring the chair closer so that the therapist can hear her better. Her voice wavers and, as this evidently entails such an effort, there are moments at which she gives the impression of gasping for air.
>
> Three years ago, she reveals, she had a polyp removed from her throat. Since then, she has had persistent problems with her voice. She has already undertaken several different therapies. She has been seen by several psychologists, who told her that the important thing was to relax. Upon getting up in the mornings she can speak normally, and even sing, shout, and scream . . . One of the psychologists told her that perhaps she feared that her throat disorder was cancerous, which was the reason she was anxious. Another remarked that perhaps the death of a significant person in her life shortly before the operation might have affected her. The therapist shows an interest in this loss.

It is clear that the adult aspect of the patient "brings" the "sick person" to the consultation, the person with the affliction, who suffers from the symptom—the chronic aphonia—which occupies the foreground. The adult aspect is also revealed by her collaborative attitude in suggesting the idea of drawing up her chair to come closer to the therapist to be better heard. Yet, she goes on to relate the failure of previous consultations, which augurs badly, pointing towards a personality with difficulties in accepting help. However, she has been able to retain the suggestions that were made to her, in the sense of associating the symptom with fears and situations of loss. The therapist makes use of this last piece of information to explore this question further.

> It is very difficult for her to respond, as at that moment her difficulty in speaking is exacerbated. The loss was of someone who was like a mother to her, and whom, in the last days and months of her life, during her illness and subsequent death, she considers she neglected. While this person was in a residence [for the elderly], the patient went on holiday, and upon her return she had already died [the patient becomes upset]. The therapist has had to make a significant effort to follow the story, as the patient's voice became almost inaudible. She asks the patient to clarify what she means by "as if she were my mother".

> She recounts that her biological mother was left widowed without any money when the patient was young, which is why her mother had to go out to work. As she could not look after her, she entrusted her care to a neighbour, who acted as her mother until she was eighteen years old. Her mother and the neighbour did not get along. She suspects that it must have been because of jealousy, since she was the only child of the former, and the latter, being a spinster, had no children. She emphasises that she feels very guilty for having gone on holiday and not having looked after this person [her adoptive mother] when she became ill. At the same time, she has a terrible relationship with her biological mother, perhaps as she contrasts her with the other [mother]. A year and a half before she died, she was taken into a residence for the elderly and then had to be moved to a hospital, where she died.

> The therapist enquires about why she gets along badly with her (biological) mother. She replies that she reminds her about everything she did not do for her [the patient] in her life. "Of course, she did what she could and what she knew how to do," she adds, "as she was left widowed without any financial resources, and I'm sure I would have done the same thing

in her circumstance." And yet she cannot escape the feelings of anger when she sees her, although she also recognises that her mother is a good person and has looked after her as far as she has been able . . . She falls silent.

The therapist asks her what else she remembers of her childhood.

"A disaster," she says. With her "neighbour" she lived well. She was a rich, educated woman, whose house was full of books and who taught her many things. Her mother, however, was illiterate and worked as a domestic cleaner in other houses. "As a child and a teenager, I was ashamed of her; most of all when I used to go out with her to public places, like to the bank, and she had to sign some paper or other, and I saw that she didn't know how to. It was really awful for me." The mother lived with one of her sisters and the sister's son. The two sisters were always fighting and screaming at each other. Her mother would criticise her for going out and having a good time. She was very strict and uncompromising. Her aunt also got along badly with the "neighbour", probably because of jealousy . . . She thinks that it could have been worse, although it was not an ideal childhood. She considers that she has always been a strong woman, who has managed to endure life's hard knocks. But now that things are going better for her, she does not feel well: she is depressed and has this problem of not being able to speak very well. She has a "marvellous" husband, and two preadolescent children, but they are good . . .

Upon talking about her children, her voice once again breaks, so she asks the therapist if she "understands" her. She means to say if she hears her, but she uses that other very significant verb, "understand". The therapist tells her that she does, and that she thinks she is talking to her about many things that are painful for her, which is why there are moments where she seems to be gasping for breath or choking.

It is clear that the symptom is related to emotional problems, since it acts as a signal for increased difficulty when the patient tackles subjects that are particularly painful to her. She immediately brings up a matter that seems to be crucial to her problems: the two maternal figures that live in conflict within her, and her feelings of guilt in relation to the adoptive mother. The contact she maintains with her childhood is very present. However, there is, arguably, a splitting of the infantile self, corresponding to each of the maternal figures, respectively. To the mother who is rich, educated, and so on, must correspond a child who has received satisfaction of her needs, who has been able to establish a relationship of healthy dependency. To the poor, limited mother, however, a plaintive and resentful child is suitable. Hence, the contradiction when she says that her childhood was a disaster, when she had all the affection and care from her "neighbour". Upon explaining her bad relationship with her biological mother, she justifies it by her being the personification of everything that a mother fails to give to a daughter, and that very fact led her to have to be strong in order to face up to the things in life that her mother was not capable of taking on. In other words, she had to take care of her own matters along with some of her mother's. This aspect might make us once again consider a personality with self-sufficient, even narcissistic, traits, which cause her to consider that needs exist in others, in people whom she is able to look after. She is, therefore, surprised that, having been so strong all her life, it should be now—just when she has a favourable family environment—that she does not feel well. Here, she displays the inadequacy of the defensive resources she has used until now, rendering it necessary for her to accept the help of a professional. It is curious that, upon mentioning her children, her aphonia is exacerbated. Perhaps when she situates herself as a mother, she enters into conflict with the split-off internal maternal objects we mentioned previously, thereby hindering identification, or, instead, signalling feelings of guilt in relation to both.

> The patient replies that yes (there are things that are very painful for her and that do overcome her[2]), in spite of the fact that she has always tried to face up to adversity. At fourteen she began work as a trainee, and later as a clerk in several different firms until she married, and the firm closed down. Now, as her children are older, in the sense that they do not need her as much, she feels stuck at home, so is taking a short course on caring for the elderly. She has had to make up some of the studies she was missing, and she has gained good marks in them. She comments that she is telling the therapist all of this so that the therapist can see the great efforts she has had to go to. She likes reading, and she is good at writing. But she hates it when she cannot read what she has written out loud. It was a "neighbour" who told her about these courses and who thought that she might like to do it. She pauses.
>
> The therapist asks, "A neighbour?"
>
> "Ah! Well yes, a neighbour, but another neighbour; one I have now [she remains pensive]. But why should I have chosen that type of work in particular? Could it be that I want to get rid of the guilt I feel about the

others? Well! You've really made me think about this now. And I don't know if I'll be able to cope with looking after old ladies, how I'll feel . . . I don't even know if it's something I've always wanted to do. But I am proud of how I'm doing."

On terminating the interview, the therapist proposes they continue with another interview and offers her an afternoon timetable if the indication of psychotherapy is confirmed. But this seems to be incompatible with the course she has mentioned. The therapist then tells her that if she cannot change the time of her classes, before going any further with the interviews she would refer her to another therapist who works at the Centre who does have availability in the mornings. The patient replies, "So lose everything I have done today? I think I'll try to speak with the course director so I can take that hour off."

The patient's attitude seems quite sincere. She is concerned to know why her discomfort occurs. She recognises that, in spite of having been strong, her strengths are now failing her, or, rather, the inadequate defences she has employed until now, such as the projection of need into others. So much so that she seems to accept the figure of the therapist as someone she has need of: she takes her suggestions on board and even admits that one of her interventions has made her think about her reason for choosing to work in caring for elderly women. This is more clearly expressed at the end of the interview, when she declares that she is in no way willing to lose the work carried out with the therapist. That is to say, she has been able to establish a sufficiently valuable link with her to go to efforts to preserve it.

In the *second interview* (one week later), the patient arrives punctually and says that she feels calmer. She has been able to rearrange her timetable to come at this time. She is very happy to have managed to do this, because she already feels she can trust the therapist, and because, besides it being hard for her to talk (literally), there is also the fact of having to ask for something, and on top of that it is so she can go to see a psychologist. This latter part she did not say like that, but rather that she had to consult a doctor. What she cannot understand is how it can be that her speech becomes worse, in point of fact, around the people who are actually closest and most dear to her: her children, her husband, and her mother. She asks the therapist what she makes of this . . . [Silence.] However, when she talks with other people—not always, but on many occasions—while she does not manage to do it perfectly, none the less she does not experience as much difficulty.

[As in the first interview, there are oscillations in the degree of intensity of the aphonia. There are times at which she has to make a tremendous effort to emit a sound, so much so that it appears that she is having difficulty breathing.]

The therapist asks her what she herself thinks.

She remains in thought for a few moments. Following this, she admits that she is confused. As she already said, it all started as a result of the operation. The fact of the matter is that she went to the hospital to see a doctor about a bite on her ear that had become swollen and, when the doctor heard her speak, he examined her larynx and vocal cords and told her that she had a cyst that would need to be removed immediately. Despite the doctor telling her that there would be no reason for her to lose her voice, she has been like this since the operation. "Sometimes I think that if I could have spoken with more ease about my difficulty, things would be different. For example, with my children and with my husband I never mention this subject. I pretend, I try not to speak, and that must make the problem worse. I haven't spoken openly to my mother either. Of course, with her it's difficult, because she immediately makes a tragedy out of every little thing; it has always been me, since I was a child, who has had to deal with every issue or problem ... Although I do understand my mother's attitude; she had a 'tragic' childhood. When she was eight years old, she was already being made to get up at four in the morning to go and work as a servant. The problem is that this has left my mother with a servile attitude towards everyone, above all towards her 'masters'" [bosses]. At Christmas time, her mother forced the patient to write her bosses a greetings card, which made her very angry. The patient has also had to work since she was very young, although doing other things. When she looks at her own daughter, she thinks about how easy she has had it.

[During this account, she has been able to speak more clearly, although at certain points her voice failed her, according to the emotional content of what she is saying.]

The patient returns, contented that she has been able to overcome the resistance offered by the narcissistic aspects of her personality that oppose her seeking help. It appears that the experience of the previous interview served to check such aspects, to the extent that now she is able to state explicitly that she has trust in the therapist. She immediately takes up the central thread of her problems once more, the fact that the symptom is particularly activated around her loved ones. When she asks the therapist her opinion, and she refers the question back to her, once more the conflict with her mother arises, with whom she has not spoken "openly". That is to say, she has not spoken with the devalued internal mother, whom she has not been able to forgive; neither has she let herself be forgiven. The patient makes an attempt to enquire into the problem, although she is currently not getting very far alone, as feelings of resentment and the efforts she had to make, through not having received adequate maternal care, quickly reappear. At the same time, the elements that shape her problems gradually take on substance, which, in turn, will enable a therapeutic focus to be established.

> After a silence, the therapist asks her about her dreams or anything else that she can think of. She says that she does not remember her dreams. Regarding her childhood, she recalls what she has already told her, although that does not seem so terrible to her either. She used to feel quite proud of her ability to solve problems. At twelve years old, when her mother and she lost their flat and were made homeless, she did not get frightened about anything. She looked for solutions; her mother, meanwhile, who was very scared, could only complain about things. She does not remember having cried, simply because her mother was always crying over everything. And even now she continues to do so: she cries about the war, the poor and hungry, street children . . . [at this point she almost loses her voice completely].

The therapist asks her about her father.

She says that she hardly remembers him. He died when she was four years old. However, she very clearly remembers the day he died, because of the constant coming and going that went on at the house. Although he had been unwell for some time, he died of a heart attack. His death caused them serious difficulties in the long and the short term, the most significant being that they were made homeless. It was then that she had to go and live at her neighbour's house while her mother went to live with her aunt. Her mother remained fixated on the memory of the father. She did not remarry. She dressed in mourning clothes and hung a very large photograph of her husband in a visible place. "My mother used to find it strange that it hadn't mattered to me . . . [the father's death]. She is very religious, devoutly so, and she wanted me to be the same. But I'm not. In any case, what I have actually thought about are the consequences of that death; of having had to take charge of so many things, being so young; of going to live away from home, of not having two pennies to rub together. But look, now that I have everything sorted out, a wonderful family, a stable economic situation and a home, that's when I feel like this, with this problem."

Now the patient tries to relativise the misfortunes of a childhood without a (biological) mother capable of looking after her, because she was strong enough to deal with things alone. Once again, the narcissistic aspect re-emerges, relativising the healthy, sane, infantile dependence at the expense of overvaluing her capacities, even when the data she provides give credibility to her version of an external mother as a somewhat limited and fragile person, which caused her to have to struggle to take on responsibilities beyond her years in order to survive. She then points out a matter that also seems to be significant—her difficulty in doing the work of mourning—when she picks up the issue of her mother finding it strange how little her father's death appeared to matter to her. Arguably, faced with the external reality of a very depressed mother, the child was not able to find the support to experience the pain at the loss of her father. In any case, the death of the adoptive mother (the "neighbour") reactivates the need to learn to go through such experiences of mourning.

> The therapist remarks that perhaps all these things that she remembers from her childhood, such as having had to take on so many responsibilities, are arousing considerable feelings of anger in her.

> She says no; she felt very strong and capable compared to other girls her age. [After a silence] "Although perhaps you are right." And upon thinking about everything that happened, she did in fact feel angry towards her mother, because of what she has suffered.

> Then she says that she is thinking about A, her husband. Two years ago, she made a real fuss over a question of jealousy, as she had got it into her head that he liked one of her closest friends, although, in reality, she had no cause to think that. And yet, that was how she felt, to the point where she stopped seeing her friend. After thinking about it for a moment, she says that perhaps she took a dislike to this friend because she was so tall, slim, and beautiful, and she, on the other hand, had put on a lot of weight after her operation, as she did nothing but eat. However, she cannot complain because the people around her help her a lot, and they are very patient with her.

> The therapist points out to her that it seems as though it is she who is now less patient with herself, with all this that is happening to her.

[The patient looks at the therapists and smiles.] "Well, yes, it's true; I am very annoyed at myself." After having struggled so much in life, to now feel bad like this, because of this voice problem. She thinks that perhaps she has done the course to help the elderly as a way of giving of herself to others. But she sees the difficulty, because how will she be able to help the elderly, who need someone to talk to, when she feels as inadequate as she does with her loss of voice? Sometimes she asks for God's help, but she thinks that instead he will punish her for not being at all religious.

The therapist tells her that perhaps it is she who punishes herself, by feeling "inadequate".

She says that perhaps she does too much. In the morning she studies, in the afternoon she has the course, and then she takes care of the house. Although she manages everything well. She remains silent for a moment, and then adds, "Well, not as well, not since my 'neighbour' died." She felt that they got rid of her when she became ill and was taken into a residence for the elderly, and then when she died . . . She always thinks about that— the fact that she didn't look after her—and she feels very guilty.

[In today's interview, the patient has been calmer; she has not needed to bring her chair closer to be better heard by the therapist, so it appears that her degree of anxiety has lessened somewhat, in spite of the fact that her aphonia persists.]

What is exhibited in this interview fragment is curious. On the one hand, the narcissistic aspect, or, rather, the narcissistic wound, continues to be evident, judging by her feeling unwell and the sense that all the efforts she has made in her life have now resulted in failure. In such a way, we may detect an attempt at maniacal and omnipotent reparation, by undertaking so many activities; although the patient herself, to some extent, questions this new activity of looking after the elderly, in the sense of whether it is authentically reparatory. On the other hand, she does not establish a narcissistic relationship with the therapist, but is able to give her recognition for her interventions. It is as if, through this dissociation of her two selves with the two maternal figures that we have seen, the one that now predominates is the self that is able to recognise healthy dependence. This might be a favourable sign for the initiation of treatment. Whether it will be necessary to integrate the other dissociated aspect of the relationship remains to be seen.

Comments on the interviews during the supervision

The symptom presented by the patient affects an organ with a relationship function: the voice. That is to say, it is an organ with an important emotional and relational significance. She cannot speak because she feels choked by the emotions she feels, particularly by the feeling of guilt, which is the prevalent emotion.

In this account of the interview, quick to emerge from her story is the significant set of problems related to the "neighbour–mother". She is the only child of a mother who, upon being widowed, is plunged into such poverty—emotional as well as material—that she is unable look after her. She speaks of a poor mother, towards whom she feels ambivalence. In one sense, she tries to understand her, since she also had a tragic childhood, but, in another, she cannot bear the narcissistic "shame" of having had such a limited mother. She shows, quite clearly, two very different female figures: first, the poor, limited, biological mother with no economic or self resources, followed immediately by the "mother–neighbour", an educated woman with considerable resources and a house full of good objects. It is curious that while she praises the figure of the latter, it appears that she interposes a certain distance by constantly referring to her as the "neighbour", as if she were not able to accept her as a mother—probably so as not to feel as though she were permanently excluding the biological mother, even in name: at least she retains her formal title. She says that her childhood was disastrous, but she seems to attribute this to the fact of having had a mother of whom she was ashamed, owing to the fact that she could not look after her and had to give up her duties to another person, the "neighbour". The patient seems to be pronouncing, "It is shameful to have a mother who is not capable of assuming her maternal role". So, to recognise the "neighbour" as a mother would mean divesting the biological mother of her title, which is the only thing she feels is rightfully hers. This would explain her ambivalent attitude towards the "neighbour", as well as her relative negligence towards her during the last years of her life, and, above all, her overwhelming feelings of guilt for not having recognised her as a true mother. Albeit, this would have brought with it another type of guilt in relation to the biological mother, who was already so devalued that it would have meant practically cancelling her out entirely.

At the same time, we can see that in the interview the patient adopts a collaborative and sincere attitude; she takes the therapist into account and is concerned about whether or not she will understand her, and whether or not she has felt heard. From the outset, the patient needs to speak and not be spoken to, because of the risk of questions being pointed out to her which might arouse her feeling of guilt—always very close to the surface.

In the second interview—the notes on the supervision proceed—the patient reveals the numerous efforts she has made throughout her life to survive and forge ahead, which has enabled her to achieve a number of things. As she says, she is in a situation where she has a family who loves her, and whom she loves; however, that does not seem to be enough to resolve her conflictive situation, which is why she seeks help. She cannot do it alone. She does not have anyone close to her who is able to "hear" her. At home, her family just does not seem to understand, and what is more, she herself conceals her feelings. In any case, the fact is that it is an internal problem the patient has with her maternal images. Her mother's personal limitations were accentuated, it appears, by the fact of not having been able to assimilate the loss of her husband, or then to take responsibility for her daughter by herself. Instead the opposite happened; it was the patient, when they were later made homeless when she was twelve years old, who would become her mother's support. Only at one point in the interview was she able to express the anger she felt towards her mother. It is not very clear what kind of relationship the patient has with her own children, bearing in mind the difficulties she has with her own mother. How does she resolve the question of identifying with a poor and limited mother, while at the same time be able to look after her own children? Does she feel that she gives them what they need, or does she think that her care falls short, through her own feelings of dissatisfaction in relation to her mother? Or, otherwise, does she triumph over her mother by regarding herself as performing her maternal role better than she? During the supervision, we comment that these might be questions to enquire into during treatment.

In the working group, we add that it might be worth thinking about the following focus: the guilt she feels over the death of the "neighbour–mother" and what bearing this has in relation to the biological mother; a guilt that she feels because of how she has experienced this relationship with each of her two "mothers". One might put it to her that perhaps she was not able to take more care of the "neighbour"—pointing out to her in passing that it is still curious that she continues to call her this when she has explained that she assumed maternal duties with her—because doing so would mean recognising everything that she has received, which would be tantamount to giving her the title of mother, thus taking this away from her biological mother. And that perhaps neither has she been able to recognise the resentment she feels towards her biological mother for not being able to give her what she needed—or, rather, what the other (mother) did indeed offer her—despite this being on account of personal and circumstantial limitations. There is, then, a very radical splitting of the maternal figures: on one side, there is the neighbour–mother, the idealised mother, and on the other, the biological mother, a poor woman and someone to be ashamed of. The comments from the supervision end here.

Brief psychoanalytic psychotherapy was indicated, lasting for one year, at a frequency of one session per week, which meant a total of forty-two sessions. As treatment progressed, therapist and patient were able to work through and to gradually close the breach between the two maternal figures. The patient was able to appreciate that her feeling of guilt was rooted in having erased her biological mother from her life in order to recognise only the idealised mother, but also, as was established in the sessions, in not having looked after this mother during her last days, since this would have meant increasing her guilt towards the former. The development and outcome of treatment confirmed that the aspects chosen as a focus for psychotherapeutic treatment had been correct. The symptom improved. This psychotherapeutic experience has enabled the patient to become closer to her biological mother, by valuing her in a more realistic way, which, in turn, has also made it possible for her to accept better both the loss of the idealised mother and her feelings of guilt for not having duly looked after her. Towards the end of psychotherapy, we were able to examine several different situations of separation and loss: in addition to the loss of her adoptive mother, there was also the loss of her treatment, as well as that of her daughter, who reached an age where she could leave home.

(Degree of) Tolerance to separation/linking anxieties

In any person's life, he will have had experiences of separation and loss, even if these are only those that are part and parcel of growth.

Each stage of development entails—to a greater or lesser extent according to the stage in question—a separation from the relationship with the people or situations that have been vital to us. But we also separate from what we ourselves have ceased to be by the same process of growth. In the development of the individual, the following losses are inevitable: the loss of the intrauterine relationship, the primitive relationship with the mother during the first years of life, as well as with the parental figures who looked after him in his infancy, and also the loss of each stage of life in order to proceed to the next, by virtue of the stage of progress attained. However, of all the losses of the various stages of human development, the loss of childhood carries particular significance. This is as a result of the relationships of dependency that were established, which enabled an organisation of the child's mental functioning to be maintained in order to cope with his life and his world in an acceptable way, thereby achieving a certain stability which, in the following stage, will have to be reorganised in a different way to deal with new needs and new responsibilities.

And, of course, we must consider any traumatic losses that might have occurred. These losses occur when, to the situations that are part and parcel of the individual's natural progression, are added certain especially adverse circumstances: a difficult birth, weaning accompanied by painful familial circumstances for the mother, resulting in her carrying out the process inadequately or even interrupting it suddenly, or any situation in the child's subsequent development which involves a separation that reactivates the pain of early separations, although, along with it, the learnt capacity to tolerate those separations. If, however, particularly negative circumstances arise in subsequent separations, this could overwhelm the fragile learnt capacity to bear them and, as a result, this new separation might be experienced as traumatic, even if the early experiences were not. This could happen in the case of a child who is starting school for the first time shortly after the birth of a brother or sister, or, indeed, that of the concomitance of organic illnesses with some of those transitional stages. In adolescence, when bodily changes hold so much significance, an accident or illness that causes irreparable physical injury or disability will be a loss that has significant consequences.

Obviously, the loss of people close to the individual will have particular repercussions, especially the earlier they occur and the more traumatic they are. But—as always—their significance will be accorded not only by the historical fact itself, but by how the person has experienced it and what consequences we perceive it has had on his mental life. By making this revision of the various situations of separation that may have tested the patient's capacity to tolerate them, it is not my intention that they should be reviewed in the diagnostic interviews as if they were a clinical history protocol. As we already discussed in Chapter Three, these are examples I have cited simply with an aim to recapitulate what I am referring to. I consider such pieces of information to be significant enough—and, moreover, the time at which they appear—to pay attention to them when they arise unprompted in the interview. It might be that the patient remembers those situations of loss upon being invited to talk about some or other aspect of his life which is apparently unrelated, but which he has associated in his mind with this loss. For example, his childhood might be tied to a certain traumatic loss which endows it with a particular significance.

However, just as we are accustomed to considering and assessing the patient's anxieties towards situations of separation, perhaps we do not take into account to the same degree the opposing factor; that is to say, the patient's anxieties towards situations of linking. In fact, however, as is clear from what we have already pointed out, the patient's response to experiences of separation will depend upon how these experiences took place when relationships of linking with his significant external objects were established. So, it follows that within the same indicator should be included the pair shaped by the anxieties and experiences arising from experiences of separation, as well as those of linking.

Just as in the exploration of the separation anxieties, I am often on the alert for the data the patient provides when he comes to relate the various stages of his life, but now I will be paying particular attention to the data relating to his personal *relationships*: his relationship with food in early childhood—whether he took the breast eagerly or reluctantly (in the case of patients who are able to provide such information); his relationship towards the affectionate gestures of his parental figures; his relationship on the whole with his parents and siblings; with school friends, and so on; and in the present day, with his work colleagues, his partner, and others closest to him.

As we have said of the indicator for "tolerance of pain/pleasure", the experience of pain is not always positive, and neither does the experience of pleasure inevitably need to be linked to defensive manoeuvres. And the other way round: neither does pain have to be something sick or unhealthy, and pleasure, conversely, something healthy. In the same way, separation is an unavoidable experience that contributes to the development of the individual, as does union, in the sense of linking with the object. Any separation beyond what is tolerable might end up being damaging to the self. However, this is something that not only depends upon the external facts but also on the capacities of the individual (sometimes, we find patients who have experienced significant situations of lack and who, surprisingly, have developed a capacity to relate to, and value, the object on the basis of the little they have received in their lives). Similarly, any relationship that entails an experience of fusion and undifferentiation with the other will also affect the individual's development, which, in the same way as the previous situation, will not only depend on the existence of an overprotecting object, but on subjective experience.

Capacity for and (degree of) tolerance to the masculine–feminine

In any patient, I think it is useful to investigate the coexistence of the feminine and the masculine elements, as well as his capacity for integration of the above. We know that in our social relationships, roughly the same thing occurs as we spoke about with regard to our difficulties in recognising the infantile in the adult: the infantile is considered to be a stage of life that is long past and, as such, must be rejected or ruled out in a person of adult age. Likewise, the elements of this indicator are often considered as being two dissociative poles, to the point where the man has to possess only those attributes and qualities that belong to his sex and the same for the woman. Anything that might mean possessing characteristics of the other sex would also mean belonging less to one's own and, in short, being less oneself. In spite of the social achievements that have contributed towards lessening this split, I believe that there is a question that has its roots in psychology, and it is the difficulty in tolerating what one is not and what the other possesses: in this case, the other sex.

It is clear that the individual's development is fundamentally achieved starting with the parental figures, man and woman, and that, consequently, we have had to receive from each one of them certain aspects or characteristics with which we have identified. Thus, very briefly, of the "feminine capacities" we might include those psychological characteristics that, in our view, are more identifiably female. A list of these, taken from general observation and clinical practice, might include, among other things, anything relating to the ability to receive and to care for, linked to the capacity to offer a form of containment in the relationship with the other and with oneself. Similarly, the capacity to be sensitive, to be responsive, to be in touch with one's emotions (it is relatively common to hear the expression that crying is something women do, as if the cry were not the expression of certain feelings in every individual, male or female). This sensitivity is often more pronounced in women, and not only when it relates to being in touch with one's emotions, but also to a particular skill in picking up levels of non-verbal communication in human relationships that are difficult to explain in words. With regard to the "masculine capacity", we might enumerate characteristics such as drive, decisiveness or determination, and strength, as well as perhaps the capacity for organisation and efficiency.

I am not seeking to establish here a catalogue of differential psychology of the sexes, but simply to point out some of the general aspects that might be more or less evident. In any case, however, what I wish to stress here is the idea held by the patient himself in terms of what the masculine and the feminine signify to him, and how he situates himself in relation to each one of these prototypes.

Even though the usual social prejudices are lessening all the time, a person might still rely on these to a greater or lesser extent, depending on his history and personal development, his psychological characteristics, and the particular vicissitudes of his processes of identification on the basis of his parental figures, first, and all of those figures resulting from them, later. Therefore, this indicator will comprise certain questions of interest, such as those relating to sexual identity and, closely linked to this, to relationships with male and female figures. Furthermore, there is another aspect that I consider to be significant in the assessment of the patient's personality. This indicator also involves the possibility of exploring the degree of integration or dissociation between the masculine and the feminine; that is to say, not only how the patient has internalised a female and a male figure, but how he has introjected the link between the two. That introjection, if it dates back to the early relationships, lays the foundations for the individual's capacity to establish links that are essential for life and for growth. To this effect, Bion indicates that one of the principal problems for the psychotic patient stems from the "attacks on linking" (Bion, 1967)—the attack on the relationship with the primitive object being one of the fundamental ones—but to which we should add, in my opinion, the attack on the link between the parental couple in particular. I think this idea may be applied to every patient, although in the most serious patients it takes on particular dimensions. Below, I have included clinical material from a young adult patient that illustrates the problems experienced by a patient in achieving a masculine sexual identity as a result of difficulties in identification with a parental couple who has serious relationship problems.

Clinical material 4: the boy confused with his parental couple[3]

Diagnostic interviews

First interview

The reason for the consultation comes from the patient's difficulties in his sexual relationships with girls. He has a small penis complex. Of his mother, he pronounces that she is a failure because of her bad relationship with his father, whom he describes as, "A fossil, a vegetable, and impotent" (according to what his mother has told him). In the interview he feels "small" (he cries inconsolably). We might consider that if he is seen to be small, including his "penis", that is to say, his mental capacities, then there will be no risk of castration.

He explains that he was an unwanted child. He wanted to know his parents' problems in order to resolve his own, but this caused him some confusion, as he identified as much with his (failed) mother as with his (impotent) father. In the patient's unconscious phantasy, not being wanted signifies that his parents did not have enough desire for each other to share an experience that might result in mutual wellbeing or pleasure, the product of that union perhaps also being him, the child. Consequently, he does not understand how his mother and father can have achieved any kind of union, not even a physical one, holding his father responsible for such a senseless act, "It must have been my father who put it in [his mother] without thinking," he says, and from that irresponsible act he was born.

So, then, it seems that the patient's set of problems are rooted in internally accepting united parents, of whose union he himself was the outcome. But the path he chooses as a route to a possible solution is that of "investigating" the reasons for that difficulty in uniting, whereby he complicates things for himself, and inevitably forges alliances with one parent (in the majority of cases, his mother), against the other parent. In so doing, he deprives himself—at the same time as evading—of the opportunity to take care of his own growth.

During the supervision, an early conclusion is reached regarding a potential focus for psychotherapeutic treatment, which involves enabling the patient to learn to release his parents, to trust somewhat more in their own capacities—whatever they might be—and in such a way be able to deal with his own life.

Second interview

The patient says that, from an early age, his mother would mistreat him, including physically, as his birth meant that she was tied to his father, a person whom, in fact, she wanted nothing to do with. With his father, however, he remembers having had a good relationship during childhood. Shortly after he started to walk, he went back to crawling, and his doctor advised his parents to ignore him as he was simply attention seeking. If they hit him, he says, it was because he was a "little rascal", a naughty child. However, his father defended him from his mother. He was enuretic until the age of fifteen or sixteen. He once spied on his mother during the time she was having sexual relations with a neighbour. He asserts, however, that his mother is an innocent and naïve woman. He also remembers having been very jealous of his younger sister. He explains a dream in which he is in bed with an older woman who says that she does not know how to do anything (in her sex life), but he wants to try it.

During the supervision, the eroticised relationship with his mother and this dream give us cause to consider the potential transferential risks with a view to the course of psychotherapy. The female therapist would need to be alert to the degree of contamination of the therapeutic relationship by the fantasy that the mother (and the therapist, during treatment) is the innocent one (the older woman who does not know) and he, the expert in whom she is (sexually) interested.

Third interview

The patient is open and honest. He had requested a male therapist, but once he has said this, now he does not mind one way or the other. He asks himself about his parents' problems and he does not understand them. He insists on wanting to explore this issue more deeply, because *he needs to know where he comes from.* One might interpret from this that the patient is implicitly formulating the following questions: how is it possible that he comes from a father who is a fossil and a mother who goes off with another man (not his father)? And how can he recognise himself with any kind of psychological identity if he thinks that he has not been (present) in the minds of his parents (in his father's, because he is a fossil, and his mother's, as she is sexually unsatisfied and has to seek relief outside the home)?

The focus—it is emphasised in the supervision—should consist of trying to cleanse the familial relationship from the patient's perspective, by helping him to distance himself from his parents' conflicts so that he can look inside himself, in his emotional life and in the relationships he establishes. For the time being, the boy is considered to possess sufficient ego capacity to carry out such a task without direct intervention in the family circle.

Brief psychoanalytic psychotherapy (BPP) is proposed, to last one year, to which the patient replies, "You think I'm really that bad?" The therapist answers that, from what they have been looking at in the interviews, this is what she considers the most suitable option for him, and she goes on to ask him how he sees himself. To this, the patient answers that he is "mixed up by his parents".

Comments on the supervision

It seems clear that the patient has a good grasp of what his problems are. The solution involves coming out of that complicated involvement with his parents, even if this means abandoning the position—to some extent a privileged one—he seems to occupy through his attitude: he places himself between his parents in order to fix their lives, because they cannot. And, in so doing, he comes out on top. By this insertion, moreover, he will achieve a pairing with both one and the other, and, in short, will triumph over both.

The treatment lasted for one year, with a total of forty-five sessions, at a frequency of one per week. The chosen focus seemed to be the right one, as is shown by these notes taken in the supervision group after session number thirty-one: "In this session (the patient) also recognises the support of a paternal figure (at work). At this point we can see that *the patient has achieved a 'more hygienic' family environment*—which was one of the aims of the treatment. This is manifest in the patient now being 'less involved' with his mother, as well him valuing his male paternal figure to a greater extent. He has initiated a few relationships with girls, where his own difficulties have been evident, thus enabling us to examine them." The patient is able to recognise, at the end of treatment, that he needs to have his own space—both physically and mentally—which he takes responsibility for, so he is assessing the possibility of going to live on his own. This is a very different situation from the one at the start of treatment, where he came "mixed up" in the relationship with his parents, there being no discrimination between functions or spaces, with the result that he was not able to take care of himself.

Notes

1. As with Clinical Material 2, used in Chapter Five, the following material has been gathered together from a supervision carried out within the same working group. I take all responsibility for the version set out below, as well as for any changes made to preserve confidentiality.

2. Translator's note: In Spanish, the word used by the patient to describe her feelings, *ahogar*, has the dual meaning of the figurative "to overcome" (with emotion) and the literal "to choke", or indeed, "to drown" or "suffocate". An approximate phrase in English might be "to be choked" with emotion, but this does not fully convey the emotional impact of its Spanish counterpart.

3. This material has been provided by the same working group as that of Clinical Material 2 and 3, although from a different therapist.

CHAPTER SEVEN

Complementary indicators

While the seven indicators described in the previous chapter might show with some degree of accuracy the suitability of a patient for psychotherapy or psychoanalysis, it is important to also take account of certain other indicators, which could help to complete them.

Response to therapist interventions

We often consider this aspect more precisely in relation to patient response to the "test interpretations" made by the therapist. However, in my opinion, a more generic approach to one that relates exclusively to interpretation might yield more reliable results. If we proceed from the idea of the existence of an intense transferential climate in the early interviews, then any therapist intervention will arouse some kind of response, which to some extent will be significant. The more neutral and open the therapist's interventions, the greater the possibility that the patient's reactions will correspond to how he experiences the transference, or, rather, to what he has projected into the therapist. Consequently, there does not seem to be any advantage to be gained from making a test interpretation. Moreover, given that the therapist does not yet possess sufficient knowledge of the patient, there remains the risk that he will make an incorrect interpretation, that is to say, one that hardly comes close to the patient's internal reality, if, indeed, it does not depart entirely from it. In such a case, clearly the patient's response will be iatrogenically falsified. For that reason, I am more in favour of observing the patient's reactions, whatever they might be, in response to the different interventions made by the therapist.

Nevertheless, in the event that the therapist opts for a test interpretation, I think it would be worth considering a number of questions. In any first contact between patient and professional there is a considerable tendency to "look outside" of one's internal world, irrespective of the degree of psychopathology. In addition, the patient will try to get the therapist to follow him by directing his attention towards the external world. And in this sense, the initial versions of relational conflicts usually offered by the patient show themselves to be indissolubly bound to the characteristics of the person to whom the conflict is linked (the partner, child, boss, etc.), to the point where it would seem that the problem could only be resolved with the presence of the other. That the patient should act in this way is not surprising, given that the "look" inside himself is something he has tried to evade throughout his life because of how painful it is for him, at least in so far as it indicates his psychopathology, and perhaps also because there is a certain magical expectation that the therapist will "see" for him, to then advise him what to do without him having to "see", or, rather, to take cognisance of it for himself.

As a result, an interpretation that attempts to make manifest conflicts that are hidden for the patient, in the first interview, might be difficult for him to accept (leaving aside any question of the therapist's tact and timeliness in making it), and could be felt to be almost like an intrusion, to a certain extent even as something violent; the more dissociated the interpretation is for the patient, the more violent it will be.

For all of the above, interpretation might not be only somewhat unreliable, but also constitutes an unnecessary risk to the therapeutic relationship. Having said that, it is always possible to put an interpretation in the form of a proposal for investigation, as a hypothesis or, instead, in the form of a plausible doubt or query, which might then be confirmed by the patient: for example, when the therapist verbalises any (unconscious) doubts the patient might have over whether this treatment will be of any use to him, or perhaps whether his problems will be tolerated by the therapist. Clearly, there is no sense in insisting if the patient responds by denying any possible interpretation made. We are at the diagnostic evaluation stage, and not in treatment proper, and, as such, we can only take note of the patient's reaction. Even in the therapeutic process itself, any interpretation is always only ever a hypothesis, which must be tested against the patient's associations and reactions. None the less, in the therapeutic session we will need to exhaust the possibility of such a hypothesis, whereas in the interview it is preferable to abandon it swiftly.

In contrast, the patient's responses to the non-interpretative interventions made by the therapist throughout the course of the interview might be equally valuable and, at the same time, less risky. In that respect, any suggestion made to the patient will be valid, such as picking up on the patient's last contribution and returning it to him in the form of a question. For example, in the case of the "Mother with difficulties in her feeding function" in Chapter Five, we saw how the therapist made reference on several occasions to the subject of the death of the mother, eliciting varying responses on the part of the patient, who began by mentioning the subject in passing, then describing the external circumstances, but without referring to how she experienced it personally, all of which was indicative of unresolved mourning. Or, in the case of the patient with conversive symptoms, upon her making reference to a "neighbour" (see p. 149), a name she had already used to allude to her adoptive mother, the therapist's brief question ("A neighbour?") enabled her to come to a realisation about the situation, if not gain a fleeting insight, by making the connection between the two neighbours, and intuiting that perhaps her caring for the elderly might have something to do with feelings of guilt. In another patient, in contrast, the response to the therapist's intervention may be a laconic, "Yes (a neighbour)," with this displaying a defensive attitude. Or, continuing with the example of the death of a significant other, we should also mention the patient who will respond with a hasty explanation that he is already over that loss, as a means of ducking the issue. As always, the accompanying emotional tone and paraverbal behaviour of the patient are signs that should be taken into account.

The brief interventions made by the therapist, as far as possible following on from the patient's account, introduce nuances into the relationship that hint at certain investigative prospects. A particular evasive reaction on the part of the patient to the therapist's intervention does not only reflect how painful or how accessible to consciousness such subjects will be when it comes to examining them, but also reflects the very fact that he has accepted the therapist's intervention. This is sometimes the case when a patient seems to be very collaborative because he has talked a great deal throughout the interview, while the therapist has remained silent, listening. And yet, at the end of the interview, all kinds of difficulties arise in trying to agree upon the time of the next meeting, which might indicate an attitude of a certain opposition to, or disagreement with, the therapist, or resistance to potential treatment. While the therapist was not even able to say "this is my mouth", the only "mouth" being the patient's (for speaking), everything seemed to be going well, until the evidence showed a different reality: that there is no "mouth" for receiving. Then things go awry. It might be conceivable that the basis for such behaviour lies in a predominantly narcissistic personality.

Notwithstanding the above, I do not dismiss the option of making an interpretation, if I have enough seemingly plausible information, as not only can it be useful in terms of assessing the patient's reaction, but it also constitutes a practical tool that can occasionally open up avenues of exploration that, up until that point, had not been revealed.

Capacity for containment in the social/family environment

This factor can effectively tip the balance of a potential indication for psychotherapy or psychoanalysis in the case of patients for whom the result of the combined basic observable indicators presents an uncertain or doubtful impression to the therapist of their feasibility for such treatments. As we know, the implementation of a psychotherapeutic—and particularly a psychoanalytic—process mobilises a number of anxieties in the patient who is still not well enough, or does not possess the tools to be able to modulate and metabolise, which leads to *acting-out*, with potentially damaging repercussions to the people in his immediate surroundings. If these people do not have any knowledge of psychoanalytical therapy, they will consider such behaviour in the patient to be the negative effect of such treatment, advising against its continuation; the patient will then dissociate with his resistant aspects, which are opposed to treatment, and will project them into these close friends and family members, confronting the therapist with them and, thus, avoiding taking responsibility for the situation. But it could also happen that because, in point of fact, the treatment is yielding good results, the patient will modify certain attitudes and patterns of behaviour in relation to the people close to him. For example, in terms of lessening his dependence upon them—if this had been the case—as he begins to feel more autonomous. In this way, his family members find themselves obliged to alter the type of relationship—usually overprotective—that they had maintained until then, and readjust it to the new situation. If they do not tolerate that progress in the patient, they will find a means to discredit the treatment and hinder its continuation. Conversely, a more containing environment in this respect will facilitate the course of the therapeutic process, simply by respecting it. If this is a very adverse indicator, we might explore the possibility of another sick member of the family group also receiving appropriate help.

It is occasionally the case that the patient who seeks help is, in fact, the sanest member of his family environment. And he is seeking help precisely because he alone cannot take on the entire burden of his family's troubles. The initial request is often that he be equipped with more strength in order to be able to continue to perform this task. But it is soon clear that these are omnipotent phantasies—of trying to occupy a place that does not belong to him in the bosom of the family—which have led him to enter that dynamic, of thinking that it is he alone who can save his family, or a particular family member. The clinical material that I shall set out below might exemplify this. At the same time, it serves as an illustration of the need to be aware of the different indicators; in this case, in spite of the adverse environment, psychotherapy was, in fact, possible.

Clinical material 5: the daughter of a psychotic mother[1]

Diagnostic interviews

A girl of around twenty years old comes for help for anxiety caused by her being overburdened by the responsibility of taking care of a mother who is psychiatrically ill with severe melancholic depression and who has made two suicide attempts. One was an act of self-aggression, by stabbing herself in the stomach with a knife, and the other by throwing herself into the sea with the intention of drowning herself. The patient does not mention her father until the third diagnostic interview. There is a sister who has lived away from home for some years at boarding school from an early age until she was fourteen, but who, upon returning home, had many conflicts with her parents, as she was always considered to be "the bad one", according to them, because she was "unruly and a layabout". Between the second and third interviews, her mother has been admitted to hospital, because she made a new suicide attempt.

During the supervision, after these three interviews, it is considered inadvisable to do weekly psychotherapy in such an adverse environment, as everything is projected into the mother's illness or into the father's and sister's reticence and lack of assertion. We formulate an early hypothesis that the patient feels indebted to her mother for having received privileged treatment (she was never sent to any institution) in relation to her sister. To this feeling is added an attitude of omnipotence as her mother's life depends on her; an attitude clearly enabled by the abandonment of the rest of the family. In the second interview, she has to come accompanied by her mother, who remains in the waiting room, for fear of her making another suicide attempt if she is left alone. On the other hand, none of the patient's valid relationships, either in the sphere of work or love, seems to be contaminated by her discomfort and anxiety in the face of the situation at home. A very radical defensive attitude is apparent, which entails a splitting-off of anything that might disturb her. In the supervision, we agree to finish our assessment of the patient, in a fourth interview, by investigating further aspects, such as those relating to her childhood and dreams. It seems prudent, by way of sounding out her response, to propose the possibility of supportive psychotherapeutic help, at a fortnightly frequency as opposed to weekly, but waiting to see her reaction and being attentive to whether she contributes new data at the next interview that might contradict this opinion.

The patient comes to the fourth interview with a less defensive attitude. As more time has now passed since her mother was admitted to hospital, it is clear to see the change she has undergone as a result of not having to look after her. Now she appears to be more willing to look inside herself and to talk about her life, as well as her relationship with her mother and her family. She also describes several dreams. In general, she appears to be more honest when speaking about herself. She relates an incident from childhood where her father tried to abuse her sister, according to what her sister told her some years later. For that reason, it was understandable that she would keep her father dissociated during the first interviews and that she would avoid relying on him to help her mother, since, in her phantasy, joining with her father for any activity could be dangerous. The dreams she provides are of a persecutory nature, relating to birds (or rats) that she looks after, but which then attack her. In the supervision, these animals are understood to represent the mother, in a different image to the one conveyed at the start. If, in the first interviews, what she contributed was the image of a sick woman who makes attempts against her own life and who, therefore, is in considerable need of the patient's help, which would correspond to a more tolerable version for her, now, by means of these oniric images, a persecutory maternal figure emerges. An acceptable image is that of the sick mother; the dream image is quite another, supported by other pieces of information she resolves to reveal in this interview when she relates that her sister (she herself cannot think in that way) told her that her mother had ruined her father's life. In response to the therapist raising the question of whether fortnightly or weekly help might be preferable, the patient replies that "she cannot stay at home, she has to make her own life, and that she has enrolled on a course in *human resources*." That is to say, the patient's reply could be understood in terms of a desire to learn in order to improve her own "human resources".

Consequently, despite there being no discernible signs of the establishment of good relationships, in which she considers the other to have satisfied her needs in some way, neither is there any actively destructive attitude present in her existing relationships. On the other hand, the data she contributes in her relationship with the therapist during the interviews are assessed to be significant and encouraging. From the first interview, to which she came with a certain degree of mistrust and very defensively, there has been an appreciable progression towards a more trusting attitude. The day of the fourth interview, the patient telephoned the therapist to tell her that because of the bad weather (it was snowing, which was very unusual in the city) she was thinking of not coming to the interview for fear of slipping, but the therapist did not cancel the session, trusting implicitly in the patient's capacity to get to the Centre by herself, which is, in fact, what happened. Here, arguably, several factors intervened in making this response by the therapist rather beneficial. In one sense, her resolve in maintaining the interview slot and, in another, her trust in the patient's abilities, and, finally, the patient having someone (the therapist) who was concerned for her. Furthermore, it was very significant that a person who was feeling so indispensable to her family, with all the phantasies of omnipotence that sustained her, should be able to express her fears of "slipping" if conditions (not only the external ones—the snow in this case—but those of her relational life) are not right. Implicitly, the patient was showing signs that the omnipotent aspect of her self did not dominate to such an extent, and that she was capable of expressing weakness; she alone could not continue to walk through life without the support of someone who is strong enough, as the therapist was at that moment by encouraging her to come to the interview; that is to say, someone who helps to keep her from "slipping". So, in spite of the doubts that were raised over her unfavourable environment, as well as over certain current relationships in which she had little trust, the data provided by the relationship formed in the interviews, however, enabled us to catch sight of certain guarantees towards the establishment of a helping relationship. The hypothesis that was supported in the supervision group was that perhaps, in early infancy, the patient enjoyed and received a good relationship, which now enables her to re-establish it in the therapeutic setting when she encounters a firm but, at the same time, receptive person.

Psychotherapy was focused on her difficulties in recognising her personal needs and meeting them, in so far as she considers herself indispensable in "saving" her mother, which implies a certain devaluation of the other family members. Treatment, of one year's duration, was carried out in weekly sessions, with a total of forty-two sessions. During the psychotherapeutic process, patient and therapist were able to work through this focus. Let us take a look at certain moments of this process and a synthesis of the end of the treatment, with the follow-up interviews subsequent to its conclusion.

In a note from the supervision of session number twenty-two, it says, "She is now beginning to see herself no longer as the saviour of the family. She feels less guilty and, as such, is able to focus more on her own life, even to enjoy more . . . although she says she feels lonely, perhaps as she becomes less responsible for other peoples' problems. She explains that she is afraid to recognise the infantile part that is inside her, because then she might become depressed like her mother." Further on, in session thirty-three, we read, "*The patient's improvement*, however, has led to her limiting her participation in those things at home that are not her responsibility, which engenders resistance in others, particularly her father, to the acceptance of this new situation. She thinks about her mother in a different way, in as much as she does not occupy her mind completely like before. She accepts that her mother has other people who love her."

In the last treatment session (number forty-two), the patient begins by explaining a situation where, "the door has been slammed in her face". The therapist relates this to the door of the treatment that is closing, not as an act of aggression against her, but as a reality that has been agreed, but which is difficult for her to accept. The patient admits that lately she had not wanted truly to come to terms with the fact that treatment was ending, because she felt well, but, at the same time, recognises that "she is not going to keep coming for the rest of her life, as if this were a drug", and she says that lately she has become anxious because she wanted to resolve all those things that were still outstanding before the end since, "coming here was like a driving force". The therapist interprets that the patient was trying to act as if she were at the beginning of treatment, in order to avoid its conclu-sion, and that to do this she would have to invalidate the entire expe-rience of help that, from what they have seen throughout the psychotherapy, she has indeed been able to experience. She recognises that this is true, and goes on to add that her parents have supported her in their own way. She is aware that she must take more care of herself and her own needs, because she, too, is a person. She admits that being so wrapped up in other people's problems was a way of not looking at her own. But now she has more of an understanding of which are her own problems. When the therapist announces the end of the session, she says, "How quickly the time has passed!" and thanks her. In this last session, first she complains that the door has been slammed in her face by the treatment being terminated. And yet, later on, she recognises that this is not true; that in fact it is difficult for her to accept the termination of treatment because it has been a good experience, and, therefore, she is able to recognise what she has learnt here, which she summarises very well. First, through her association to the implicit help of her parents, in such a way that they are no longer so devalued, in spite of the external reality of a sick mother and a father with a history of sexually abusing her sister; second, through the recognition that looking after others was a pretext for not attempting to understand her own problems.

Just as was agreed, according to the conditions of the setting for this type of psychotherapy, the patient would attend a certain number of *follow-up interviews* after the termination of treatment, amounting to two or three over the course of one to two years. After three months, the patient requests the first interview. She sets out what she has achieved as a result of treatment, and also expresses her gratitude. By allaying her guilt, *her omnipresent worry over her sick mother has decreased*, as well as that felt for her sister, which has enabled her to *widen the field of her personal interests.* She has taken several courses related to her chosen career path, which have helped her to find a job. She has resumed her relationship with her boyfriend, whom she had left towards the end of treatment, partly as a consequence, we believe, of her difficulties in working through her separation from treatment. However, she considers him to be a somewhat infantile person and thinks that it would be good for him to have treatment "like the one she did", as she does not think he will be able to mature otherwise. But she understands that she has to accept him for what he is, and not try to change him, if he really does not want to change. With these manifestations, the patient's transformation is made evident, in accepting that change in others (the boyfriend) does not have to depend on her. So, either she accepts him as he is, or he does psychotherapy like her, whereby she is once again valuing the treatment that she has received.

Five months after the previous interview, and eight months after the end of treatment, she requests a *second interview.* She seems happy to see the therapist again. Her mother is still in hospital, but her father has increasingly dealt with the interviews with the doctors, something that he did not do before. She still sees her boyfriend, although as friends. In this interview the following may be noted: (a) the patient has been able to recognise the help received in the psychotherapy, and she values it; (b) she has some difficulty in doing the work of mourning for the loss of something she values. It is for this reason that she is not often able to allow herself feelings of sorrow, and never those of anger for "having the door slammed in her face", as she commented in the last session. However, there is a partial acceptance of that reality. The fact that she has come to the follow-up interviews, and the fact that the value she places on the therapist is maintained, lead us to think that this prevails over her negative feelings engendered by the termination of therapy. Incidentally, neither are these feelings particularly dominant, as she did not need to act out these feelings in other relationships, as she had attempted to in the final stage of her treatment, by means of breaking things off with her partner. She understands that this is not, in point of fact, the best time to leave him, despite seeing the limitations of that relationship, and she needs to give it time.

So, this case demonstrates several things to us. While we have to take into account the patient's immediate environment, we cannot assess it exclusively without considering other facets of her personality. Without professional intervention on her external circumstances, the patient has been able—thanks to the psychotherapeutic experience—to modify her perception of the family dynamic and its potentialities, with the resulting personal benefit.

The psychotherapist

Indeed, it is debatable whether the factor of the "psychotherapist" can be regarded, strictly speaking, as an indicator. The rest of the indicators are orientated towards observing the patient, even when we are considering them in relational terms. Even if we start from the premise that the therapist possesses the necessary training to undertake the task in hand, there is scope within the professional's personal and psychopathological characteristics (although, to a large extent, these will have been resolved by his own therapeutic experience) for fewer or greater difficulties when it comes to "pairing" with the patient's personality and psychopathology, with a view to carrying out psychological treatment.

As a result, while the confluence of some of the indicators we have noted offers a degree of reliability in terms of a patient's suitability for psychotherapy, we could say that that same criterion is applicable to the "average" psychotherapist, in terms of training, experience and skills in psychotherapy and whether it is feasible that they will syntonise with the personality and psychopathology of a particular person. Thus, a patient might possess a somewhat unreliable level of indicators, and, consequently, he is not accepted by one particular psychotherapist, whereas he is accepted by another, who, owing to his experience or skills, or otherwise to his interest in certain psycho-pathologies, is willing to make the indication for psychotherapy or psychoanalysis.

The impression the therapist forms of the possibilities of doing therapy together with a particular patient, bearing in mind the experience he has acquired in the diagnostic interviews, is also significant, partly because it is essential to know if that particular patient will be able to do therapy with that particular therapist, and vice versa. That said, if the patient is capable of collaborating and working in a psychotherapeutic relationship, he will, generally speaking, be able to do this with any therapist. Perhaps this requirement of the "therapist" factor should be something to be aware of during the initial periods of training, when insufficient experience on the part of the therapist would necessitate a patient who is very well suited to psychotherapy. In any case, as soon as a new therapist is offered some experience, he often sets about his work with an excitement, an enthusiasm, and a dedication which, unfortunately, might be lacking in the therapist who has been in the profession for years.

Other matters regarding the indicators

Use of indicators: convergence of the three dimensions—the biographical, psychopathological, and interview data

As I have already said, I do not intend the indicators to be considered as targets to be sought in the patient. It is precisely the fact that we are able to detect them only as a result of the interplay between the data provided by the three areas of investigation in the diagnostic inter-views (the psychopathological, the biographical, and that of the rela-tionship in the interview itself) that prevents us from treating them as if they were a medical record to be filled in. They are, instead, the product of the process of reflection and elaboration that has been taking place in the therapist throughout the course of the interviews.

Moreover, neither must we demand that all indicators be fulfilled in order to assess the indication for psychotherapy, as I have pointed out in due course, although we might have to take into account the combination of several indicators, as well as the degree of intensity of each one, in order to obtain the final result. We might consider the list of indicators to be a little long still, and that there remains the risk of doing what we were trying to avoid; that is to say, that we are not sufficiently avoiding the conceptual artefacts "present" in clinical practice, thus to be more open to what we observe in the patient, his relationship with the therapist, and the thoughts he suggests to us. In this respect, it can never be repeated too often that all of the conceptual apparatus the therapist has at his disposal, the theoretical and the technical, must be put to the back of his mind, so that it "saturates" his field of observation as little as possible, while, on the other hand, still always being available to him. In any case, I believe that once the effort of obtaining as many indicators as possible has been made, it is well worth prioritising, or, better, summarising those we consider indispensable for psychotherapy to be feasible.

In a nutshell, I would say that *the person who is likely to be most suitable for psychoanalytic psychotherapy or psychoanalysis is the person who comes to the therapist because he recognises emotional suffering in himself, shows that he is, to some degree, in touch with his infantile levels, is basically sincere during the interview, and is curious to know what is happening to him.* In the next chapter, we shall examine the issue of making the decision between psychoanalytic psychotherapy and psychoanalysis.

In more descriptive terms, the degree of availability of a person for psychotherapy or psychoanalysis is determined by the degree to which we are able to detect, in that person, the *adult* who comes to the consultation with the *patient* and the *child* that exists inside him, along with a desire to know what is wrong with him in order to alleviate his suffering as far as possible. I have italicised the words *adult*, *patient*, and *child*, as these indicate the aspects existent in every person; that is to say, the *adult* self, *infantile* self, and the *patient* self.

Use of the countertransference: "countertransferential dramatisation"

The compilation of the data that we have been listening to and observing in the patient clearly does not take place in an aseptic way, but will have repercussions within the therapist. They will stimulate his interest, boredom, wish to help, rejection, erotisation, paternal or maternal feelings, and so on; in short, a wide range of emotional impressions that will make us feel close to, or distanced from, the patient. All of these reactions are stirred up throughout the course of the interview and are not always immediately recognisable, given their intensity at the time they are being experienced. And, at times, they do not become clearly manifest until the interview is over and the patient has gone. Then, certain feelings that we had previously not been able to recognise will emerge in a clearer, more distinct way. At first, they will be very general impressions of acceptance, rejection, confusion over not having understood what the patient meant, or, conversely, the impression of broadly understanding the dynamic of his functioning.

These early overall impressions occurring immediately after the termination of the first or the second interviews are useful provided they can then be measured against the data we have obtained. Hence, the countertransference might be a useful instrument in the collation and comparison of the data we have gathered in the three previously mentioned areas in drawing the resulting indicators from them. I do not need to warn here of the dangers entailed by the abuse of the countertransference, in so far as those impressions might be contaminated by the therapist's own emotional state or by a lack of ability as a result of his level of training. But as long as these impressions are checked—even to a minimal extent—against the rest of the data, I believe they are rather valuable, above all when we begin to weigh up the decision of whether or not to take the patient on for treatment.

So, in the case of the patient with whom a good relationship has been established and where there has been collaboration on his part, at times the therapist will not begin to take cognisance of this until the interview is already over, when he tries to transcribe or take note of the most essential data and realises that these data are surfacing in his mind quite freely. Conversely, in other patients, we face great difficulties in remembering what they said to us or the significant events of their lives until we realise, after having gone to lengths to reconstruct the interview, that it is anodyne in its entirety, and of very little significance in terms of understanding the functioning of the patient's mind, in spite of the fact that he had been talking at length throughout the interview.

Those early impressions will arise in the therapist in a spontaneous way, perhaps during the interview itself, although, as I said before, it is likely that they will take shape with more clarity once the interview is over. These *impressions, vague at first, and which gather up isolated aspects of the patient's problem(s)* (from the account he has given us of his life, together with the psychopathological data and that contributed in the interview), *at a certain point will gel together and form an image or scene that is often rather expressive of one or other of the individual's central conflicts.* Normally, the image in question will come from the memory of a childhood episode or a dream mentioned by the patient. This *countertransferential dramatisation of the patient's conflict,* as we might call it, has a visual, sensory character, which gives it its expressive potency, and often marks out the pattern of the patient's dynamic conflict, which is repeated in different life situations, including his relationship with the therapist. On occasion, they might be very simple images; for example, the information contributed by the patient that he was a baby who fell asleep when it was time to feed, which was why his mother had to keep waking him up and stimulating him. Perhaps the patient has commented on this in passing—even as a humorous anecdote he has been told at home while reminiscing about his early childhood—in such a way that, although we pick it up, we do not quite realise the importance of this piece of information at that precise moment. But, once the interview has been concluded, the visual image, of a mother struggling to stimulate her child to feed, comes to us. And then we realise that, in the interview itself, we often had to ask the patient questions, perhaps more than we would have wanted, owing to his apathy, and, likewise, we remember other situations in his life where others had to motivate him, to stimulate him, and so on.

Owing to their great expressive force and their power to dramatise internal conflicts, *dreams* provide valuable data, by giving form to the dramatisation of which I am speaking. We must consider, moreover, that the dreams related in the early interviews hold particular value in so far as they condense significant aspects of the patient's mental functioning. So, an oniric image might be relevant, especially if we easily imagine it in a visual way, which means that the version the patient has given us possesses those sensory characteristics of pervading and penetrating into the other that prove so communicative.

Certain authors have described phenomena similar to the counter-transferential dramatisation I am describing. For example, Balint and

Balint (1961) use the term *flash* to describe the instantaneous intuition that a doctor has of a patient's fundamental problem, whom he has known in a long-term context, although they assume that this "flash" is experienced by both doctor and patient. Malan (1963) describes the phenomenon he calls *crystallisation of a focus* as something that emerges gradually between patient and therapist. But in both cases— and I stress—these refer to something that is experienced jointly by patient and therapist, while the countertransferential dramatisation to which I am referring clearly concerns only the therapist and is comparable to a precursor to the elaboration of the feasibility of the patient's being taken on for psychotherapy. On the other hand, in terms of the type of psychological process underlying it, the countertransferential dramatisation is probably closer to the concept of Malan's *crystallisation*, as it implies an element of elaboration, than to that of Balint and Balint's *flash*, which could carry a connotation of magical intuition and, therefore, runs the risk of becoming a reaction with omnipotent elements. I shall now cite several vignettes that illustrate what I mean by "countertransferential dramatisation".

The first is the case of a patient who remembers that, as a child, she had always imagined that her mother must have some kind of "metal pots" for breasts. The possible impact of these—clearly devaluing— phantasies can be inferred from the fact that the patient is seeking help for the psychical consequences, including depression and anxiety, resulting from having one of her breasts removed because of cancer. Another case is that of the patient whose family told her that from an early age she had problems feeding because "pus pockets" formed on her gums. We do not know if, in fact, the information was conveyed to her in these terms, but the patient does not question it in the interview and takes the description made in this way to be correct. We could cite as a third case the patient who recounts the childhood memory of when his father tried to teach him to ride a bike, so began to help him by holding the handlebars and then proceeding to hold him steady by the rear mudguard. One day when he was going along fine, confidently and with assurance, it occurred to him to look behind him, whence he was devastated to find that his father had long ceased to be holding the bike: he promptly fell off on to the ground, furious.

Although these brief accounts have been taken out of the context of the interviews in which they took place, I mention them because their dramatic and evocative power are sufficiently eloquent to give the idea of expressiveness I mentioned before, thus having a considerable impact on the interlocutor, which might fix in his mind the field of observation. The image of the pots stirred up in the therapist's mind by the patient who had recently been operated on for breast cancer indicates to us straight away that the violence of her devaluation of the maternal breast is linked to the violence of the cancer. We are not seeking to introduce an argument about the genesis of the cancer, but to establish the hypothesis that, in the patient's internal world, one and the other have become connected. Furthermore, we should be able to extrapolate that factor to the patient's interaction with the therapist in the interview; thus, we might find some confirmation of this in her difficulties, for example, in valuing and accepting the interventions of the "therapist–breast", as did, in fact, occur. The scene of the girl who remembers the child with a mouth full of "pus pockets" is also illustrative of oral problems that we would expect to find in the account she gives of her life and, likewise, to a certain extent, in the relationship formed during the interview. And let us look finally at the recollection of the third patient, where the image of the child whose confidence in his bike-riding skills "fall flat" upon discovering that he was making use of his very own resources, without his father's support. In this last case, his dependency in relation to figures of authority is a piece of information that seems relevant, and which will have to be confirmed against other data from the patient's life and those drawn from his relationship with the therapist.

Note

1.   The material belongs to the same supervision group as before. Therefore, sometimes I shall make recourse to the remarks noted at the time.

CHAPTER EIGHT

Specificity of psychoanalysis and psychoanalytic psychotherapy

Definition of the problem

Before studying the subject of the decision as to the best kind of treatment for the patient, which we shall see in the next chapter, I think that the consideration of a previous issue—upon which this decision is based—is inevitable. Whatever options are chosen will depend on the therapist's idea of the specificity characterising each one of them, particularly concerning the choice between psychoanalysis and psychoanalytic psychotherapy. As no unanimous agreement exists in this respect, I think it is necessary to include this chapter, in which I shall go over the state of the issue and define my position.

The need to mark the boundary between psychoanalysis and psychotherapy was noted by Freud in 1914, in order to differentiate it from the other psychological techniques of the time, such as suggestion and hypnosis. That which defines psychoanalytic method, he says, are those techniques that attempt to understand *transference* and *resistance*, and he adds,

> Any line of investigation which recognises these two facts and takes them as the starting-point of its work has a right to call itself psycho-

analysis, even though it arrives at results other than my own. (Freud, 1914d, p. 16)

But a few years later, concerned by the insufficient expansion of psychoanalysis to reach the most socially needy, he proposed what was to be the first definition of psychoanalytic psychotherapy:

> It is very probable, too, that the large-scale application of our therapy will compel us to alloy the pure gold of analysis freely with the copper of direct suggestion . . . But, whatever form this psychotherapy for the people may take, whatever the elements out of which it is compounded, its most effective and most important ingredients will assuredly remain those borrowed from *strict and untendentious* psychoanalysis. (Freud, 1919a, p. 168, my italics)

On the one hand, Freud defines the specificity of psychoanalysis, and, on the other, he gives birth to the concept of psychoanalytic psychotherapy. Both quotations reflect two fundamental concepts that are to be found as bases of arguments that are still discussed to this day.

One of these concerns is the need for psychoanalysis to be firm in establishing its specificity. And the second is for psychoanalysis to reach the largest number of people possible through the psychotherapy derived from it, with corresponding firmness. Debate is sparked, however, when we seek to define whether it is possible to continue to maintain the differentiation between psychoanalysis and psychoanalytic psychotherapy.

In order to differentiate today between psychoanalysis and the psychotherapies, we should consider to what extent these Freudian definitions are still valid. Since they were established almost ninety years ago, developments have taken place both in psychoanalytic theory and technique, and in the psychotherapies derived from them, which render it necessary to redefine the relationship between them. At first, psychoanalysis was a therapeutic procedure exclusively for adult neurotic patients. Application of the original method was later on extended to children and to serious cases: narcissistic personalities, seriously disturbed, and even psychotic patients (Bion, 1967; Rosenfeld, 1964, 1978; Segal, 1957, to quote a few examples). Although fifty years have passed since the latter contributions, none the less it must be stated that psychoanalysis is not likely to be chosen as the treatment for these more serious pathologies nowadays. Even so, it is still a tool that is available for certain cases fulfilling particular conditions, as we shall see later on. But, above all, it has been the greater depth of psychoanalytic understanding of the mind in general, with the introduction of observation and a certain understanding of its primitive and psychotic levels as a base of the psyche in every individual, which has opened up psychoanalysis for these serious patients. Consequently, the concept of transference has undergone a considerable modification in comparison with the concept implicit in Freud's quotation. Now we no longer understand it as an exclusively neurotic kind of link, but as a more complex relationship, being also made up of those psychotic and primitive elements, even when dealing with a neurotic organisation of the personality. In this way, the "analysis of transference", to which Freud refers as a basic principle, nowadays has a different meaning to the one implicit in the above Freudian quotation. Another aspect recognised today in psychoanalytic practice is the use, on a smaller or larger scale, of other psychotherapeutic techniques besides those that are specifically psychoanalytic, in what has been called the "infiltration of psychotherapeutic techniques" (Wallerstein, 1989). However, we should have to clarify if such an "infiltration" responds to the acceptance of an inevitable fact: that it is not possible to work exclusively with transference interpretation, or if this is due to not firmly maintaining the psychoanalytic method.

Furthermore, current psychoanalytic psychotherapies have evolved in two ways. First, as they make less use of "direct" suggestion and introduce other technical elements, such as clarification, confrontation, and non-transference interpretation (Bibring, 1954). Second, and above all, due to the progressive use of elements taken from psychoanalytic technique, such as transference interpretation, in accordance with the Freudian indications in the previous quotation (Freud, 1919a), and the taking into account of the "here and now" in the therapeutic relationship, following later psychoanalytic development in the sense of "total transference" (Joseph, 1989).

Thus, in the history of the relationship between psychoanalysis and psychoanalytic psychotherapy, the distance between the respective techniques has lessened, as Wallerstein describes (1989). In this author's historic account, he studies almost exclusively the North American tradition, except for the first phase, and, consequently, the line of this development is determined by a conception of the classic "analytic cure", which entails considering only the neurotic patient.

Wallerstein contemplates a *first prehistoric phase*, which takes as its subject the life of Freud, in which the author, together with Jones and Glover, establishes the differences between psychoanalysis (characterised by the already-mentioned analysis of transference and resistance) and other psychotherapies which use suggestion. There follows a *second phase*, which Wallerstein defines as "psychoanalytic consensus", covering the period from the 1950s to the end of the 1970s. In this phase, two groups emerge: one a minority, represented in particular by Alexander, French, and Fromm-Reichmann, who defended the dissolution of the boundaries between psychoanalysis and psychotherapy; and the other—a majority at the time—which, although accepting a psychoanalytic theory common to several therapeutic procedures, advocated differences in technique and aims between psychoanalysis and other psychoanalytic psychotherapies. The representatives of this tradition were Gill, Rangel, and Stone. Twenty-five years later, these three authors met up again to re-examine the state of their theses. The latter two adhered to the initial position, although with slight modifications, while Gill had evolved radically towards the assimilation of psychoanalytic psychotherapies into psychoanalysis. The criteria upheld by Gill to defend this evolution were rooted in his new emphasis on the analysis of transference as a specific characteristic of the psychoanalytic method. But, according to him, this would be a technique that would be feasible regardless of setting conditions. He justified this position owing to the limited possibility of fitting with the classical conditions of the so-called "extrinsic criteria" necessary for the practice of psychoanalysis (i.e., high frequency sessions, the couch, unlimited length, etc.) This third phase, which continued until the period in which Wallerstein's work was published in 1989, is called *fragmented consensus*.

Other recent texts refer back to this debate, discussed by several panels, such as one that considers the question, "What does a psychoanalyst do when he/she says or thinks he/she is doing *psychotherapy*?" (Adams-Silvan, 2002, my italics)—an issue discussed within the context/framework of the International Psychoanalytical Association; similarly, the panel that outlines the conceptual differences between psychoanalysis and psychoanalytic psychotherapies (Wallerstein & Hoch, 1992), the therapeutic technique corresponding to each one (Tyson & Morris, 1992), and the indications and contraindications for each (Bachrach & McNutt, 1992). These last three issues were discussed in the American Psychoanalytic Association. In Europe, the volume edited by the European Psychoanalytic Federation (Frisch, editor, 2001) is a collection of very different geographical and theoretical positions.

Most authors agree that there is a range of psychoanalytically based therapeutic procedures. At one end we might find psychoanalysis itself, and at the other, supportive psychotherapy (Kernberg, 1999). Or, according to my classification, psychoanalysis at one end and, at the other, the psychotherapeutic interview, with brief psychotherapy and psychoanalytic psychotherapy somewhere in between (see Tables 8.1, 8.2). There is, however, an intermediate zone, in which it is difficult to establish the differences, and this is the case with intensive psychoanalytic psychotherapies, based on a three-session-per-week, face-to-face relationship, with frequent use of transference interpretation (probably the most eloquent example is given by Ruszczynsky and Johnson, 1999). Nevertheless, it seems to me that it is possible to make efforts to stipulate certain criteria in order to define when a procedure is closer to one end of the scale or the other. This is what I attempt to do in this chapter, my aim being to lessen the confusion, if possible. I will briefly recapitulate the common ground for both therapeutic practices—psychoanalytic theory—which does not offer any particular difficulty as there is general agreement on this subject. Later, I will go through some of the technical elements which are also common to both, but where discrepancies between authors begin to emerge, and I will finish with what I consider to be the specific core of psychoanalysis and of psychoanalytic psychotherapy, respectively, thus entering into a clearly controversial area.

Theory and technique common to psychoanalysis and to psychoanalytic psychotherapies

As I said in Chapter One, I support a conception of the organisation of the mind based on the theories of Freud, Klein, and Bion. To summarise, mental life is determined by unconscious conflicts between destructive tendencies and life tendencies, which are externalised in object relationships, through projective processes, and later introjected. The history of this interplay between projection and introjection settles a nucleus, or core—the self—and its internal referents (objects). Together, they make up what Klein called the "internal world" of the individual, or Freud's psychic reality. The inherent vicissitudes of this history give rise to basic anxieties, which, in turn, generate defences: from the most primitive and pathological to the most evolved, resulting in particular states and organisations of the mind. Such processes are sustained in unconscious fantasies, an important concept for understanding and approaching psychic reality. From this point of view, what we are—our identity—is constituted by different aspects of our internal world separated, to a greater or lesser extent, from each other according to the degree of psychopathology: those aspects that we recognise as our own, and those that we reject and attribute to other people (through projections into external objects); not forgetting those aspects which we believe belong to us when, in fact, they are characteristics of others, and which we have appropriated, through omnipotent introjection.

Another assumption of psychoanalytic theory is that the knowledge of our own mind (or aspects of it), along with strategies to acquire that knowledge and the possibility of introducing changes to its dynamic, provide some relief. One of the sources of this relief is being able to avoid the repetition of destructive patterns, in the widest sense. Paradoxically, however, the task of knowing our own psychic reality is a painful experience for two reasons: in itself, because it means having to accept those aspects which were projected into others, a process which involves reintrojection, or reintegration, and having to give up what does not belong to us. It is also painful because of the narcissistic wound, which involves having to recognise the need for the object. So, in order to create a psychoanalytic therapeutic modality we need to establish methodological conditions in order to facilitate access to the knowledge of the psychic reality, but, at the same time, we need to make bearable the inevitable pain resulting from the experience itself. Now I will give an approximate description of what I consider to be the primary conditions.

A psychoanalytic method of observation

This is based on the listening attitude established by Freud under the concept of "evenly-suspended attention" (Freud, 1912e, p. 111), deepened by Bion through his conceptualisation of the term *reverie* (Bion, 1962, p. 36, 1967, p. 116), which allows a psychoanalytic understand-
·ing of the experience observed. Connected to this, the therapist needs to adopt a neutral attitude, so as not to interfere with the emergence

of the patient's spontaneity: his free associations and projections. Although this observation focuses upon verbal and non-verbal behaviour, particular attention is paid to the unconscious manifestations. This is possible because implicit to this kind of observation is the therapist's emotional participation, owing to the fact that he is the receptor of the patient's projections. One of the advances in psychoanalysis in recent decades has been the development of the concept of countertransference as a useful element for knowing those projections, although, as I have already said in other parts of this book, we should avoid confusing any emotional reaction on the part of the therapist with a countertransferential response. The deepening of the concept of countertransference is due in large part to the concept of projective identification, introduced by Klein (1946) and developed by post-Kleinian analysts, such as Bion.

Settling the setting

This means establishing external conditions that facilitate the task of observation of the psychic reality. The setting is an important element for two reasons: first, to reduce to a minimum the variables interfering with this observation, and second, as a medium that helps the therapist to tolerate and to "modulate" (Meltzer, 1967) anxieties arising from this task. In other words, the setting contributes towards the creation of a framework of containment able to bear the experience shared by patient and therapist.

Understanding and working through the vicissitudes of the link between therapist and patient

This is based on the patient's previous experiences of separation and links, with the concomitant anxieties. To these, I would also add integration anxiety, arising from the mental state achieved each time new knowledge is incorporated, because this demands an adjustment to the old equilibrium in the mental organisation. In each of these experiences we find, to a greater or lesser extent, the basic anxieties as already described: depressive, paranoid and catastrophic.

The importance of the "here and now" in the therapeutic situation

As I have been saying in several parts of this book, I think that the "here and now" "vertex"[1] constitutes one of the seminal advances in psychoanalysis over the past few years. We are far from the Freudian idea of searching for the infantile trauma as the source of the patient's psychopathology by filling in the amnesic lagoons of childhood. We know today that the patient's versions of his history, relationships, and conflicts are inevitably determined and, in some way, distorted by the permanent interplay between projection and introjection; between external reality and internal reality, as it is subjectively experienced. One prominent way to approach knowledge of the patient's psychic reality is by observing how it is manifesting now, in the relationship with the therapist. It is in this present relationship, here and now, when faced with the therapist, that we can observe how the internal relationships unfold.

An interpretative work

This sets off, in the patient's internal world, the integration of split and projected aspects of his self and internal objects. The extension and depth of this task constitute, in my opinion, one of the capital elements in the discussion of differentiation between psychoanalysis and psychoanalytic psychotherapies, depending on whether we include the interpretation of the transference as a primary technical principle, as well as the level and extension of the splitting transferences that are analysed.

This psychoanalytic comprehension of mental life has led, to a large extent, to an extension in its application to a great variety of areas other than the psychoanalytic session, although with the corresponding technical modifications, both in individual psychotherapies and in group and family therapies (see Ávila & Poch, 1994, for a conceptualisation of psychoanalytic psychotherapies; Coderch, 1987; Pérez-Sánchez, 1996a, for the psychotherapeutic practices in national mental healthcare; Tizón, 1992, for its application to primary healthcare).

Elements for differentiation between the psychoanalytic method and the psychotherapeutic method

By "method", I understand a set of technical elements that make up a certain therapeutic procedure, and by "process", the development that is set in motion by the above-mentioned method. I will deal now with the former.

As the purity of the psychoanalytic method has been demythologised, "pure gold does not exist" (Hinshelwood, 2001), and as I said before, the distance between the two has diminished, this has given rise to the debate as to whether it is valid to perpetuate the limits that separate the method used in psychoanalysis from the one applied to the psychoanalytic psychotherapies. The matter under discussion, regardless of the formal conditions—that is to say, of the type of setting—is whether it is possible to maintain the compulsory Freudian indications for psychoanalysing, that is to say, of analysing the transference and the resistance. Or whether, on the contrary, this is not the case, and it would be necessary. to include, as part of the psychoanalytic method, a specific setting to distinguish it from the psychotherapeutic method, which has its own corresponding setting.

It is generally accepted that the use of the couch and the frequency of the sessions are not, in themselves, elements that lend specificity to psychoanalysis. But such an obvious matter has led some authors to diminish its importance. Experience certainly shows that the mere fact of lying a patient down on the couch for four or five sessions a week does not constitute a condition enough to develop a psychoanalytic process, since it can be used defensively against the development of an authentic contact with psychic reality. The fact of lying down can turn into simple routine, and this is something that does, in fact, happen, inevitably, at some moments of the psychoanalytic treatment. The patient gets accustomed to a defensive use of the couch as a place of rest for the body, transforming a condition conducive to facilitating "looking inside oneself" into its antonym: corporal wellbeing is the only relief that is achieved; in this way avoiding any psychic restlessness and the need to understand it. The number of sessions can also be used defensively, in the sense that the intensity of the contact with the analyst can promote a passive dependence when the relationship turns into a situation where the analyst is "used" as a container in which to evacuate the anxieties of the day, or as a kind of auxiliary self, from whom the patient expects orientation or advice, which has very little to do with the development of an authentic psychoanalytic process.

Nevertheless, the defensive use of the "extrinsic conditions" does not justify, in my opinion, that both elements of the technique (the

couch and the high frequency of sessions) should be deemed irrele-
vant in defining the psychoanalytic method. On the contrary, I believe
that they are necessary to fulfil the fundamental function of facilitating a primordial field of observation: the internal world of the patient,
through the transferential experience. The use of the couch, having
deprived the patient of visual perception of the analyst, is a condition
that facilitates direction of the *look* inside his mind, to then communicate what is observed through free association. In psychoanalytic
psychotherapy, the use of free association is limited by the face-to-face
presence of the therapist. Similarly, the latter is restricted by having to
control his corporal reactions when facing the patient, not feeling able
to look inside himself in the same way as when the patient is on the
couch in order to gather what the impact of the interlocutor's projections has produced inside him.

Therefore, in my opinion, the use of the couch and a high frequency
of sessions, despite being insufficient conditions to define the psychoanalytic method, are necessary, provided they are accompanied by
other specific elements, particularly the "systematic" interpretation of
the transference. However, rather than "systematic", we should say
prioritised interpretation, since other interpretations, and even non-
interpretative interventions, are also necessary, as I have already said.

In order to clarify the differences between psychoanalysis and
psychoanalytic psychotherapies, and even within these groupings,
according to my classification, between psychoanalytic psychotherapy
(PP), brief psychoanalytic psychotherapy (BPP), and supportive
psychotherapy (SP), I will use four arguments that are based, respectively, on four other aspects of the conception of the mind from the
psychoanalytic perspective. These are, in my opinion, the characteristics of psychic life: *the existence of the unconscious component, its resistance to change; the pain concomitant to any attempt at change*, and—as a
result of the latter—*the need for working-through.*

The first argument rests on the most representative premise of the
psychoanalytic conception of the mind: its unconscious character, or,
rather, its relative determinism for the unconscious. If we consider
that the unconscious motivations of the individual determine his
behaviour, it is obvious that we need to establish contact with the
patient's unconscious in order to know these motivations. This is the
first difficult task we face: communication with the patient's unconscious, for which not only is it necessary for the analyst's perceptive

apparatus to be available, but also for his own unconscious to be receptive. This is related to what we have already said about "floating attention", or *reverie*. The second task consists of transforming the experience we have had with the patient into words accessible to him. In other words, interpretation, or, more precisely, the *interpretative work*. As for the first, the unconscious communication, there are two factors that should be borne in mind: the personal factor and the method. As for the therapist's personal factor, experience shows that it is necessary to have personally experienced psychoanalytic treatment, not only to mitigate one's own psychopathology so that it does not interfere in the relationship with the patient (a previous fundamental point), but also to familiarise oneself with unconscious content in general, and with access to one's own unconscious. In other words, with the "integration" of one's own unconscious with one's mental life, in the sense of "making it available".

But it is also necessary to have the ability to put oneself in touch with the other's unconscious, and this could be said to be the capacity for empathy and tolerance towards the patient's projections. Although this argument is common to all therapeutic psychoanalytic procedures, the difference resides in the intensity of the manifestation and the analysis of certain unconscious content, especially the primitive and psychotic aspects, which might vary depending on the method used. Their degree on the therapeutic scale would rise the closer we come to psychoanalysis in its strictest sense, and would be of lower intensity the further we move away from it.

Another indispensable factor for access to communication with the patient on unconscious levels is the *method*. The use of the couch and a high frequency of sessions will facilitate the contact between the patient's unconscious and that of the analyst. As for the frequency, in psychoanalysis I would consider valid the criterion by which the number of sessions should be superior to half the days in the week, that is to say, four or five (de Saussure, 1988). In this way, the presence of analysis in the patient's life will be sufficient for the routine separations and other events in his daily life not to excessively interrupt the contact with his unconscious aspects and with the process under development. In psychoanalytic psychotherapy, holding sessions at a rate of twice per week allows for an experience of a different intensity from that of psychoanalysis, and, in turn, different from that of a one-session-per-week psychotherapy. Another aspect of the method also mentioned, the interpretative work, will be studied later on.

The second argument relating to the nature of the mind from the psychoanalytic perspective would be that of *resistance to psychic change*. The mind is organised in such a way that the *self* of the individual consolidates forms of incorporation (introjection) and of projection of object relationships throughout his entire life, which provides a certain mental balance, and which is also why any modification to this gives rise to serious resistance. Any proposal for change does not guarantee a better balance—however pathological the current one might be and however much suffering it might cause—because there is always the risk that, while this new "order" is taking shape, psychic catastrophe (catastrophic anxieties) could break out. Thus, the proposal for change implicit to any psychoanalytic treatment must take place in conditions that are sufficiently strong and stable for the patient to consider the possibility of change to be feasible, with a minimum guarantee that they should be able to bear these catastrophic anxieties. As I said before, such changes include the reintrojection of split, separated, and projected aspects—"as if they were not ours"—as well as the giving up of those other aspects that we consider as belonging to us and that, in fact, do not. In psychoanalysis proper, the prospects for change would be *wide*; that is to say, it aspires to explore *all the transferences* and *different levels of the mind* of the patient that could emerge in the analytical process. (Here, I intentionally avoid the expression "structural change", which is open to debate.) In psychoanalytic psychotherapy, I would speak of a *zonal* change, meaning that it is subordinated to the treatment of those zones of the mind and the patient's personal life which he brings to the sessions, depending on the conditions of the setting, and which are presumably more restricted than in psychoanalysis. In brief psychotherapy, the change would be *focal*, since there is a delimited area of the patient's mental life and personal relationships to treat and to try to change. To sum up, the methods need to be adapted so they are consistent with the prospects for psychic change.

The wider the field of exploration and treatment, the greater the effort demanded of the therapeutic couple. For the therapist, this means a *laborious task of containment and interpretation*, and for the patient, the persistent task of *working through*, which will require frequent and prolonged contact between them, if we consider the above-mentioned difficulties for psychic change. In this respect, I would agree with the statement that one of the things that distinguishes psychoanalysis from psychoanalytic psychotherapy is the intensity of the experience between patient and analyst, plus the capacity for understanding the transference: first by the analyst, and, later on, after interpretation, by the patient—something that would be more limited in psychotherapy (Willick, in Tyson & Morris, 1992, and Gillman in Bachrach & McNutt, 1992). In a similar way, the intensity of psychoanalytic psychotherapy (PP) will be greater than in brief psychoanalytic psychotherapy (BPP), and in the latter, in turn, greater than in supportive psychotherapy (SP).

The third argument, linked to the one above, is the *psychic pain* concomitant to any attempt to attain knowledge of oneself and, consequently, any attempt at change. As I have already indicated, both in psychoanalysis and in psychoanalytic psychotherapies, there are some more or less common basic conditions in place to contain the pain of the therapeutic experience. But it will depend on the scope of the aim of the treatment ("wide", "zonal", or "focal") as to whether the resultant pain will be greater or lesser. As a consequence, the conditions of the setting to tolerate, understand, and work through it will be different in each therapeutic procedure.

Another way of distinguishing between the different types of psychoanalytic therapy depends on the *field* to be observed, or rather the *vertex* from which we observe it. I would distinguish between two vertices: one referring to the scope of the field to be observed exclusively in the mind of the patient, which I call the *intrapsychic vertex* (IV), and the other referring to the scope of the field to be observed in the relationship between patient and therapist, which I call the *transferential vertex* (TV). I would also specify a third position, which avoids these first two and would be presided over by the primitive defences of denial of one's own psychic reality, in which case the focus would be directed particularly on the external world, or on the past as something foreign to the person. This is a vertex in which not only the patient can take part, but also, by collusion, the therapist, if he is not cautious. Generically speaking, we might call this a *defensive vertex* (DV).

From the *intrapsychic vertex* of observation, the area of attention centres on the patient's internal world. The patient's verbal communications and accounts of his current and past experiences allow us to make conjectures and interpretations on the way he functions in his mind and in his relationships. Both participants—patient and therapist—direct their attention, as a priority, to this field of observation.

From the *transferential vertex* of observation, attention is directed at the immediate experience of what is happening in the relationship between patient and analyst. Paradoxically, when the area of attention is concentrated on the "here and now" between the two, we delve deeper into the mind of the patient (so, in short, we broaden the field of observation). This might be the key to the "psychoanalytic perspective", since the patient, *through* the relationship that he establishes with the therapist, transmits or communicates aspects of his mental life of which he is not even aware. The fact that this interaction between patient and analyst is an object of examination—or, to be more precise, of analysis—makes the experience all the more painful. (It is easier to speak about problems suffered with others than about those arising with the very person one is talking to.) Besides, we try to analyse this interaction from a psychoanalytic perspective, which is to say, it is coloured, to a greater or lesser degree, by the relationships that the patient has with his internal objects—relationships that are a product of his personal history. In other words, it is an interaction that is particularly determined by the transference. Taking this into account, the dilemma as to whether we should focus our attention on the patient's intrapsychic life, or on the interaction established between patient and therapist, seems, to me, to be avoidable. From the transferential vertex, they are both included.

However, both vertices are present in all psychoanalytic treatments (psychoanalysis and psychotherapies), in the sense that the therapist directs his attention to both intrapsychic and transferential fields. But, there again, it is the setting in which the therapist places himself which will favour one vertex or the other, or the scope of what is to be observed. It is also this setting that might or might not allow the patient himself to manage to adopt the "transferential vertex", as a complementary route to extending the intrapsychic vertex.

We were saying previously that, once the experience of the patient's psychic reality and/or the transferential relationship has been observed and understood, the second task takes place: the *interpretative work*. This is an important element in the distinction between the different types of psychoanalytic therapy and psychoanalysis proper. The possibilities of the interpretative work are determined, once again, by the scope of the field of exploration, whether it is "wide", "zonal", or "focal", according to the terminology we have been using. In psychoanalysis, for all the reasons stated above, the interpretation or analysis must be as a priority transferential, whenever possible, even including the most primitive and psychotic transferences. Nevertheless, psychoanalysis also needs other "psychotherapeutic" techniques such as "extra-transference interpretations"[2] or other interpretations, together with non-interpretative interventions such as clarification, confrontation, support, and even suggestions—although implicit in a positive transference (Bibring, 1954; Coderch, 2000; Kernberg, 1999). In PP, the interpretation of the transference will be limited to transferences close to the conflict zones, that is to say, the conflicts most frequently mentioned and treated in the sessions; in BPP, although transference might be admitted on many occasions, it will be limited to moments at which the treatment reaches an impasse and to the final phase of the therapy.

The fourth argument is the *working-through task* that falls to the patient, which, in turn, corresponds to the analyst's interpretative task. This concept of working through has been defined as the work necessary for the patient to carry out in order to overcome resistance and to assimilate the interpretation or insight offered to him, for which he needs time (Coderch, 1995, p. 474). The analyst's interpretation contributes to the creation of insight in the patient, that is to say, the analyst offers some elements that allow the patient an understanding of aspects of the functioning of his mind, and this constitutes the first intellectual process. But this step is not sufficient to produce internal modifications. Meltzer, in *The Psycho-analytic Process* (1967), points out that, apart from this intellectual insight, there is also a need for the insight that comes as a result of a double process. First, the internal objects will supply themselves, so to speak, with the elements contributed by the interpretation, in such a way as to allow modification in infantile structures and diminution of infantile omnipotence. In addition, the working-through task involves the introjective identification of the adult part of the personality with the already modified internal object, which will allow the exercising of control over the infantile structures (Meltzer, 1967, p. 157).

Freud speaks for the first time of this in "Remembering, repetition and working-through" in these terms:

> One must allow the patient time to become more conversant with the resistance with which he has now become acquainted, to *work through* it, to overcome it, by continuing, in defiance of it, the analytic work according to the fundamental rule of analysis. (Freud, 1914g, p. 155)

These words well describe the "painful" experience that results from any attempt at change for the patient, and the "patience" with which the analyst must be armed in order to accompany him in this task. But, in addition, they show that the above-mentioned task is a key distinguishing element. Although Freud was establishing the *difference* with reference to suggestion therapies, it seems to me that we can apply this to the present situation and establish the differences with regard to psychoanalytic psychotherapies. And this remains the case in spite of the fact that, nowadays, PP is a far cry from the rudimentary procedures of psychotherapy through suggestion.

But the current developments of psychoanalysis in access to, and understanding of, the psychotic and primitive levels of the personality are evidence of an extremely difficult, painful task of working through, which requires much patience. In this respect, Klein declared herself a supporter of Freud's ideas:

> I have always been convinced of the importance of Freud's finding *that "working-through" is one of the main tasks of the analytical procedure*, and my experience in dealing with splitting processes and in tracing them back to their origin has made this conviction even stronger. The deeper and more complex the difficulties that we are analysing, the greater the *resistance* we are likely to encounter. (Klein, 1957, pp. 231–232, my italics)

Bearing in mind everything I have set out, in my opinion, only certain specific conditions of setting and method render the above-mentioned task feasible.

A synthesis of the distinctive technical characteristics between psychoanalysis and psychoanalytic psychotherapies is reflected in the tables below. Nevertheless, they should be taken as a mere approximation, and with certain reservations, since their very schematic nature brings about a certain measure of reduction and distortion of the psychic reality, as always occurs with any attempt at synopsis of matters relating to it. In Table 8.1, I propose a specification of the characteristics of the psychoanalytic method, compared to several types of

Table 8.1. Differentiation between psychoanalysis and individual psychoanalytically-based psychotherapies: method and setting.

	Psychoanalysis	Psychoanalytic psychotherapy (PP)	Brief PP (BPP)	Supportive psychotherapy (SP)	Psychotherapeutic interviews (PI)
Therapist's attitude	Technical neutrality and evenly-suspended attention	Neutrality (limited by face-to-face)	Relative neutrality	Active, and based on listening	Active, and based on listening
Patient's attitude	Free association	Free association (limited)	Relative free association for purposes of focalisation	Centred on immediate problems	Centred on problems specified by consultation
Therapist's interventions (in order of priority and frequency)	Interpretative (T, pT, & psT), IC. Other interpretations and interventions	Interpretative EC, IC, T, other interventions	Clarification, confrontation, interpretation, EC, IC, T, other interventions	Non-interpretative interventions, interpretations, EC	Non-interpretative interventions, interpretations, EC
Working through	EW, "wide", repeated insights, IW	EW, "zonal", insights less frequent.	EW "focal", sporadic insights, IW	IW	IW
Position p/t	Couch	Face-to-face, couch, rarely	Face-to-face	Face-to-face	Face-to-face

Notes: IC: internal conflict; EC: external C.; T: transference; pT: primitive T; psT: psychotic T; EW: emotional working through; IW: intellectual W individual psychotherapy, on the basis of my experience.[3] In Table 8.2, I take the factor of time as a parameter to establish the differences. Although time as a delimiter forms part of the setting, for the sake of explanatory clarity I have also devoted a separate space to it, in another table (Table 8.3). The items corresponding to each cell are arranged in order, according to the priority that I grant them, on the strength of their importance and respective feasibility for each of the therapeutic procedures. For example, with reference to the therapist's interventions, in the "Psychoanalysis" column, I mention them in the following order: transferential interpretation (T) (i.e., of the transference experienced with the analyst); still within transferential interpretations, I distinguish between primitive transference (pT) and psychotic transference (psT)[4] (as, although on many occasions they might approximate one other, I believe that conceptually and technically we must make a distinction); interpretation of internal conflicts (IC); other interpretations of external conflicts (EC), owing to personal relationships (and extra-therapeutic transferences), and so on. Continuing with the interventions of the therapist, in the "Psychoanalytic psychotherapy" column the order of priority of the interpretations should be, in my opinion, first, the interpretation of external conflicts (those concerning personal relationships) and second, internal conflicts and later interpretations of the transference in the therapeutic relationship itself.

As for working through, I have followed the same distinctions as those I made for the aims: "wide", "zonal", and "focal". I believe that in psychoanalysis proper, a "wide" working through takes place, which includes repeated insights (and here I understand this as encompassing both cognitive and emotional elements of the interpretative experience). That is to say, intellectual insights alone do not suffice. The "wide" working through is described further back in Meltzer's terms: it implies an introjection of the experience which modifies the internal objects, with the consequent repercussions to the infantile aspects of the personality in order to diminish their omnipotence, and an introjective identification on the part of the adult self with such internal modified objects (or with aspects or characteristics of them). For the sake of simplicity, I refer in the table to "emotional" working-through (EW), meaning by this authentic (or true) working-through. Intellectual working-through (IW), in contrast, may be more limited since there is an absence of the process of modification of aspects of the internal world as a result of not sufficiently having undergone the experience.

Obviously, we are not attempting in this chapter to give a detailed description of the technique required in psychoanalysis or the various psychoanalytic psychotherapies. Nevertheless, some mention should be made of the most important questions, in order to offer a basis for the distinctions that we are proposing between them. With regard to the question of time, in Table 8.2, I have devoted four columns, respectively, to the duration of the whole therapeutic process, the length of each session, the frequency of the sessions and, finally, to whether or not a time plan is used in each specific treatment.

If in a particular patient we find sufficient fundamental indicators as to whether he should receive psychoanalysis or psychotherapy, at the time of making the choice of treatment it will be necessary to consider the time factor. If the aim of psychoanalysis, as we have commented, is to promote a "wide" psychic change, it is likely that this will involve more time than is needed in the case of a course of psycho-

Table 8.2. Time as a factor in psychoanalysis and in psychoanalytic psychotherapies.

	Duration	Session time	Frequency of sessions	Time planning
Psychoanalysis	Several years (more than in PP)	45–50 min	4–5 per week	Not established
Psychoanalytic psychotherapy	Several years	45 min	1–2 (up to 3) per week	Not established
Brief psychoanalytic psychotherapy	12 months (approx.) (sometimes 6 months or even 3 months)	45 min	1 per week	Established at the beginning
Supportive psychotherapy	Several months or longer	30–45 min	1 per fortnight (or more frequent in urgent situations)	Not established or established
Psychotherapeutic interviews or interventions	4–6 weeks More than 4–6 weeks	30–45 min	1 per week Every 3–4 weeks	Established Not established

analytic psychotherapy, where the change is "zonal"—although a "sufficient" period of time is also necessary for the latter. "Sufficient" as we well know, is an adjective that must become personal for each patient, but, as experience shows, this generally means several years. In other types of psychotherapy, such as *brief psychotherapy* (BPP), one of its characteristics is precisely the limitation of time, which in my experience has been estimated as approximately one year, although it is possible to plan a shorter period, depending on the possibility of focusing on more attainable aims. In *supportive psychotherapy* (SP), the duration depends on the possibility of delimiting an area of work. If this is the case, several months may be long enough. If it has not been possible to establish a definite focus, supportive psychotherapy may need a longer period of time, up to several years. I use the term *psychotherapeutic interviews or interventions* (PI) (see Chapter Four) for a procedure that is able to concentrate the help on certain conflictive aspects in the patient, as does supportive psychotherapy, but in which the therapeutic relationship does not last long enough (several encounters) to develop into a therapeutic process.

In terms of the *frequency* of the sessions, it is my belief that psychoanalysis requires a high frequency of sessions, with a possible maximum of four or five per week, as I said before. As for psychoanalytic psychotherapy, the ideal frequency is two meetings per week, although it is also possible to develop a psychotherapeutic process with one weekly session, if treatment lasts a "sufficient" time.

Therapeutic aims and analytic aims

Let us recall, *grosso modo*, the two types of aim that I have already indicated in Chapter One. By "therapeutic aims", I mean those that attempt to obtain symptomatic relief of, or improvement in, the emotional suffering of the patient. By "analytical aims", I understand the aspiration to an improved knowledge of the patient's mental life in order to favour psychic changes, in the sense of a growth in the complexity of the internal world. Within the analytical aims, I would also establish a few differences according to the scope of the field of observation and exploration, as I have mentioned previously.

I consider that both aims, analytical and therapeutic, are legitimate both in psychoanalysis and in psychoanalytic psychotherapy. The difference is rooted, as far as I can see, in the fact that, in psycho-analysis, we implicitly try to cover a "wide" field of observation of the patient's intrapsychic life and of the interaction between patient and analyst, whereas in psychoanalytic psychotherapy, the aim covers a "zonal" field, and in brief psychoanalytic psychotherapy the field is "focal".

Psychoanalytic process and psychotherapeutic process

Many authors consider the psychoanalytic process to be a sign of identity for psychoanalysis (Kernberg, 1999; Smith, 2002; Weinshel & Levy, in Tyson & Morris, 1992). Starting from the definition of pro-cess, which I gave in another study (Pérez-Sánchez, 1999), I can now state the following. The psychoanalytic process is structured around two axes of reference: the (sub)process of the experience of linking and the (sub)process of the experience of separating from the object (the analyst). The recognition of the need for the object is one of the foundations for establishing the bases of *learning through experience*. And if, as I believe, all psychopathology—taken in a wide sense—is the psychopathology of narcissism, one of the primal therapeutic tasks is to obtain from the patient an acceptable dependence on the object, the analyst or the therapeutic situation. On the other hand, the expe-rience of separation is indispensable in order to complete this learn-ing, so that, through first tolerating differentiation from the object, and then recognising the loss of the valued object, the fundamentals for building self-identity are established. The interaction between the two processes, of linking and of separation, is, in my opinion, the element that determines the development of the general psycho-analytic process.

As I see it, the clinical material that gives content to the psycho-analytic process is determined by the characteristics of the method. In the psychoanalytic process, in a prominent position will be the content referring to the transference with the analyst and the history of the relationship with him as it is experienced in the sessions, where there are kaleidoscopic images of projections of the different internal objects on to/into the analyst, plus the analyst's particular idiosyncrasies. All of this will be largely present in the material of dreams and in the unconscious fantasies underlining the patient's communications in the session. Through the psychoanalytic process, the patient is able to correct his different distorted versions of the analyst, and, as a consequence, this will lead to a modification to the similarly distorted versions of the internal primordial objects—particularly parental figures, or others in the patient's history.

In psychotherapies, a process also develops, one which I will call a *psychotherapeutic* process, in order to distinguish it from the psychoanalytic one. Such a process consists of acquiring, through learning, a certain capacity for observation of the psychic reality and relationships on the part of the patient, in the "zonal" area, which is possible to explore. The experience of linking and separation also takes place, although not with the same intensity as in the psychoanalytic process. The most frequent clinical material will be that of the extra-therapeutic transference. The analysis of dreams and fantasies, although present, is more frequently related to current and past external objects, and not so much to the therapist. In the psychotherapeutic process, that which is "reconstructed", although partially, is a corrected version of the most fundamental internal objects and the relationship with them.

It has been said that the aim of psychoanalysis consists of the internalisation of the psychoanalytic process (Weinshel & Levy, in Tyson & Morris, 1992). I believe that it would be more appropriate to speak of the internalisation of a method, although this would not be completely exact either. As I have said, in my opinion, the method is made up of a set of technical elements that facilitate the development of a process. Therefore, it is not enough to state that what characterises the psychoanalytic method is exclusively the interpretation or the analysis of the transference, since other conditions are also necessary; that is to say, high frequency meetings (four or five per week), using the couch, and a personal and technical ability to bear and to understand such an experience. All of these conditions offer the opportunity to explore the patient's mind through the analytical relationship, at its different levels and areas, including the most primitive and psychotic aspects, even if we are dealing with "*minor* pathological organisations",[5] commonly known as "neurotic". An internal coherence exists in the psychoanalytic method, since the intensity of the sessions corresponds to the intensity of the experience to such an extent that the interpretations directed at the analytical relationship stimulate intensification in the link between patient and analyst, and vice versa, mobilising the respective internal objects. And it is this special link between patient and analyst, through their unconscious communication, as Freud said—or as we would now say—of the communication between the patient's internal objects and those of the analyst, that constitutes one of the basic characteristics of the psychoanalytic method. So, strictly speaking, it cannot be said that the method is internalised, since the experience of knowledge will never be the same with the help of the analyst as knowledge achieved by oneself. What is internalised, I believe, is the ability to link some aspects of the mind with others, certain aspects of the self with others, the self with internal objects, and the self with external objects. Likewise, what is also internalised is the ability to tolerate separation from an object whose autonomy has been accepted; particularly to tolerate the experiences of separation from the analyst, which will be more complete once the analytical "process", which the two have shared, is over.

The psychotherapeutic process[6] also needs its own internal coherence, by adapting the method to its area of exploration and intervention. Otherwise, giving priority to the interpretation of the transference in a once-weekly psychotherapy, for example, involves mobilising in the patient primitive and/or psychotic anxieties which are difficult to contain and to resolve in the psychotherapeutic setting. And I think this is valid regardless of whether the therapist is a psychoanalyst or not, in opposition to the authors who think that psychoanalysis is any treatment directed by a psychoanalyst (Aisenstein, in Frisch, 2001). As I have been maintaining, *it is the method used and not the analyst or the therapeutic couple that defines an experience as psychotherapeutic or psychoanalytic.* Whether the therapist possesses the capacity and preparation necessary to carry it out is quite another matter, in terms of the appropriate training required to be able to undertake psychoanalysis.

Table 8.3 summarises the differences between psychoanalysis and psychotherapies depending on the aims and the process.

Provisional conclusions

Nowadays, the use of psychoanalytic psychotherapies is on the increase, exceeding that of psychoanalysis. Many patients benefit from the former to a considerable degree, although probably far fewer than those who actually need them, without taking into account the different applications of the psychoanalytic foundations in a wide

Table 8.3. Differentiation between psychoanalysis and individual psychoanalytically based psychotherapies: aims and process.

	Psychoanalysis	Psychoanalytic psychotherapy (PP)	Brief PP (BPP)	Supportive psychotherapy(SP)	Psychotherapeutic interviews (PI)
Aims	1. Internalise analytic "method" and "process" 2. "Wide" psychic change. Clinical improvement	1. Internalise psychotherapeutic - process 2. "Zonal" psychic change. Clinical improvement	"Focal" psychic change. Clinical improvement	Clarification of conflicts in relationships Symptomatic improvement	Symptomatic relief. Some understanding of relationships
Process	Psychoanalytic	Psychotherapeutic	Psychotherapeutic	No process. Assitencial advisory relationship	No process. Assitencial advisory relationship
Session	Dreams, fantasies (referring to or understood within the therapeutic relationship), also to present and past life events	Present and prior life events. Dreams and fantasies.	Focused on present life events (less on past). Fantasy and dreams a little)	Present life events	Consulting problems

variety of therapeutic and welfare practices, as I have already mentioned. Nevertheless, I believe that it is necessary to continue to make an effort to define the specific nature of psychoanalysis, and, subsequently, that of the psychotherapies, for the sake of both. In order to achieve progress in psychoanalytic technique and theory, we need the best conditions in our "laboratory": the clinical setting (Segal, 2007). In this way, we will help to avoid spurious forms of psychoanalytic or psychotherapeutic practices that give rise to pseudo-psychotherapies and pseudo-psychoanalysis, respectively, to the resultant detriment of patients and therapists. For the patient, as he will be subjected to contact with emotional suffering without the conditions and tools necessary for bearing or understanding it, and for the therapist—as the analyst's mind is his principal therapeutic instrument—if he does not have the optimum conditions offered by the appropriate method to protect him, he might come out of it personally affected.

Revisiting the Freudian analogy of pure gold for psychoanalysis, and that of a gold–copper alloy to obtain psychoanalytic psychotherapy, we can state that this does not conform to the current clinical reality. We should say, rather, that this "gold" (in inverted commas, since we know that there will always be "impurities", starting with our own limitations and the use of therapeutic elements other than those which are strictly psychoanalytic), as we have seen, consists of the use of the right method, be it psychoanalysis or psychoanalytic psychotherapy, adapted to the needs and what is possible of the patient and the therapist. If the corresponding method is used, in a "strict" way, as Freud says in the quotation at the beginning of this chapter, and if it is used coherently, this "noble metal" will be both what is used in psychoanalysis and what is applied in the psychotherapies derived from it, at the same time accepting that these are two different procedures.

Notes

1. A concept introduced by Bion (1970), taken from mathematics. I understand it as a "point of view" that rates some perceptions of reality above others.
2. In fact, this expression does not sound right, if we consider transference as a universal phenomenon, and therefore present in every relationship.

Nevertheless, tradition in psychoanalysis has established that "transference interpretation" alludes to the patient's transference in the relationship with the analyst and "extra-transference interpretation" to the relationship outside of the therapeutic relationship.

3. To simplify the debate, I limit myself to the individual psychotherapies, which does not mean that I exclude other psychoanalytically based psychotherapeutic modalities, such as group and family therapies, to which I refer in another publication (Pérez Sánchez, 1997).

4. Primitive transference is the externalisation of primitive forms of object relationship, and implies a more preserved self. Psychotic transference is a type of primitive but pathological object relationship involving, therefore, a more damaged self.

5. I use this expression in reference to the one used by Steiner (1993), "Pathological organisations". I develop this idea in another publication (Pérez-Sánchez, 1996b).

6. For a more detailed description of psychotherapeutic process, see Pérez-Sánchez, 1996a.

CHAPTER NINE

The choice of indication: psychotherapy or psychoanalysis

Factors determining the choice of indication

Psychodynamic indicator factors

The psychodynamic indicators, as described in Chapter Six, attempt to provide elements that might be of assistance when it comes to assessing the suitability of a patient for the psychoanalytic psychotherapies in general. In the previous chapter, I attempted to set out my position to the effect that not all of the psychotherapies will attain the same therapeutic aims, and neither do they use the same method. While it has always been easier to make this distinction between the supportive and the brief or focal psychotherapies in relation to psychoanalytic psychotherapy, as we have seen, it is not always so easy to do so between this latter practice and psychoanalysis. Taking into account what we have noted in the previous chapter, it is worth examining, from the point of view of the psychodynamic indicators, whether it is legitimate to make a choice between either or both therapeutic practices.

Put another way, when a patient, after being examined for the psychodynamic indicators, tests positively in terms of meeting the conditions to benefit from a psychoanalytically based treatment, we wish to elucidate which treatment to choose: brief or supportive psychotherapy, or otherwise psychoanalytic psychotherapy, or psychoanalysis.[1] In this chapter, we shall look at the indication for psychoanalytic psychotherapy, which then becomes an indication for psychoanalysis,[2] with the arguments supporting this choice, for which I have drawn on clinical material.

Below, I have included verbatim an excerpt from the notes I wrote after the first interviews with a patient for whom I indicated psychoanalysis, at a rate of four weekly sessions, which we carried out over several years. I have preserved the telegraphic style of the original as it expresses very well my first impressions, in which I was attempting to highlight the most significant elements. Considering that at that time I had not yet begun to formulate the psychodynamic indicators, the brief paragraph seems particularly illustrative to me, as I believe that within it are already encompassed some of the indicators. The roman text between square brackets is a recent addition made for the reader's ease of understanding. My remarks are as follows:

> [Patient] *Willing to do analysis. Good contact* [with the analyst and with herself]. *Speaks about her childhood* [she gives a good description of her infantile aspects]. *Responds to my suggestions by providing new data* [which are illuminating]. *Collaborative. Presence of suffering. Unsatisfied with the defences that have served her for a long time (narcissistic defences).*

In the first instance, the patient's motivation is underlined by the expression, "willing to do analysis". In order to make this affirmation, the analyst has had to draw on various factors that are apparent in the course of the interviews. This includes a sincere desire, a curiosity, to know herself and a certain excitement about realising this process together with the person with whom she is carry out the interviews. Linked to this is the fact reflected by the remark that the patient establishes "good contact", both with herself and with the analyst. The good contact with herself is made evident by the good description she gives of her childhood, but in a way that enables the interviewer to gain a rather accurate impression of significant aspects of her internal "child", of the patient's infantile self. With regard to the good contact with the analyst, this is illustrated by the explanation that she "responds to the (analyst's) suggestions by providing new data", which helps him in his diagnostic task. While implicit in these comments is the participative attitude of the patient, this is then underscored by the adjective "collaborative". Immediately after-wards, the notes add that there is the "presence of suffering", that is to say, that present is a request to be treated, not as a result of intel-lectual curiosity, given that the patient is a highly qualified profes-sional, but through necessity. Finally, it is observed that "(she is) unsatisfied with the defences" used until now. Several things could be inferred from this. One is her awareness of some of her defences, and, therefore, a certain capacity for self-observation and insight; another is the recognition of their inadequacy, which carries particular signif-icance, as the text in parentheses makes clear, as these are, in point of fact, narcissistic defences, which she will have to fight against in order to accept a helping relationship coming from another person (the analyst).

Put in terms of the indicators, though also grounded in what I call the "classical approach", I would summarise this case by saying that this is a person with adult capacities, or, rather, with an adult *self* who is able to "bring" the sick person (who is suffering) and the child (whom she describes well), who recognises the psychological basis for her discomfort, and who is curious to know herself, as well as a degree of personal or self-knowledge, although not enough, for which reason she needs and accepts the help of a professional.

And yet, while a person might be eligible for psychoanalytical treatment on the basis of the factor of the psychodynamic indicators—unlike the vignette above—this is not always enough, for which reason I consider it necessary also to take into account other factors, as we shall see further on. But continuing, for the moment, with the factor of the indicators, we may assert that the choice of the type of help is determined by the patient and by the method. By the patient, in those cases where the request is relatively confined to certain psychic and relational conflicts which enable the therapist to define a treatment focus, and which are not derived from wider personality problems, whence we might deduce the indication for *brief psycho-analytic psychotherapy*. In other cases, it is not possible to establish a focus and, moreover, there are existing personality problems, for which reason the indication for focal psychotherapy would not be adequate and, consequently, the treatment of choice would be *psycho-analytic psychotherapy*. In cases such as these, the patient himself, on the basis of the conditions offered by the psychotherapeutic method, will be unconsciously shaping or outlining those problems that are most "repeated" in his psychic and relational functioning, and will afford the therapist—along with himself—certain possibilities for exploration of particular areas or *zones* of his personality, and yet, at the same time, the method itself will restrict access to others. As I already said in the previous chapter, the zones that are less accessible using the psychotherapeutic method, in the psychoanalytic psycho-therapies can be summed up as those relating to the primitive infan-tile levels and to the psychotic aspects of the personality.

A patient with a very poor indicator for tolerance to separation–linking anxieties will hardly gain any benefit from brief psycho-therapy (which, in my understanding, means of one year's duration, let alone if the timeframe is less). Whether this is because his incapac-ity is linked to primary anxieties, those of separation, by forming highly dependent relationships that render the absence of the other unbearable to him, in which case the brevity of the course of the ther-apeutic process would not enable this dependence to be resolved, or, otherwise, because the predominant anxieties are those resulting from the very fact of the linking itself, to his poor tolerance to the recogni-tion of linking relationships, as occurs in narcissistic personalities, in which case neither will it be possible to treat his impediments or barriers to the linking in that short space of time. In both cases, at the very least, long-term psychoanalytic psychotherapy would be req-uired at a frequency of twice per week. With regard to the choice for psychoanalysis, I consider two questions to be salient. The first is the existence of a certain curiosity, experienced as something that is felt to be needed, to know oneself, which we can correlate with the indicator for "love/(hate) for the search for the truth" about one's own psychic reality; that is to say, when there is a predominance of a cognitive–emotional stance of esteem, enthusiasm, and, in short, even love, for that search. The other question I consider to be crucial in making the choice for psychoanalysis, as we already saw in the previ-ous chapter, is that patient has the capacity to realise the essential task of working through of the insights acquired. And this working through demands two things: the capacity to tolerate the concomitant pain, and time. For that reason, the indicator for "tolerance to pain/pleasure" deserves to be highlighted in deciding the feasibility of psychoanalysis, although the conditions of the psychoanalytic method at once provide a framework that enables mental pain to be tolerated more successfully than the psychoanalytic psychotherapies.

Psychopathological factors

Traditionally, the not very serious neurotic and character pathologies have been considered to be subsidiary to psychoanalysis and the psychoanalytic psychotherapies. We have already asserted, however, that progress in psychoanalytic technique has enabled us to approach the treatment of more serious patients, including psychotic patients (Bion, 1967; Rosenfeld, 1964; Segal, 1957), in such a way that, nowadays, a number of psychoanalysts have had the experience of directing psychoanalytic treatment with serious patients (psychotic and borderline patients, or *major pathological organisations*, as we might also call them (Pérez-Sánchez, 1996b)). Some time ago, I had the opportunity to carry out the analysis of a schizophrenic patient, at five sessions per week for five years (Pérez-Sánchez, 1989) where, with the appropriate help of the supervision and the antipsychotic drugs prescribed by another psychiatrist, what I consider to be a psychoanalytic process was able to develop. In this case, it was not the psychopathology that induced me to carry out this process, as this was a person who had undergone psychiatric confinement several times as a result of episodes of psychic decompensation with manifest psychotic psychopathology, delusions, reality perception, and thought disorders. But, notwithstanding the above, I would say in spite of the patient himself—in spite of his sick part—there was a strong desire in him to know what was wrong and a constant dissatisfaction with the treatments he had received until then. And although his tolerance to pain clearly was very low, through being able to rely on a collaborative family environment it was possible to realise the psychoanalytic experience over five years, in which time the patient was able to achieve personal gains that beforehand had not been possible. By this, I wish to make the point that it is not the psychopathology which makes the definitive decision when it comes to making the indication for psychoanalysis, even in very serious patients; rather, other factors also combine, which hold specific weight and should be taken into account. In any case, these cases are the exception, given that the emotional strain, as much for the patient (even the slightest insight will bring significant painful experiences in its wake) as for the analyst (who will have to be available to sacrifice part of his free time and his holidays to deal with the emergencies that, inevitably, will arise with a patient with these characteristics), as well on his family surroundings, is not always seen to be compensated in terms of justifying continuing treatment. There are authors who propose a modified form of psychoanalysis for psychotic and borderline patients (Kernberg, 1976) and others, among whom I include myself, as we have seen, who do not share this view (Rosenfeld, 1978), considering that it is possible to maintain the psychoanalytic setting even in such cases. As we have been saying, I think it is the assessment of the specific individual by a particular analyst, who also has an interest in undergoing that difficult experience, which might decide whether it is possible to carry out a treatment according to the psychoanalytic method, or, otherwise, whether psychoanalytic psychotherapy is preferable.

Social factors

Even when the factors relating to the psychodynamic indicators and the psychopathology combine sufficiently favourable elements to establish the indication for psychoanalytic psychotherapy or psychoanalysis, it is still necessary to consider the social factors. In the clinical material I have included in previous chapters up until now, the patients came from the sphere of public healthcare and, as I have attempted to demonstrate, fulfilled the necessary requirements to indicate them for brief psychotherapeutic treatment, which was then carried out. It was a suitable treatment choice, depending on the assessment made in the working group, and was not bound by the restrictive conditions of the public institution. We also met with other patients who were not suitable for this psychotherapy, and, thus, supportive psychotherapy or psychotherapeutic interviews were offered to them. Similarly, we interviewed others for whom the indication of choice was long-term psychoanalytic psychotherapy, and, in a few cases, the suitable therapeutic recommendation was even psychoanalysis.

Whatever the circumstance, the therapist should possess the freedom of choice to make the therapeutic indication that he considers most suitable for his patients. But, given that long-term psychoanalytic psychotherapies, and especially psychoanalysis, are very consuming of both time and resources—financial and emotional—we should adopt certain guiding or illustrative criteria, bearing in mind the combination of the psychodynamic, psychopathological, and social factors to establish an indication that balances the potential benefit against the cost (in all of the senses mentioned above).

One of the factors that intervene in that assessment is the social factor, in the sense of taking into account that the purported benefit of treatment might have repercussions not only on the person who is receiving it, but also on the other people who are linked to him by the work he does in a professional context. This is the case with all patients, whose professions fall within the purview of taking care of the sick or needy (the social and healthcare professionals: doctors, social workers, educators, nurses, etc). While the realisation of such work demands, *a priori*, a personality that is strong and motivated enough to tolerate it, it is desirable, in addition, for there to be a technical and emotional support structure in place to aid in the performance of these tasks: known as the Balint Groups, these were initially set up to help general practitioners, but have now been extended to encompass other professionals, the supervision of clinical cases in the field of the psychotherapies, or treatment of difficult patients. At times, however, either because such a support structure does not exist, or because the professional's personality is not strong enough, or perhaps because of the addition of other circumstances of a personal nature, a breakdown occurs which requires psychological help. In such cases, for these people, a more intensive treatment choice is preferable to a more intermittent form of help, be this psychoanalytic psychotherapy or psychoanalysis. In terms of deciding which of the two latter options would be the optimum one, we should jointly assess the psychodynamic, psychopathological, and social indicators, with an estimate of the predictable results. In my opinion, however, the greater the emotional involvement in one's professional work, the more necessary the choice of psychoanalysis becomes.

Resistance to the indication for psychoanalysis

As we may have gathered from what has been said in several chapters of this book, in view of the psychotherapist or psychoanalyst's inevitable emotional involvement in deciding which indication he considers the most suitable, the countertransferential component acquires considerable significance. This component might engender resistances to establishing the indication for psychoanalysis or, conversely, might prompt one to make the indication in an inadequate and hasty way. But, in the event of prevailing difficulties of an external nature, the greatest risk lies in the emergence of these resistances. Both personal factors and general or overarching factors, including social and, if you will, historical factors—tied to the particular moment at which psychoanalytic practice finds itself—might have a bearing on the countertransference. The personal factors allude to the impact that the patient's psychology and psychopathology will have had on the professional in the diagnostic interview: whether it has stimulated reactions of conscious—but especially unconscious—rejection, for whatever reason, or he has felt overwhelmed by the problem(s) the patient presents, or it has brought up blind spots in the personality of the therapist himself that have not been adequately elaborated. It is assumed that all of these countertransferential vicissitudes shall be assumed and worked through by the therapist, thanks to his own personal psychoanalysis and aided by the supervision of another colleague, if necessary. However, and I stress, the problem comes about when these unconscious difficulties are very dissociated, so that the therapist does not have sufficient knowledge of them or, consequently, the need to supervise them, with the result that they act in the form of resistances, leading him—for example—to dismiss the indication for psychoanalysis when it would have been the most suitable option. It is to be hoped that this resistance to making the indication for psychoanalysis does not occur very frequently, as, if this were the case, it would constitute a personal difficulty of the therapist's in relation to psychoanalysis, and would arguably be related to poor achievement in his personal therapy, or might also be owing to a limited capacity to carry out the task of the psychoanalyst. For example, in the case of some therapists with years of experience in professional practice in the field of psychotherapy who do not encounter suitable patients who might benefit from psychoanalysis, they are likely themselves to constitute the very source of resistance; however, even in some analysts we might encounter this.

The second factor that might have a bearing on the countertransference is of a broader nature: the social factor. By this, I mean the assessment that is made within the immediate environment of the practice of psychoanalysis and the psychoanalytic psychotherapies. We know that, today, there are few requests made for psychoanalysis. This might be owing to several different circumstances. Nowadays, there are innumerable treatment choices, on the whole, in the field of mental health, and in particular this has increased enormously within what we might describe as the "psychoanalytic" field, in inverted commas, as this description comprises very different practices both with regard to the various theoretical foundations upheld, and by the precarious, and occasionally almost non-existent, professional training of the people who do them. There are plenty of treatments that are called "psychoanalytic", even though—for example—they take place at a frequency of once a week, in such a way that, understandably, the choice of different psychoanalytic treatment of at least four weekly sessions, such as we are defending here, has initially less chance of success, unless the patient truly has an interest in delving deeper into his conflicts and difficulties.

Be that as it may, what I wish to highlight here is the resistance in the professionals themselves, who know that psychoanalysis is an activity that requires considerable effort. If they are psychotherapists whose job includes doing psychotherapies, excluding psychoanalysis proper, it is clear that they will need to overcome certain resistances owing to the fact of having to make an indication for something that they themselves will not carry out, even though it is close to what they do. Unresolved envious and competitive aspects might act as a prime mover for resistance when it comes to failing to make the indication for psychoanalysis in a patient who perhaps meets the conditions for this treatment. To this are added reasons of a purely pragmatic nature: a patient who is eligible for psychoanalysis will undoubtedly also make progress in psychoanalytic psychotherapy, even if it falls somewhat short. Nevertheless, many other honest psychotherapists have considered, on the basis of the diagnostic interviews, that the optimum indication was for psychoanalytic psychotherapy and did not duly weigh up that the indication for psychoanalysis might have been the more suitable option, as the aforementioned unconscious aspects hindered them from doing so. And yet, during the course of the psychotherapeutic process, they become aware of having reached the limits of what the psychotherapeutic method is able to offer and, therefore, establish the indication for psychoanalysis, thus referring the patient. Furthermore, it must be said that in some of these cases, if the indication for analysis had been made from the outset, it would have been the patient's own resistances that would have rejected it, since until the therapeutic experience had familiarised him with a method close that of the psychoanalytic—though, of course, the psychotherapeutic method differs somewhat—he would not have been able to accept the indication for psychoanalysis.

Still yet, we must make mention of the resistance to indicating psychoanalysis among psychoanalysts themselves. Although this might seem surprising, it is a reality we sometimes come up against, as a result, in point of fact, of the impact of social conditions. So, in the analyst who is too "understanding" with his patient, he will not wish to expose him to strain that might seem excessive by making an indication for psychoanalysis, so instead will offer him a psychoanalytic psychotherapy. Thus, instead of working through the resistances of the patient, who is using the external reality to avoid strain, he forms an alliance with these resistances. Clearly, I am not suggesting that we should be insensitive to the real external difficulties, which amount to serious obstacles to committing to psychoanalytic treatment (from the financial to the emotional, including the time-consuming element), but I wish to draw attention to the need to examine them thoroughly in order to assess when they are insuperable, and when, as I suggested above, they are at the service of the resistances to the necessary emotional work. I think that one of the most important elements leading to the analyst's resistances to recommending psychoanalysis is a *lack of conviction in the psychoanalytic method*.

I should like now to set out certain clinical material relating to the indication for a psychoanalytic psychotherapy, which, subsequently, after one year, became psychoanalysis.

Indication for psychoanalytic psychotherapy: clinical material 6

Diagnostic interviews

A colleague requested my intervention for a patient who has made a suicide attempt by ingesting certain drugs that her psychiatrist had prescribed for her. She had allegedly been diagnosed with endogenous depression, although in the hospital where she received emergency treatment they questioned the validity of the diagnosis. As she was a young adult, my colleague considered—even though he had not seen her himself—that it might be possible to consider some kind of psychotherapeutic help.

In the light of the information with which my colleague provided me, my initial impression was not favourable. This seemed to be a difficult and complicated case. A patient who makes a suicide attempt denotes a considerably severe condition, either as the result of a particularly unbearable circumstance, or because she herself has perpetuated a situation that was damaging to her until, out of desperation, she opts for suicide. In both cases, the prospects for psychotherapeutic help, as requested by my colleague—also a psychoanalyst —did not seem particularly promising. On the other hand there was still a certain interest on my part in the case, in terms of it involving a challenge for me, as a psychoanalyst and psychotherapist, to address such a situation in order to help this young person. Clearly, here, I found myself assailed by certain preconceptions that were not by any means rational, as they are indefensible consciously. In principal, there is no reason to exclude the possibility of a person who has made a suicide attempt being able to benefit from psychoanalytic psychotherapy, and even from psychoanalysis. In fact, we have seen above that patients with a more serious psychopathology might be eligible for a psychoanalytic process, provided that certain external and internal conditions are met. In fact, at that time, I was undertaking the psychoanalysis of the psychotic patient I mentioned before. But I am setting out the situation just as I experienced in order to show the various countertransferential reactions that emerge from a request, from the very first instants, before one has even met the patient. So I agreed to see her, but with the implicit predetermined idea that I was expecting to do little more than some supportive psychotherapy to contain the immediate severity of the situation. In any case, I had left a small margin for other possibilities until I had a "better" knowledge of the patient. Later on, I thought that the source of these prejudices might have been conveyed to me in the manner (the words, the tone of the voice, and so on) with which my colleague referred to the patient.

The patient is a woman in her thirties who comes to the first appointment in a clearly depressed state. She adopts a very passive attitude. She gives an explanation of what has happened to her as something that is almost wholly determined by the people around her, in such a way that she has suffered the consequences of their inadequate actions; that is, she was the victim. She says that in the hospital where they treated her for her suicide attempt following the ingestion of a bottle of pills prescribed by her psychiatrist—some forty pills—she was advised to seek psychological help. She has undergone psychiatric treatment for several years, with monthly appointments and antidepressant medication that had been progressively increased to the current dose of 150 mg of imipramine hydrochloride with a further 150 mg of clomipramine hydrochloride per day. The psychiatrist treating her had diagnosed her with endogenous depression, but the professionals at the hospital were not very happy with this diagnosis—while still recognising that she was depressed—so they lowered the dosage and suggested to her that she might require psychological help.

The patient comments in this same interview that she has decided to leave her psychiatrist as a result of the loss of confidence brought about by him having upheld for so long a diagnosis that is now revealed to be incorrect. Furthermore, she explains, this has had damaging effects, as the psychiatrist told her that the diagnosis of endogenous depression is something that will be with her throughout her life, although it might be alleviated with medication, which she will have to take permanently. This placed the patient in a passive position; since any struggle against the illness would be useless, her only recourse was to obediently follow the medical prescription, which in turn—above all towards the end—contributed towards her condition of substantial impairment of mental functioning, with drowsiness and confusion, restricting her from carrying out her work. Her partner, with whom she had lived for some time, reproached her for her passive attitude, and thought that she could do more to get herself out of her depressive states of lack of drive and apathy, which caused her to stay in bed at the weekends and when she did not have to work. All of this gave rise to arguments and confrontations with her partner. She felt incapable of coming out of the situation by herself, which her partner did not accept, and who still pressed her to try harder, thus causing her to experience feelings of intense loneliness and desperation. She reveals that, in addition, the problem was getting worse, not because he did not understand her, but because she was incapable of expressing her disagreement to him. Their last argument brought her to a state of helplessness and desperation, which led to her suicide attempt.

At that point in the interview, we stop to explore the relationship with her partner, which seemed to be the core issue, being the immediate trigger for the patient's breakdown. Her partner is a man who is separated from his wife, with two children who are already in their teens. She asserts that at one stage she agreed to one of the children coming to live with them, thus demonstrating her willingness to assume the function of "the mother" of this "family". But she realised that this was not the case, and that she was an addition to the true family made up of her partner and the mother of both of their children; that, in fact, her partner was not interested in constructing a new family with her, and was explicit in his wish to have no more children, which involved a certain frustration that apparently she was prepared to bear in order to continue to be with him.

Previously, the patient had lived with another man for several years, from whom she decided to separate. The reason was that he was very close to his family of origin, who did not accept her at all. This relationship came about from a group of friends "constructed" (a word the patient uses at various points during the interview, in different contexts, which I understand to mean an expression of interest to perform a task of "construction" in her life and in herself, at this juncture) in the academic field in which she studied. This brought together various people who came from outside the city, although she realises that they formed a kind of ghetto, which hindered their integration into other circles within the city. She was an important component of the group, for which reason, when she separated from this first partner, the group broke up. A few months later, she met her current partner.

Before moving to Barcelona, she had been in a committed relationship with a boy for some years. The families knew each other and approved of the relationship, for which reason it was expected that they would end up getting married. When she was nineteen years old, she started work, and thought about the possibility of getting married in order to become more independent. But her mother advised her against it, considering her to be too young, and suggested that she go to finish her education away from the town. Shortly before this, her father had died. She chose Barcelona because of the type of studies she wished to do.

Once she was there, the relationship began to cool with her boyfriend, who was also travelling a lot because of his job, so they saw little of each other. This was the reason, according to her, that precipitated the end of the engagement. It was difficult, because the boy found it hard to accept, as did the respective families who, on the other hand, were very close.

I now express an interest in the death of her father. She comments that the year before her coming to Barcelona there were a number of deaths of people with whom she had had some type of link, culminating in the death of her father. She cites five or six losses: the parents of two friends with whom she was very close, the brother of another friend, and two more to whom she was less connected.

She is the youngest of several brothers and sisters, with a large age difference in relation to the eldest. She admits that this fact is significant. For example, her brothers and sisters talk to her about two parents who have little in common with the ones she knew, as they were already older when she was born; it is as if they were talking about different people. Her brothers and sisters experienced a very restrictive and strict parental upbringing, while with the patient, the parents were more permissive. In any case, as a child, she remembers her father with some fear, although she adds that this must have been more as a result of the image formed of him on the basis of what her brothers and sisters explained to her. Her brothers and sisters formed a group that she was never able to be part of, as she was too small. However, she says that they (the siblings) were not brought up by her parents, but by a *tata* (a nanny), whom they thought of like a mother.

I make a remark to her to the effect that it seems as though she formed a separate group with her parents, while her brothers and sisters constituted another group. They did not have their parents, but a substitute. I also remark to her, later on, that in Barcelona she was able to collaborate in forming a new group, in which she felt included, being, furthermore, an important part of that group, as evidenced by its dissolution when she left after separating from her partner. That is to say, something similar happened to what she might have felt occurred at home: that she was the central figure in the group formed with her parents, as she now was with her friends. She smiles, and shows she accepts this, at the same time as expressing surprise over the connections established between an old situation and a current one, implying, however, that she has understood.

In spite of these differences, she maintains that she has a good relationship with her brothers and sisters. As for her mother, she is a woman who has suffered ailments and maladies, primarily migraines, that cause her to take to her bed relatively frequently. The patient herself also suffers from them, as well as one of her brothers. She is able to manage them with analgesics.

She later connects this with the reason she first went to see the psychiatrist, three years ago, on the recommendation of her current partner. At that time she had started to feel depressed. Previously, she had never undergone psychiatric treatment. The appointments involved monitoring her medication and a chat, at a frequency of once per month. She believed that this was "therapy" (psychotherapy), but, although she talked about her problems, because of what has been explained to her now, she says that this cannot have been psychotherapy because of the infrequency of the appointments. It also bothered her that, upon coming out of hospital, she was trying to locate her psychiatrist but he did not return her calls, which made her entirely lose her trust in him, which had already dwindled when his incorrect diagnosis was discovered. Finally, she was able to talk to him and they arranged to meet on the same day as she had an appointment arranged previously, since their last consultation.

She maintains that when she took the pills she had no intention of killing herself, but of sleeping the whole weekend away, although the psychiatrists who treated her in the hospital say that the quantity of tablets ingested suggests that she did, in fact, intend to commit suicide. She admits that there have been other times when she has had thoughts about dying, before she was under medication, but that she did not do it as she did not have any pills to hand, and that other methods, like cutting her wrists or throwing herself out of the window, seemed very violent to her. The tone in which she explains all of this appears to be sincere and undramatised.

She remembers her childhood well. Her mother was able to be there for her, which she did not do for her brothers and sisters. She (the mother) is a very religious woman, and, as such, the patient's upbringing was very strict, although her father was not. Sometimes, she had the impression that her parents were abandoning her, because when the weekend arrived and she was able to be left in the care of her brothers and sisters, apparently during her latency, her parents would go to their house in the country to be alone and do everything that up until then they had not been able to because of the children. The patient, however, experienced this as a kind of abandonment, despite the psychiatrist making it clear to her, when she told him about these experiences, that this was not so. She thinks she must have been breastfed. She considers that she is the one who has broken the mould in relation to the family norms, owing to the fact that she left home early and chose a kind of life that does not conform to the formality of the family.

I ask her about her dreams. She has many, she says, in which she is being pursued or chased. There is one that is repeated, in which some person or animal appears, for example a snake, in the last one she has had recently (she went through a period of scarcely dreaming at all, which she attributes to the effects of the medication that made her sleep deeply). In these dreams, she has a good relationship with these people or things or animals, until there comes a point where she begins to apprehend that the other party is adopting a hostile attitude towards her, something that is not manifest or obvious, and the problem lies in that if she externalises her fear towards the snake—for example—then it will attack her. So, she has to be quiet and endure the fear, which causes her to suffer, turning the dream into a nightmare.

Comments on the first interview

At the beginning of the interview, the unfavourable impression I was given by my colleague's information is confirmed. This is a woman with a considerable depressive symptomatology, who adopts a passive attitude. She is referred for psychotherapy and, obediently, she follows the recommendation, as if she had not asked herself what this will entail. The psychiatrist and her partner are the ones, according to her, who have put her in a situation with no other way out than the suicide attempt, as she has not been capable of expressing her disagreement in any other way to either of them. This submissive and passive attitude concerns me, and I even wonder whether such passivity leads her to effect an inhibition of her cognitive and intellectual capacities, which would render psychoanalytic psychotherapy impracticable. As the interview goes on, however, and her paranoid anxieties, due to being faced with the new situation with an unknown professional, start to diminish, a more open attitude emerges and she is more able to syntonise with herself and with the therapist. The therapist's interventions are well received by her. She provides meaningful information, which helps us to understand aspects of her functioning. Both the description she provides of the mutual relationship between herself and her family, including parents and siblings, and her difficulties in her relationship enable us to formulate a profile of a particular type of mental and relational functioning. She repeats the history of feeling that she does not belong in the family group, as a result of having arrived later than her brothers and sisters: in adult situations, with her group of friends, however, it is she who demonstrates a certain leadership. This is a group that is, after all, made up of people from out of town and who do not "fit in". With her partner also she has arrived late, as he had already formed his family. In the interview, it is clear to see an interest in "constructing" something new in her life that is not as damaging as some of the things she has built until now. She is in touch with her childhood. She recognises that there is a mother who gave her the breast, or, rather, who cared for her, and perhaps with more dedication than she did her brothers and sisters, as, having been born so close together, they had to be looked after by a *tata*. In other words, it is clear that there is a person who is suffering and who is in contact with her infantile self. Little by little, during the course of the interview, she has been demonstrating a greater adult capacity, in terms of taking responsibility for her communications and providing new information. She is in touch with her internal world through her dreams, in which I think she is illustrating the situation she is experiencing in the present with her partner, and perhaps with the psychiatrist, in conformity with a pattern of behaviour that is repeated. She relates to a person of whom she is afraid, but who will not attack her provided she silence the panic he generates in her; this is what she has been doing until now. But that position is not beneficial to her health, even though she is able to sustain the relationship with such person (creature or thing).

In terms of the psychodynamic indicators, we can say that this is a person who is bringing the "patient" (she expresses her suffering) and the "child" (she is in touch with her infantile aspects), as well as feeling a strong need to come out of an unhealthy functioning, of which she is partly aware (the relationship she sustains with her partner). She is sincere, collaborative, and possesses certain ego capacities that it seems she does not sufficiently utilise, in so far as she establishes dependent relationships where she is submissive before figures that represent some degree of authority. The content of her dreams reveals the presence of certain frightening internal objects, faced with which she has to give the appearance of "normality", that is to say, submission or compliance, while repressing the panic she feels.

For my part, while expectations improved in relation to my initial impression, I needed to know what would happen during the next encounter. Would this positive progress, seen during the first interview, be maintained, or would she regress to her initial position? What aspects of the image she had given me of herself up until that point would change, if they did at all, and in what way?

The second interview

This takes place one week later. The patient has parted with the psychiatrist, who continues to uphold the diagnosis of endogenous depression, upon which, he explained to her, stressful circumstances might have had a bearing. Today, she further expands upon the difficulties in her relationship with her partner. She describes her companion as someone who does not want to feel stifled by her requests and demands, above all with regard to the need to talk about the things that are wrong between them, as he is quite a reserved person. She recalls that the psychiatrist told her that her partner is a man who has problems and who has not helped her in her illness, or something similar.

I do not think that this reasoning, of "laying the blame elsewhere", convinces the patient at all, even though, in fact, she is now using it with me. Accordingly, I try to be cautious in this respect. The type of relationship she establishes in the interview is one of considering that the therapist is someone in whom she trusts and whom she needs, having placed a great many expectations in him. Her attitude is somewhat submissive for the purposes of getting the other to collude with her in relation to her projections. It is likely that this is what happened with the psychiatrist, which leads me to be alert.

The patient is able to accept what I point out to her about her difficulties in assuming or taking responsibility for feelings that might perhaps be her own, but that she attempts to attribute to her partner, as could occur when she feels discomfort as a result of how she experiences their relationship. Instead of expressing it thus, she disguises it by asserting what is wrong between them and that they need to talk, as if this were something that was equally shared.

As she already disclosed in the previous interview, another of the questions that has been cause for conflict with her partner is the fact that, as he has two children from his previous marriage, he does not need any more. That is to say, he does not feel a lack or a need to form a new family, for which reason she feels as if she is an "addition", that the partner's true family is the other one, and that she will not be able to form a new one with him.

We return to the theme of this feeling of exclusion in connection to her family of origin, where being the youngest, with many years' difference in relation to her brothers and sisters, made her feel a little excluded. With her partner's children she claims she has a good relationship. Furthermore, on one occasion, one of them came to her defence upon seeing his father's unfair attitude towards her. She recounts that, some time ago, this particular son had problems at school and with his friends, which made it necessary for her partner to hold conversations with his ex-wife. The patient believes that this situation must have stirred up a number of issues in her partner which he then did not have the opportunity to assimilate, and that it is likely that this also contributed towards making living with her difficult, as he must have already felt very stressed and then had to put up with her bouts of depression.

Likewise, she talks about the feeling of insecurity she has been experiencing lately at work, which is something she has not felt since adolescence. She scarcely participates in meetings, as if she were fearful of saying inappropriate or inadequate things. She considers that her bouts of depression might be also linked to the fact that her mother did not agree to her coming to the parental home with her partner, as they were not married. Thus, she was not able to include her partner in the family (as represented by her mother, as at that time her father had already died), and, consequently, neither was she accepted at all, even though her brothers and sisters did, in fact, accept him.

When we are reaching the end of the interview, I explain that the type of treatment I consider to be suitable for her is psychotherapy at a frequency of two sessions per week, and add that there are other options for help, such as weekly psychotherapy and psychoanalysis at four to five sessions per week. I clarify the differences in method between both, with regard to the use of the couch and the level of understanding of mental life, which is different in each case, but add that I have chosen the first option as I consider an indication for therapy to be sufficient for her at that stage. With this information, I want the patient to be aware of the existence of psychoanalysis, in case this possibility were to present itself later on, as, by the end of this second interview, I already feel that she is a person who could benefit from it. When I mention to her that it is preferable to have two weekly sessions rather than one, she says that she agrees, because the week that has gone by since we had the first interview has seemed like an eternity to her.

General impression and therapeutic indication

In the second interview, the first matter the patient clears up is the fact of having parted with the psychiatrist. This seems to me to be a good indication of her desire to clarify the situation: if she has to begin a new therapeutic relationship, she must finish with the previous one, even before deciding upon the level of therapeutic involvement here, which, in some way, indicates that she does not make that termination conditional upon this beginning. What is more, she does so by facing up to this parting, rather than simply leaving without further ado and "legitimately" abandoning the "bad object". Neither does she use this encounter to reproach him and, in so doing, take her revenge. Furthermore, she then relates the type of relationship she had with the psychiatrist to the therapist, as a way of warning him, unconsciously, about the risks of collusion involved in relating to her, at the same time as another part of her seeks this in the interview. When, however, she communicates the psychiatrist's remarks condemning her partner's abandonment in the face of her illness—roundly placing the blame on him—she does not seem to be very convinced that this is the best way to help her. Perhaps it is for that reason, also, that she dedicates a good part of the second interview to talking about her relationship with her partner, giving a version in which she makes the partner's inadequate way of acting patently clear, not only in order to relate a problem that worries her, but also to sound out or test the therapist. What will be his response to this? Will he side with her, as the psychiatrist did? Will he take the partner's side, accusing her? Or, there again, will he respond in other ways, and if so, how?

The patient has shown a growing interest throughout the course of the first interview and proceeding to the second. We can say that she is motivated by the need to come out of a state of suffering that has already lasted long enough by the curiosity to know why all of this is happening to her, and, in particular, how this relates to her, and by the expectation of beginning a treatment approach that differs from the one carried out up to now. By the second interview, I can see that the adult aspects of the patient are richer than was evinced in the first interview. She responds well to the indications made to her, collaborating and contributing further associations that enrich the information. In the few interpretations I make, she seems to agree, although this aspect is relativised, in point of fact, because of her tendency towards submission faced with authority figures.

Finally, all of this leads me to choose psychoanalytic psychotherapy as the optimum proposal, at a frequency of twice per week in a face-to-face relationship. That is to say, I have dismissed my initial impression, which I thought was the most feasible option when I was told about the patient: supportive psychotherapy. It was clear that she had sufficient resources for a somewhat more intensive therapeutic treatment. Although I mention the once-weekly frequency of treatment to her, I also dismiss it, as I do not consider this sufficient to treat her problem of dependence in relation to authority figures. I also think that the problems she presents in her romantic relationships are very much rooted in old unresolved conflicts with her parental figures, for which reason I consider psychoanalysis to be the most suitable indication. That is why I wanted to make her aware of it as another option, as the patient had no prior knowledge of it, although psychoanalytic psychotherapy was the treatment that seemed most appropriate at that stage. I had not even expressed the possibility of subsequently reviewing the indication, in relation to psychoanalysis proper, as, while I see potentialities in the patient to gain access to certain insights, I have doubts about the psychical strength she has to tolerate them. I prefer to keep this possibility to myself and to observe the evolution of the psychotherapy in order to see if it is sufficient or if, subsequently, it will turn out to be necessary to move on to psychoanalysis.

I am concerned by the excessive idealisation the patient might make of the treatment and of the therapist, as already in these diagnostic interviews she has made me feel something akin to her "saviour", while she settles into a passive attitude by depositing all responsibility in the therapist. But I hope we can count on the resources I have noted in the interviews: her capacity for self and hetero-observation, for reflection, and the need to look inside herself, in order to get round these risks.

With regard to the management of her ongoing pharmacological treatment, the patient makes some reference to it, as if waiting for the therapist's decision. I tell her that I will not take charge of this, in order to make a separation between each type of help, which, in my practice, I think is advisable. With some preoccupation, I wonder what psychiatrist will take on this task, in case it is someone who is not in favour of psychoanalytic psychotherapy. The patient herself suggests that she can contact one via a friendly society (for health-care). I accept her initiative precisely because by this she is displaying a different attitude to the passive one, the problem that concerns me. I shall wait for her news on the appointments with the new psychia-trist in case any problem arises, but I also trust that the patient is suffi-ciently motivated to defend this treatment. Some weeks later, she informs me with relief, a feeling I in turn experience, that the psychi-atrist knows me, and I him, and whom it is hoped will be respectful of the psychotherapeutic treatment. So, we begin psychotherapy under the aforementioned conditions, lasting approximately one year, at which time it seemed like an appropriate juncture to suggest the need to proceed to psychoanalysis.

Indication for psychoanalytic psychotherapy (PP) as a preliminary phase to psychoanalysis: transforming PP into psychoanalysis

Over the past few years, for those professionals who accept the distinction between psychoanalysis and psychotherapy, it is quite common to begin by carrying out psychoanalytic psychotherapy—at two sessions per week—and then to go on, after a period of time, to psychoanalysis at four or, more unusually, five. Previously, this was not considered to be common practice; on the contrary, it was thought inadvisable to do so. The indication for one thing or another was established from the outset. If, during the course of psychotherapy, the need to do analysis was noted, the termination of the psychother-apeutic stage was prepared for and the patient would be referred to another psychoanalyst.

Among the reasons adduced to support this view is the argument that, within the psychoanalytic field, the therapeutic relationship that must prevail is one which is fundamentally determined by the trans-ference (and countertransference), and that while such phenomena are manifest and are taken into account in psychoanalytic psycho-therapy, as we have seen in the previous chapter, the factor of the face-to-face arrangement of therapist and patient means that the former will take on a very real physical presence, which contaminates and restricts the transferential experiences of the latter. Furthermore, in those cases where, even with two weekly sessions, use is made of the couch, the relationship will have been shaped by external events in the patient's life and not to the same extent by the internal and transferential world, given the lower frequency of the sessions.

Nowadays, numerous arguments have served to modify this stance. One of them, as we have already said, is the shortage of patients who request psychoanalysis, owing primarily to the considerable expansion of treatment choice in the field of mental health, even with the purview of the "psychoanalytic" itself, and, moreover, as a result of the powerful influence of the pharmaceutical industry. The factor of resources—of money and time—that need to be invested into the achievement of psychoanalysis is, likewise, often a deterring factor. And it is even more so within the context of the prevalent ideology—in the broadest sense of the term—in our western societies, one that we might call the *ideology of immediacy*, of the urgency to obtain and attain things in life, be it food (*fast food* would be the most eloquent metaphorical expression of what I seek to describe) or the resolution of personal problems.

This is not the place to examine the matter in more depth, but it is opportune, at least, to point out some ideas, since this question is often implicit, as I was saying, to the initial practice of much psychoanalysis. The fact that a change in technical position is owing to factors extrinsic to those typical of an indication, should this discourage the indication from being made—that is, the progression from PP to psychoanalysis with the same analyst? Is this the only way of making the indication for psychoanalysis feasible, in the light of precisely these external conditions? Does this alter, and to what degree, the conditions of psychoanalytic practice, that is to say, the development of the transferences in the analytic relationship?

Without going into details, we might give some approximate answers by taking into account our experience of the last few years. In principal, I do not think it is necessarily an insuperable issue. First, it depends on the type of "psychotherapeutic" relationship that has been established prior to the transition to a "psychoanalytical" relationship, in the strict sense of the term. If the relationship has been developed keeping in mind certain conditions that approximate those established in the analytic setting, albeit apart from the differences we mentioned in the previous chapter, it will not be especially difficult to make the transition between one modality and another. Furthermore, when this transition—as we would hope—has been elaborated in the last stage of psychotherapy, we will be able to see that the change in rhythm of the sessions, the transition to the couch, as well as a greater predominance of transferential interpretation and, in short, the establishment of an analytic setting, will effect in the patient a further degree of involvement in the relationship, as well as a greater interest in the observation of his internal world. Now the patient will have a better understanding of the references to the transferential situation which might have been noted and might have even arisen at certain points during the psychotherapy, and he will also be more willing to access more primitive levels of his mind.

I can cite the case of a patient whom I treated in psychoanalytic psychotherapy at two sessions per week, face-to-face, for a period of two years. Towards the end of this time, we were noticing that the patient's capacities for collaboration were stagnating, owing to his tendency to rationalise, given his intellectual and discursive resources. While some symptomatic and relational progress had been made, it was evident that an even greater therapeutic work, at deeper levels, remained to be done. The insights he obtained shared little of the experiential component, for which reason they became merely "interesting" rationalisation—rather brilliant ones—both on the part of the patient and the therapist, but with little impact on the potential for internal change. For that reason, I put to him the need to consider the transition to psychoanalysis, and, in order to do so, we would, in the first instance, have to terminate psychotherapy and then begin psychoanalysis, which he should do with another psychoanalyst. I argued that it was, in point of fact, the type of therapeutic relationship that we had established—one that was very influenced by rationalisations—which would be disadvantageous to him starting psychoanalysis with me. The patient accepted the proposal and, after I had provided him with name of a colleague, we parted ways.

After several years, the patient returned, asking for help with some urgency, as the symptomatology for which he had consulted me at the beginning had been reactivated. I explained to him that, as we had discussed at the time, it remained for him to do a more intensive treatment than the one we had realised until then. I do not recall what circumstances of an external nature were put forward to account for him not having started psychoanalysis with the professional I recommended; perhaps he did not have appointments immediately available. He expressed to me that he was still interested in starting psychoanalysis and asked me if I could take charge of his case myself. I considered it, in terms of weighing up if the fact that we had had the previous psychotherapeutic relationship would constitute a disadvantage; my opinion was that several years had gone by and, in any case, during psychotherapy, I had tried to maintain certain conditions approximating the psychoanalytic, in the sense I mentioned above. So, I told him that I would be willing to, but that at that time I did not have any availability in my schedule until the following January (it was June); that is to say, some six months later. But as the patient had sought to carry out the diagnostic interviews before the summer to then start treatment in September, I also remarked to him that if this seemed like a long time to wait, perhaps it would be worth referring him to another psychoanalyst. So, I gave him the details of a colleague, in this case a woman, whereas the first had been a man, thinking perhaps that this fact—the masculine gender of the analyst—had contributed towards increasing the patient's resistances.

A couple of months later, he once more requests an interview, explaining that he met with the colleague, who seemed fine, two or three times, but he would prefer to wait until I was available. And so, when I was available, we started psychoanalysis at four sessions per week. For myself, I cannot say that the transition from one treatment to the other offered up any particular difficulties. On the contrary, we confirmed what was predicted, that under the conditions of the couch and with a greater frequency of sessions the patient was able to access more primitive levels of his mind, and in such a way other transferences emerged, which had not been possible in the face-to-face relationship as a result of his very defensive, intellectualising and pseudo-adult attitude, as I have already pointed out. Analysis was able to progress over several years.

This experience made me reconsider my previous position as to what extent does it constitute a counter-indication that the same analyst take on the transition from psychotherapy to psychoanalysis. I think a key question is whether, during psychotherapy, the therapist adopts a stance or attitude, as I have already said, that "approximates" the analytic stance, despite this being face-to-face and without the prevalence of transferential interpretation, yet still maintaining the attitude of neutrality and of listening. When this is the case, the power of the transferential relationship quickly prevails, in the course of the psychoanalytic process, over the kind of therapeutic relationship that would have been formed in the stage of psychotherapy where understanding based on events of external reality would have predominated.

Another case is that of a patient for whom I assessed the indication for psychoanalysis as the treatment of choice from the very first diagnostic interviews. According to the patient, in the light of the economic circumstances he was going through at that time, he was not able to assume the cost of analysis. However, his financial difficulties in themselves did not appear to be sufficient grounds to rule out undertaking psychoanalysis, as when we later began—his financial reality being comparable to what it was prior to starting—he did not have any objections to coming to an arrangement whereby I adjusted my fees to an amount which would be feasible to him, and to me as well. Consequently, it seems clear that this external difficulty served as a pretext to a certain resistance he had, at that time, in relation to intensive psychological treatment. Even so, I respected this initial resistance and agreed to start psychotherapeutic treatment at a frequency of twice per week, face-to-face, with the condition that during the course of treatment—I might have specified a period of one year—we would be able to review the possibility of making the transition to psychoanalysis of four weekly sessions. In this case, unlike before, both the patient and the analyst knew from the outset that the indication for analysis had been given; consequently, in my attitude as a therapist, I tried to be more mindful of this, in the sense of venturing a little more in the transferential interpretative work, whereas, in the case of the patient for whom I indicated psychoanalytic psychotherapy, which I have talked about on previous pages (Clinical Material 6), although it seemed to me that it would be possible to make the indication for psychoanalysis, I did not do so at the beginning because of certain doubts, which made it advisable to wait and see how the psychotherapy progressed. Below, I shall set out the transformation to psychoanalysis of that very case.

Transformation of psychoanalytic psychotherapy to psychoanalysis: clinical material 6 (continued)

Evolution of the psychoanalytic psychotherapy

Just as we had arranged in the diagnostic interviews, as I have already set out above, we had been carrying out psychotherapy at two sessions per week for one year. During this time, the patient has experienced a notable clinical improvement. Her depressive symptoms have abated considerably, and she has regained the ability to carry out her work at a level at which she feels satisfied. In spite of this, from time to time intermittent depressive episodes reappear, which might be understood by linking them to some conflictive aspect she is experiencing: specifically, her relationship with her partner, and, to a lesser extent, other relationships, especially in her working environment. Shortly after beginning psychotherapy, after her suicide attempt, her partner suggested to her that it might be best if they separate, as he did not feel able to continue the relationship given the sick condition she was in. Very painfully, the patient accepted this. Not only was the loss of her partner painful for her, but also his selfishness, as he left her just when she was feeling so awful. It was apparent, from the start of the psychotherapy, that the patient experienced the last weeks and months of the relationship with her partner as a situation with no way out, as she was not able to explain what was wrong with her and took refuge in passivity at the same time as being tormented by her helplessness to emerge from such a situation. It was this passivity that drove her partner to leave her.

The patient went to live on her own. Gradually, she overcame her fears of not being capable of getting over her loneliness. She rebuilt her friendships; in fact, she had many relationships that responded well. Nevertheless, at the beginning she was very sensitive to the fact that people did not call her more often, which she attributed to the little that she meant to others, accentuating her feeling of self-devaluation.

We were able to look at the type of relationship that she experienced in her relationship, which was linked to conflict faced with authority figures. Her position had always been one of submission and passivity, that is to say, she has related to these figures at the cost of invalidating part of her personality. In the psychotherapy sessions, she recalls episodes linked to her family of origin and to her childhood. She remembers an elderly father, who treated her with care and gentleness, although he inspired respect, almost fear, but at all events she presents an image that is very different to the one her brothers and sisters remember. They talk about a demanding and strict father who was severe to the point of punishing them physically.

During the course of psychotherapy, her fears also emerge—tied to that problem with authority figures—that the same type of relationship will be repeated in this treatment as that established with the psychiatrist with whom she was being treated for several years. The patient needs to remember the conversations with that professional, when he maintained that she had an endogenous depression, that it is something she will have all her life, that she will require continuous medication, that, in addition, it is an illness that is particularly reactivated by the changes in season, which, indeed, she had been able to confirm, so that when she went back to feeling depressed, she thought that this tallied with it being the beginning of spring or autumn. This "awareness" of illness was something she was deeply marked by, in the sense that it enabled her to surrender herself to a passive attitude—as she was now able to recognise herself—under the pretext that nothing could be done in the face of her illness except take the medication prescribed by the psychiatrist, of which the side-effects, especially the drowsiness, restricted her ability to perform and to be effective at work and in her relationships. Her bouts of depression were increasing in the frequency with which they appeared, which was interpreted as a need for more medication, thus increasing the dosage of antidepressants. This also exacerbated the patient's side-effects, as well as her emotional state in terms of her passivity and feelings of helplessness, in a vicious, never-ending circle. These problems were compounded by the dissatisfaction of her partner, who reproached her for not making enough effort to overcome her condition. As there was an element of truth to this complaint, the patient felt guilty. While she felt her partner's attitude to be unfair, as he did not take into account the opinion of the psychiatrist, who had passed the judgement that she was suffering from an endogenous depression, that is to say, an illness "for life", and that she would need medication permanently, at the same time, however, she knew that she was settling into that attitude of passivity. At some point, the fleeting thought crossed her mind that perhaps she needed another type of help, or she struggled to accept that her problem was something that was irreversible and irremediable, for life. But then, having to confront the psychiatrist in order to question her treatment method distressed her even more. The progression of this state of affairs reached its climax, as we saw in the diagnostic interviews, with the ingestion of the tablets at a point when she felt desperate, helpless, and that the people close to her—her partner and her psychiatrist— did not understand her.

Hence, this was one of the questions we needed to deal with quite frequently during the first months of psychotherapy, transferred to the new therapeutic relationship with me. The patient feared not meeting the demands the therapist expected of her, that she should get better clinically, and do so quickly, and when improvement did occur, she could not then return to subsequent sessions exhibiting discomfort, sadness, or other signs which might indicate a certain backward movement, as the therapist would not tolerate it.

During the course of psychotherapy, the capacity and the need of the patient to air her emotional difficulties, to put them into words, is revealed with greater clarity. She continues to make use of her good capacity for self-observation and insight; she grasps the interpretations made to her and, all in all, she is collaborative. In short, she is a person who benefits from psychotherapeutic treatment. This is evinced after a few months, and then is maintained throughout the following months, until we arrive at the present time, approximately one year later. During the last sessions, the patient recognises that the achievements she has attained are being consolidated, such as making use of her ability to carry out her work, as well as to confront the vicissitudes that have arisen in her relationship with her partner. After several months where she did not see him, the patient met with him, and he, upon seeing her in a better condition, suggested they go out again from time to time. She accepted. This was taking place close to the summer holidays (it would be the first long holiday to take place during this psychotherapy). They met. She went back to her home town, where she had not been for some time—since before her suicide attempt—in part, because her mother, with her religious principles, did not accept her partner without them being engaged, but also because her partner did not want that contact either, not even with her brothers and sisters, which the patient submissively accepted. Upon returning from these holidays, she finds out by chance that he has a girlfriend, in spite of the fact that in the brief contact that took place between the two of them they seem to have left open the implicit promise of resurrecting the relationship. This saddened her, but most of all it made her furious, as she was now feeling stronger and this helped her to take full account of the situation and be advised against any attempt at reconciliation on her companion's part.

A couple of months later, the partner has broken up with that girl-friend and is showing signs once more of wanting to reconcile things with the patient. They resume their relationship, although each living in their own houses. As the patient begins to lessen her idealisation of the partner and is able to also see the difficulties he has, she admits that she finds it difficult to relate to people who have his characteristics.

In spite of all of this improvement, the patient complains that there are periods when she feels depressed. And although there are things she is able to relate to certain facts or events that have taken place, particularly with her partner, she thinks that there are others that seem to exist on another level and that prevent her from feeling satis-fied. For example, sometimes during session she suddenly becomes moved by something, to her surprise, as there was no apparent motive to account for it, and although we would try to understand what this emotional lability might correspond to, it is not always possible.

At the same time as the insufficiency of the psychotherapy is brought into sharp relief, I see that her potentialities in terms of the indication for psychoanalysis noted in the interviews are confirmed, as it seems to me that the patient could tolerate emotional and psycho-logical therapeutic work on a much deeper level than we have been doing. At times, she relates her dreams or memories from childhood, which allude to primitive levels of her mind that we are hardly able to examine, above all in the transference setting, or, if I am encouraged by the significance of the material, I have the impression that the outcome are interpretations and understandings that are almost purely intellectual, but with little impact on her fundamental person-ality structures. In order to do this, we would require psychoanalysis. I explain this to her. I tell her that it is clear that she has improved in her personal achievements, but that there remains an undercurrent of discomfort, sadness, and dissatisfaction which has not been resolved, and if she is willing to look at it, we would need to undertake a more in-depth treatment, or, rather, psychoanalysis.

The patient agrees. We have had to review the economic condi-tions in terms of what she would be prepared to contribute, at this time, in agreement with the analyst; to do this we have readjusted the fees she was paying for the two psychotherapy sessions to a lesser rate, which enables her to assume the cost of the four sessions of psychoanalysis. We agree to start the analysis two months later, when a little over a year of psychotherapy will have elapsed. Meanwhile, we continue the "face-to-face" psychotherapy of two sessions per week.

Detailed description of two sessions

I should like to describe two sessions from around the time of taking this decision, in order to illustrate the process of change from psycho-therapy to psychoanalysis and the *working through* of the indication for the latter. In Monday's session, the patient arrives annoyed and rather agitated by the irresponsible attitude of some of the people around her, who have not sufficiently borne her in mind or have not assumed the responsibilities that should fall to them. One of the issues is related to her work and the other to her partner, with whom she continues to maintain a relationship, though they do not live together and there has been no decision, on her part, to get back together.

At the following session, Thursday's, the second of the week— the reader is reminded that we had still not proceeded to four—the patient comes to the session in the intermittent state of depression that we are already familiar with, with the sensation of having touched upon deep-rooted issues that she does not fully understand. For example, she gets up late, when she has been awake since nine in the morning. As a matter of fact, it is not that it is especially difficult for her to do the jobs that are outstanding, such as those resulting from her work; on the contrary, it is something she likes doing. If she stops to think about it, what bothers and depresses her is the fact of having to get up to do things that are given to her, or imposed upon her, as she perceives it, as if these tasks were not her own, that have not come from herself, feeling that she is lacking that internal moti-vating force that causes her to experience them as though they belong to her and, as such, might excite her. I think that it must have been this kind of symptomatology that led to the diagnosis of endogenous depression.

In the same session she explains two dreams. One dream is from Monday, or rather, after the first session this week.

"I found myself in some kind of big ship. There was like a big woven net or mesh, of the type with pieces of glass set into it to form a kind of mosaic [in my consulting room, just on the space on the wall between where the psychotherapy chairs are located, hangs a tapestry with figures of animals in geometric drawings, each one of them framed by a rectangle, and the predominant colour tone is blue]. It looked like a work still in progress, unfinished. The predominant colours were soft blue tones. Then, I found myself on the ceiling, swinging on a trapeze, but really hard, so that I hit my feet against the wall in front; and then I am scared that, when I swing back again, the blow will also be really hard, and as I am going backwards I will fall, so before I fall I grab on to the net, and from tugging on it a large number of the little glass pieces that had been mounted on it come away and the net winds around until it forms something like a liana that I cling on to. Just on the other side of the ship there was another girl on a trapeze. I am able to identify her as a classmate. Well, because of the to-and-fro motion I am going to stop just beside where that girl was, and as I get close to her, when I am level with her face, I give her a kiss. But it was as if they were shooting a film, and so all of that, including the kiss, was part of the scene. But the surprise, as much for the girl as for me, was that I gave her a kiss for real, not just pretend, like a performance, but a kiss on the mouth. I woke up a little unsettled."

"I had the other dream last night," the patient continues, "it turns out that I was in a place where only I see myself, next to a small wooden table [she describes certain dimensions that call to mind the table I have in my consulting room, between the chairs we sit on during the sessions]. On the table there was one of those old telephones, those black Bakelite ones, with the handle and all that. It was as if I were waiting for a phone call from you to remind me of the time, I think it was seven thirty, to come to the session. The telephone rings and it is a deep man's voice who is calling me, who says, 'M, please . . .' I was so panicked by it that I hung up, and then I woke up." [M is the diminutive form of her name.]

She says that the issue about seven thirty must have been because her partner asked her to set the alarm for that time. That is to say, he has slept at her house, which is something that the patient has omitted to say until then, despite in the last session complaining about "the schemes he is up to" sometimes, by taking for granted that the relationship is rather more consolidated, such as relying on her to accompany him somewhere he is invited. We clarify this point, how she also takes that situation for granted, in spite of the fact that at other times she is aware that they are going through a stage of mutual exploration, of uncertain expectations, attentive to what potential the relationship has before taking the decision to resume it in a more definitive way.

I go on to explain to her what I make of her dreams. First, I tell her that each dream seems to reflect the state she was experiencing when she came to the session to which each dream corresponds. That is to say, on Monday she came annoyed and agitated, complaining about how irresponsible people are and in a determined attitude not to get swept along by the idleness of others and to take charge of things herself when they affect her. That agitated state might be exacerbated, as occurs in the first dream, in such a way that she ends up flying on the trapeze. But this is a perilous activity, one that might end up ruining the patient and laborious work of the net: I think that the scene has something to do with the idea of constructing something of her own self, such as the work we have been doing here in the psychotherapy, along with what she is able to do on her own, all of which could come tumbling down by that state of agitation. This culminates in the kiss with the beautiful girl, to her surprise.

She then associates that the girl who appears in the dream was "all woman"; very beautiful, very feminine, although at the same time she was someone who carried out a type of activity that was rather more masculine, in so far as the physical strength it demands; someone who looked after her body, in the sense of making it strong.

In other words, I add, that she comes together with this woman who might represent an aspect of herself, and who, while being very feminine, "all woman", at the same time possesses a masculine strength. So, it appears that when she is agitated, when she feels that she is "flying", that she is so capable she would not need a male partner, neither her companion in her external relationship nor her therapist in the treatment, as she has everything herself.

As for the second dream, the patient explains that the diminutive form (M) used by the man who calls her on the telephone is only ever used by close friends and, moreover, by people in her home town, but not here. And in any case, that voice frightened her.

I admit that it is not clear to me at that point what that menace involves. She reveals that she was hoping to hear my voice to help her to remember the time of the session, as if she did not trust herself to see to it. But the dream takes place, according to what she then explains to me, while she is in bed with her companion, or, rather, it appears that her relationship with him could distract her from coming to the session and for that reason she needed me to assume that responsibility. In any case, there is some interference from a voice—the therapist's—that calls her and proves persecutory.

I believe that this persecutory element must refer to a split-off aspect of the transferential relationship. The positive aspect of the figure of the therapist, in whom she trusts to take charge of what she is not able to, coexists with another who is able of persecuting her—a rigid and severe superego—that does not tolerate the relationship with her partner without having authorised it. Thus, she projects into the therapist her own jealousy and feeling of exclusion. However, I do not mention all of this. Although I have kept it in mind, neither do I make any reference to the connection of the dream to the immediate perspective of starting the analytic relationship, that is to say, a more intensive relationship. Incidentally, the depressive state in which she awoke this morning, with a feeling of helplessness, might this not reveal that she feels punished by the "therapist"—or a part of him—owing to the fact of "having" to come to his sessions, and that the prospect of more treatment will mean further subjugation, in spite of this being a subject we have been dealing with?

At another moment during the same session, we take up the subject of the first dream once again, and I say something to the effect that it seems to allude to her problems in the construction of her *female identity*. To my understanding, the net that is suspended and contains pieces of coloured glass that become encrusted into it reflects the psychotherapeutic work in relation to her own self or mind, as I said to her at the beginning, although, in a more specific way, it also seems to refer to questions about her female identity. The kiss with the beautiful girl, who is "all woman", might be an attempt to unite with that image of woman; however, leaping through the air to achieve it, because attempting to do so by means of the constructive work of the mosaic net, which is patient and laborious, as is treatment—or, rather, relying on the therapist, becomes arduous and difficult for her.

In response, the patient announces that she remembers another fragment of the first dream, following what has been explained to her.

"I am going shopping to buy myself some clothes. And I am, in point of fact, looking at feminine clothes, in soft colours, such as light blues, beige and the like, which also remind me of the colours of the glass pieces of the mosaic. I stop in front of a garment, which is a trouser-skirt I like. But seeing as at that moment there are not many people in the shop, I think that I can carry on walking around looking at other things. Finally, I decide to take that first garment, but when I go to look for it I can't find it any more. I am too late. In that time more people have come in, and it seems as though they bought it."

I point out to her that, in fact, her preoccupation with the question of her female identity emerges here. (Several weeks ago, she recounted a dream in which there was a pair of trousers that belonged to her. I do not remember the content, but it causes me to connect it with something I had observed; that she always wears trousers and hardly wears garments that are strictly speaking feminine; neither does she wear makeup, though she does not have a masculine demeanour or manner. In fact, in her way of dressing, she looks like a teenager, obviously a girl, but with a style that, without being overtly masculine, neutralises that femininity. On that occasion, we discuss the issue of her femininity. She associated it with her family history: at home she always wore trousers, like her brothers and sisters.) We also look at her problem in accepting femininity, as it is something that is linked to fragility and weakness. That is why she admired the friend in the dream, who, at the same time as being beautiful, was also strong. Hence, also—I now understand—the issue of the trouser-skirt that she was anxious to buy in the second dream, but through deferring her acquisition she loses it, as in that garment are united both elements of each sex.

The second session I wish to discuss follows the previous one, that is to say, the following Monday's. The patient says that she has had a violent dream and that it has worried her. But this time she specifies from the outset that when she had it she was sleeping with her companion, so as not to repeat her omission of the last session, in which the fact appeared indirectly. The dream went like this:

"I was in a house with S [her partner]. Suddenly, four men come in and start to set upon him; they were coming to kill him. I tried to defend him; I even confronted one of them. But it was as if they were ignoring me, as if I wasn't there. I pick up a bottle of cava that was to hand, as it looks as if there was a party going on. I break the bottle in order to have a weapon to attack them with, but once I am holding it in my hand I say to myself, 'And now what?' I felt incapable of assaulting anybody with that. So I took off towards another room, next to the one in which the violent scene was unfolding, and I found myself with four women. I imagined that they must have been the partners of each of the four men. Although they could hear what was going on next door, they didn't bat an eyelid and carried on in their party atmosphere, calmly drinking cava. I thought that if they were the men's partners, there would be no sense in asking them for help. So I decide to return to the other room, and I confront one of them, but I feel helpless. At that moment I wake up."

She associates the dream with something that had happened the night before when, while walking down the street with her partner, an older and seemingly somewhat drunk man came towards her, making flirtatious remarks. The patient stopped to avoid the collision that would have occurred, but her companion leapt to confront the man in a very violent manner, for which she reproached him. She told him that she was able to stand up for herself alone and that, besides, there was no danger, so it was uncalled for to get like that.

I interpret the dream as a fear at the prospect of the psychoanalysis that we will soon be beginning, after the Christmas holidays—we have two sessions left, including today's. I tell her that the four men must refer to the analyst, multiplied into as many men as sessions of psychoanalysis we have planned; the four women might be herself in each one of these four session, forming a couple with each of the respective analysts. I indicate to her that there seems to be a fear that the analysis and the analyst are competitively against her relationship. I also tell her that, according to that fear, the companion will be an obstacle to the establishment of these four analytic "couples", for which reason it would be necessary to eliminate him. In this way, the obstacles to beginning analysis—rooted in her fears, ambivalence, and resistances—would not be in her, but in her partner; what is more, it is the analyst who has to confront him.

The patient smiles and replies that it must be something like that; she has thought that coming four times a week will mean dedicating more time to her treatment and that, as her companion is very demanding of her, she will not be able to be with him as much. She relates that this weekend they spent every night together, and today at midday he has already left her a message arranging to see her again. That is to say, admittedly she also feels a little overwhelmed and would like to have a bit more time for herself. In her opinion, the problem is that he can become very demanding and possessive when he needs the other.

She goes on to add that she remembers *another piece of information about the dream,* and it is that *the four men who attack her partner seem to have something to do with drugs.* I put it to her that perhaps she fears that the problem of the other being possessive towards her will also arise here. Indeed, *it was the analyst who proposed that they proceed to four sessions.* Although she seemed to understand the case put forward, and accepted it, ultimately it was the psychoanalyst who raised the question. It might, therefore, seem like a demand on his part, a need of his. And in that sense, she might fear that now it will be the analyst who will be demanding and possessive with her, in clear competition with her partner. Even more, the analyst could be "addicted to" this relationship with her. The patient agrees.

And so we started psychoanalysis on the arranged date, which we carried out over several years (nearly ten), during which the development of a true psychoanalytic process was made possible.

Comments on the two sessions

I have described these sessions from the last stage of psychotherapy in order to illustrate the transition from this to psychoanalysis. I think that this material successfully illustrates the prospects for the work of psychoanalysis that had already begun in the psychotherapy sessions themselves, in the sense of approaching the understanding and interpretation of the transference in a notable way. So, in the case above, it was important to reveal the anxieties and defences of the patient engendered by the indication for psychoanalysis having been agreed upon. Only psychoanalytic work, in the strict sense of the term, through the interpretation of the transference, would be able to gain access to these.

When we make an indication for analysis in the diagnostic interview, we consider that the patient meets sufficient conditions and potentialities in order that his need and his interest in clinical improvement and psychic change prevail, despite his resistances, and this enables us to start treatment, but when resistances are strong, it is not easy to work through them. Furthermore, it is also at this moment when it is likely that the therapist or analyst himself could collude with them as a result of his own resistances, as we saw earlier on.

But in those cases where the patient is in psychotherapy and, either because the option of reviewing the indication for analysis during treatment has been agreed upon, or because such a treatment makes it evident, as in the case of the material I have just presented, that psychoanalysis is indeed the suitable indication, conditions are present to work through the resistances.

The sessions I have transcribed here attempt to show both the attitude of the patient, who is in touch with her internal world by means of her facility to provide dreams, among other things, as well as to evoke certain associations and fantasies on the basis of the therapist's interventions, and that of the analyst, in his work of gathering together and interpreting the material that alludes to the transference.

*   *   *

I wanted to end the book with this case where, after a number of doubts and elaborations, the course of the therapeutic relationship led to the beginning of psychoanalysis. However, as we might gather from the book as a whole and as is clear, we do not expect that all interviews will result in a similar indication. I have endeavoured to offer up some of the possible outcomes—once we had noted and discussed the elements and dynamics of the interview from a psychoanalytic perspective—towards which the interview might turn. Starting with the interview, where the aim, beyond the diagnostic, is to be an end in itself, on account of its therapeutic effect—always present in any interview—leading up to the interview that enables the indication for psychoanalysis to be established, including the other psychotherapeutic indications, such as supportive psychotherapy, the brief psychotherapies and psychoanalytic psychotherapy, as well as the elaboration of the indication for psychoanalysis proper after a period of psychotherapy.

So, the case set out above seeks to illustrate not only the vicissitudes of the transition from psychoanalytic psychotherapy to psychoanalysis, but also the different options available to the therapist for a patient who needs psychological help. These are options that the analyst should scrutinise internally in order to rule out some and select others. Once the treatment choice he considers to be suitable has been made, he should propose it to the patient if he truly has made it his own, that is to say, if he has some degree of conviction that this proposal will be one that enables work to be done together and from which the patient will derive certain benefits. As we have seen in the case above, the analyst oscillated somewhat in terms of the optimum therapeutic indication. At the beginning, based on the scant data from the colleague's telephone call, the most sensible option seemed to be a supportive psychotherapy. A large part of the first interview confirmed this impression—turned partly into a preconception or prejudice that then (unconsciously) contaminated the analyst's capacity for observation. Later on, this approach was modified to include the prospect of psychoanalytic psychotherapy, until the possibility of psychoanalysis was conceived. This was an indication that, ultimately, was confirmed during the course of the psychotherapy and especially over the years during which the psychoanalytic process took place. However, I would like to emphasise that this is possible only if the analyst relies on a specific method, psychoanalytic, or psychotherapeutic, which differ from each other, as I explained in the previous chapter.

Notes

1. As might already have been noted, I include the supportive psychotherapies within the purview of the psychoanalytically based psychotherapies, consonant with other authors (Kernberg, 1999), as the theoretical basis is the same despite the method and aims being different.
2. For a clinical illustration of the indication for psychoanalysis in the first interviews, please refer to my book *Análisis Terminable* (Terminable Analysis) (Pérez-Sánchez, 1997), which is devoted to the comprehensive account of an analytic process of five sessions per week for several years.

REFERENCES

Aguilar, J., Oliva, M. V., & Marzani, C. (1998). *L'Entrevista Psicoanalítica. Una investigación empírica.* Barcelona: Columna.

Adams-Silvan, A. (Reporter) (2002). Psychoanalysis and allied therapies: what does a psychoanalyst do when he/she thinks or says he/she is doing psychotherapy? *International Journal of Psycho-Analysis, 83*: 229.

Ávila, A., & Poch, J. (Eds.) (1994). *Manual de técnicas de psicoterapia.* Madrid: Siglo XXI Editores.

Bachrach, H. M., & McNutt, E. R. (1992). Panel reports. Psychoanalysis and psychoanalytic psychotherapy—similarities and differences: indications, contraindications and initiation. *Journal of the American Psychoanalytical Association, 40*: 223–231.

Balint, E., & Ornstein, P. H. (1972). *Focal Psychotherapy: An Example of Applied Psychoanalysis.* Redwood Press: Salisbury.

Balint, M., & Balint, E. (1961). *Psychotherapeutic Techniques in Medicine* [reprinted London: Routledge, 2001].

Bibring, E. (1954). Psychoanalysis and dynamic psychotherapy. *Journal of the American Psychoanalytical Association, 2*: 745.

Bion, W. R. (1959). Attacks on linking. *International Journal of Psycho-Analysis, 40.* Reprinted in *Second Thoughts.* London: Heinemann [reprinted London: Karnac, 1984].

Bion, W. R. (1962). *Learning from Experience.* London: Heinemann [reprinted London: Karnac].

Bion, W. R. (1967). *Second Thoughts.* London: Heinemann [reprinted London: Karnac, 1984].

Bion, W. R. (1970). *Attention and Interpretation.* London: Tavistock [reprinted London: Karnac, 1984].

Bion, W. R. (1977a). Emotional turbulence [reprinted in *Clinical Seminars and Other Works*. London: Karnac, 1994].

Bion, W. R. (1977b). *Two Papers: The Grid and Caesura*. Rio de Janeiro: Imago Editora [reprinted London: Karnac, 1989].

Bion, W. R. (1992). *Cogitations*. London: Karnac.

Bleger, J. (1971). La entrevista psicológica: su empleo en el diagnóstico y la investigación. En *Temas de psicología: Entrevistas y grupos*. Buenos Aires. Nueva Visión.

Coderch, J. (1987). *Teoría y Técnica de la psicoterapia psicoanalítica*. Herder. Barcelona.

Coderch, J. (1995). *La interpretación en psicoanálisis. Fundamentos y teoría de la técnica*. Herder. Barcelona.

Coderch, J. (2000). Les motivacions del pacient i de l'analista per passar d'una psiccoterapia psicoanalítica a una psicoanàlisi. *Revista Catalana de Psicoanalisi, XVII*(1–2): 27.

Corominas, J. (1976). *Breve Diccionario Etimológico de la Lengua Castellana*. Madrid: Editorial Gredos.

De Saussure, J. (1988). The psychoanalytic setting: frequency and duration of sessions. *Psychoanalysis in Europe, 31*: 119–125.

Etchegoyen, R. H. (1999). *The Fundamentals of Psychoanalytic Technique*. London: Karnac.

Freud, S. (1900a). *The Interpretation of Dreams. S.E.*, 4–5. London: Hogarth.

Freud, S. (1904a). Freud's psycho-analytic procedure. *S.E.*, 7: 249–256. London: Hogarth.

Freud, S. (1905a). On psychotherapy. *S.E.*, 7: 257–270. London: Hogarth.

Freud, S. (1912e). Recommendations to physicians practising psychoanalysis. *S.E.*, 12: 109–120. London: Hogarth.

Freud, S. (1914d). On the history of the psycho-analytic movement. *S.E.*, 14: 3–66. London: Hogarth.

Freud, S. (1914g). Remembering, repeating and working-through. *S.E.*, 12: 145–156. London: Hogarth.

Freud, S. (1919a). Lines of advance in psychoanalytic therapy. *S.E.*, 17: 157–168. London: Hogarth.

Freud, S. (1937c). *Analysis Terminable and Interminable. S.E.*, 23: 211–253. London: Hogarth.

Frisch, S. (2001). *Psychoanalysis and Psychotherapy. The Controversies and the Future*. London: Karnac.

Hinshelwood, R. D. (2001). Surveying the maze. In: S. Frisch (Ed.), *Psychoanalysis and Psychotherapy. The Controversies and the Future* (pp. 123–136). London: Karnac.

Joseph, B. (1989). *Equilibrium and Psychic Change*. London: Routledge.

Kernberg, O. F. (1976). Technical considerations in the treatment of borderline personality organization. *Journal of the American Psychoanalytical Association*, 24: 795–829.

Kernberg, O. F. (1999). Psychoanalysis, psychoanalytic psychotherapy and supportive psychotherapy: contemporary controversies. *International Journal of Psychoanalysis*, 80(6): 1075–1091.

Klein, M. (1935). A contribution to the psychogenesis of manic-depressive states. In: *The Writings of Melanie Klein, Vol. 1* (pp. 262–289). London: Karnac, 1992.

Klein, M. (1946). Notes on some schizoid mechanisms. In: *The Writings of Melanie Klein, Vol. III* (pp. 1–24). London: Hogarth, 1987.

Klein, M. (1957). Envy and gratitude. In: *The Writings of Melanie Klein, Vol. III* (pp. 176–235). London: Hogarth, 1987.

Liberman, D. (1980). *Evaluación de las entrevistas diagnósticas previas a los tratamientos analíticos*. En C. Paz: *Analizabilidad y Momentos Vitales*. Valencia: Nau llibres.

Malan, D. H. (1963). *La psicoterapia breve*. Buenos Aires: Centro Editor de América Latina, 1974.

Meltzer, D. (1967). *The Psycho-analytic Process*. London: Heinemann [reprinted London: Karnac, 2008].

Mitjavila, M. (1994). La iniciación del tratamiento. In: A. Avila y J. Poch (Eds.), *Manual de Técnicas de Psicoterapia* (pp. 265–289). Madrid: Siglo Veintiuno Editores.

Moliner, M. (1979). *Diccionario de uso del Español*. Madrid: Editorial Gredos.

Møller, M. (2011). L'angoscia dell'analista nel primo colloquio. *Psicoanálisis*, 15(1): Gennaio–Giugno.

Money-Kyrle, R. (1968). Cognitive development. In: *The Collected Papers of R. Money-Kyrle* (pp. 416–433). Strathtay, Perthshire: Clunie Press, 1978.

New Oxford English Dictionary (1998). New York: Oxford Press.

Parsons, M. (2006). The analyst's countertransference to the analytic process. *International Journal of Psycho-Analysis*, 87: 1183–1198.

Paz, C. A. (1980). *Analizabilidad y Momentos Vitales*. Valencia: Nau Llibres.

Pérez-Sánchez, A. (1989). Realidad y proceso psicoanalítico: enfoque clínico. *Anuario Ibérico de Psicoanálisis*. Madrid.

Pérez-Sánchez, A. (1996a). *Prácticas psicoterapéuticas. Psicoanálisis aplicado a la asistencia pública*. Barcelona: Paidós.

Pérez-Sánchez, A. (1996b). Perspectiva psicoanalítica de los trastornos de la personalidad: organización patológica de la personalidad. *Temas de Psicoanálisis*, I: 145–170.

Pérez-Sánchez, A. (1997). *Análisis Terminable. Estudio sobre la terminación del proceso psicoanalítico*. Valencia: Promolibro.

Pérez-Sánchez, A. (1999). Indicadors per a l'acabament del procés psico-analitic. *Revista catalana de psicoanàlisi, XVI*(1): 35–55.

Pérez-Sánchez, A. (2001). Ansiedad: vértice psicoanalítico. *Temas de Psico-análisis, VI*: 185–197 [translation: Catalán Revista Catalana de psico-análisis, *XVI*(1)].

Rosenfeld, H. (1964). On the psychopathology of narcissism: a clinical approach. *International Journal of Psychoanalysis, 45*: 332–337.

Rosenfeld, H. (1978). Notes on the psychopathology and psychoanalytic treatment of some borderline patients. *International Journal of Psycho-analysis, 59*: 215–221.

Rothstein, A. (1998). *Psychoanalytic Technique and the Creation of Analytic Patients*. London: Karnac.

Ruszczynsky, S., & Johnson, S. (1999). *Psychoanalytic Psychotherapy in the Kleinian Tradition*. London: Karnac.

Segal, H. (1957). Notes on symbol formation. In: *The Work of Hanna Segal. A Kleinian Approach to Clinical Practice*. New York: Jason Aronson, 1981.

Segal, H. (1993). On the clinical usefulness of the concept of the death instinct. *International Journal of Psychoanalysis, 74*: 55–61.

Segal, H. (2007). *Yesterday, Today and Tomorrow*. London: Routledge.

Smith, H. (2002). Creating the psychoanalytic process incorporating three panels reports: opening the process, being in the process and closing the process. *International Journal of Psychoanalysis, 83*: 211.

Sullivan, H. S. (1954). *The Psychiatric Interview*. New York: W. W. Norton.

Thomä, H., & Kachele, H. (1985). *Psychoanalytic Practice* [reprinted London: Karnac, 1994].

Torras de Beá, E. (1991). Entrevista y diagnóstico en psiquiatría y psico-logía infantil psicoanalítica [revised edition: Barcelona: Paidós, 1997].

Tizón, J. L. (1992). Atención primaria en salud mental y salud mental. In: *Atención primaria*. Barcelona: Doyma.

Tyson, P., & Morris, J. L. (1992). Psychoanalysis and psychoanalytic psychotherapy—similarities and differences: therapeutic technique. *Journal of the American Psychoanalytical Association, 40*: 211–221.

Wallerstein, R. S. (1989). Psychoanalysis and psychotherapy: a historical perspective. *International Journal of Psychoanalysis, 70*: 563–591.

Wallerstein, R. S., & Hoch, S. (1992). Psychoanalysis and psychoanalytic psychotherapy—similarities and differences: a conceptual overview. *Journal of the American Psychoanalytical Association, 40*: 233–238.

INDEX